IMAGES
of America

HANOVER
NEW HAMPSHIRE
VOLUME II

I0810271

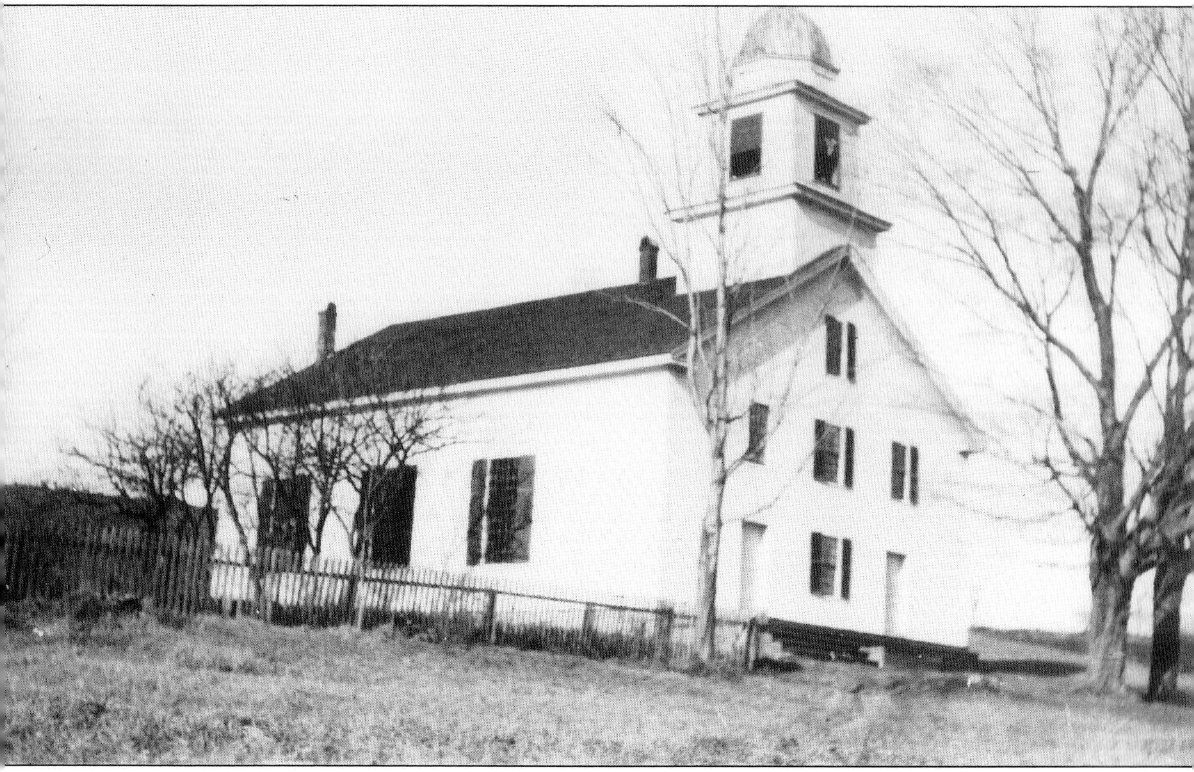

A late-nineteenth-century view of the "First Church of Christ Congregational Establishment in Hanover," situated facing the Parade Ground in Hanover Center. The facility was erected in 1840, and is shown here prior to a turn-of-the-century vestry addition placed on the rear of the building.

IMAGES
of America

HANOVER
NEW HAMPSHIRE
VOLUME II

Frank J. Barrett Jr.

ARCADIA
PUBLISHING

Copyright © 1998 by Frank J. Barrett Jr.
ISBN 978-0-7385-6340-4

Published by Arcadia Publishing
Charleston, South Carolina

Printed in the United States of America

Library of Congress Catalog Card Number: 97199065

For all general information contact Arcadia Publishing at:
Telephone 843-853-2070
Fax 843-853-0044
E-mail sales@arcadiapublishing.com
For customer service and orders:
Toll-Free 1-888-313-2665

Visit us on the Internet at www.arcadiapublishing.com

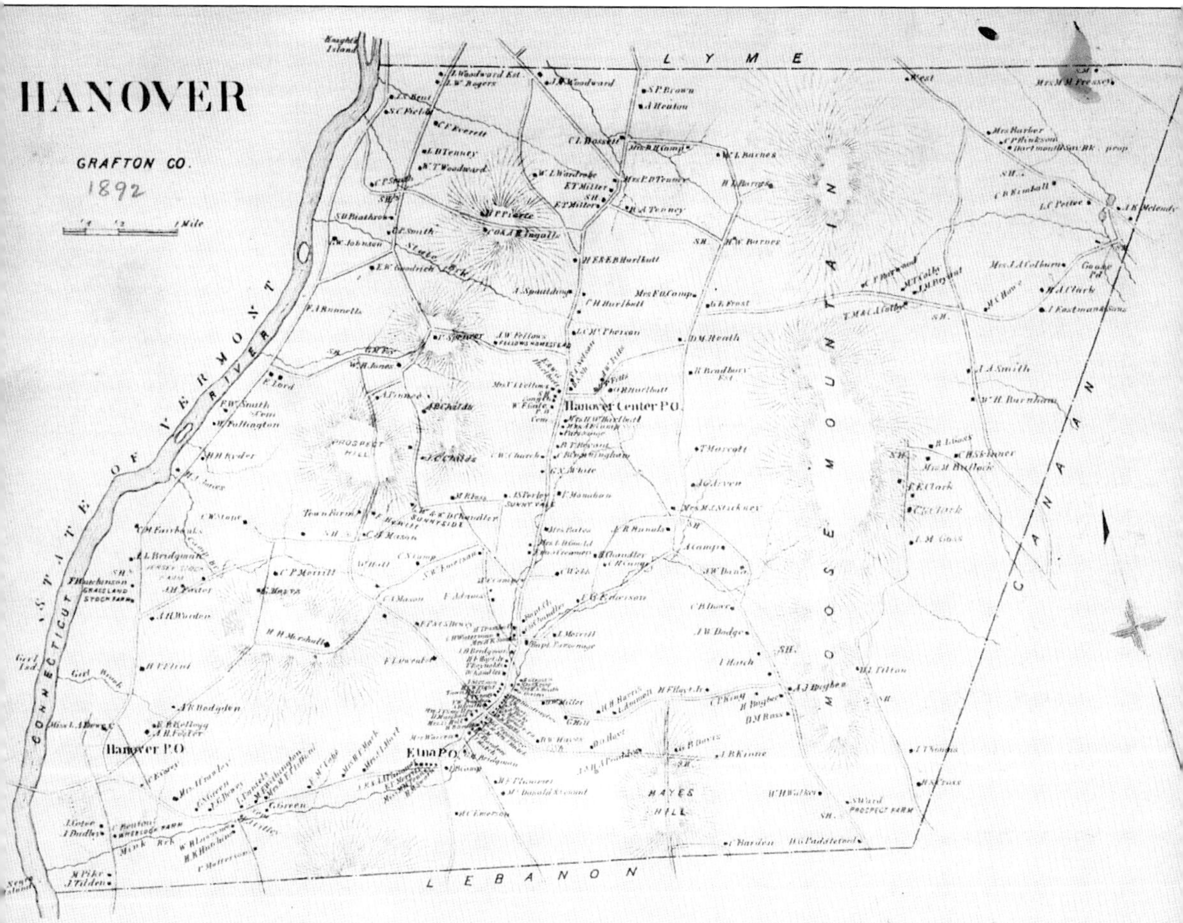

An 1892 map of Hanover, New Hampshire, showing the entire town and its three village areas.

Contents

Acknowledgments

The author would like to thank the following people who have so generously made pictorial material available for my use in compiling this book: Ethel (Elder) Hayes, Gordon Hayes, Tim Bent, Richard Baughman, Elaine Bent, Phoebe (Storrs) Stebbins, Velda (LaBombard) Dickinson, Valma (Fogg) LeBrun, David Nutt, Lois Gardner, Hallie Buskey, Divina (Croall) Dana, Helen LaCoss, Peter Shumway, Edgar Mead, Gladys (Trumbull) Bacon, Barbara Pelton, Macky (Bolleo) Clark, Regina Stanhope, Lois Stanhope, Margaret Boyd Braman, Holly (Fullington) Forward, Glenn Elder, Lester LaBombard, Eunice (Poland) Ballam, Dexter Pierce, Millie (West) Farnham, Sam Doyle, Dorothy Hood, the Hanover Water Works Company, the State of New Hampshire Department of Transportation, and the Dartmouth College Archives.

Hanover: The Rural Community

Armed conflict between Britain and France would continue to rage for several more years on the battlefields of Europe, a continuation of the so-called North American French and Indian Wars; however, by the winter of 1760, New Hampshire's Royal Governor Benning Wentworth thought the Upper Connecticut River Valley safe enough to start once again laying plans for its permanent settlement.

Wentworth, colonial governor from 1741 to 1766, considered as part of New Hampshire, all of present-day Vermont; and towards that end, commissioned a survey of the Connecticut River Valley that winter, roughly laying out towns on both sides of the river in 6-mile square blocks starting at Fort Number 4 (present-day Charlestown, New Hampshire), and stretching as far north as the "Great Co-os Meadows"—today Newbury, Vermont, and Haverhill, New Hampshire.

At about that same time, in December 1760, two gentlemen from Mansfield, Connecticut, Joseph Storrs and Edmund Freeman Jr., laid before the governor a petition seeking land in the Connecticut River Valley, in what would eventually come to be known as Hanover, New Hampshire. By early summer of 1761, Wentworth acted; and on July 4, 1761, five town charters received his provincial seal—the first of more than 100 that would soon follow. In addition to Hanover, the adjacent towns of Lebanon, Enfield, Hartford, and Norwich were created on paper that day in the far off capital at Portsmouth, in the British colony of New Hampshire.

The name Hanover was taken from the Connecticut town of Norwich that had a parish within its borders commonly referred to as "Hannover." Although the original charter had the town's name spelled with the double "n," the superfluous letter was soon dropped.

Prior to the spring of 1765, the newly chartered town had only been visited during the more seasonable months of the year by surveying groups and work parties from the lower Connecticut colony, whose job it was to start dividing the town into lots and begin the arduous task of clearing certain small areas of the densely wooded terrain. The first permanent settler was 28-year-old Edmund Freeman III, who journeyed up the river from Mansfield with his wife and two children—one of them three years of age and the other an infant of eight months. The Freemans assumed residency in a hastily constructed log house about a half mile from the river in the northwestern corner of the town, not far from the border with the neighboring town of Lyme. Soon other settlers followed, and by 1770, five years later, there were about 20 families busily clearing land and calling Hanover their home.

The earliest settlement did not take place at the village that grew up around the college, now referred to as "downtown" Hanover, on the banks of the Connecticut River, but rather out in the area of town adjacent to the westerly slopes of Moose Mountain, out where the headwaters of Mink Brook came together with enough velocity to power the first saw and gristmills that Hanover's settlers so urgently required. It was these upland, hardwood-covered slopes, overlooking the river valley below, that Hanover's first families, mostly from lower Connecticut, settled. Huntingtons, Hayes, Spencers, and Lords established farms on hills that to this day still bear the families' names. Tenneys, Wrights, and Emersons settled on the slopes of Moose Mountain; while Chandlers, Bentons, and Wests built in the high foothill area of Moose Mountain, later referred to as the Arvin District. Masons, Curtices, and Thomases established their claims to the gently rolling slopes around Pinneo Hill that more then a century later would become part of Hanover's reservoir. The high land near to the village of Hanover Center was cleared by the Freemans, Camps, Hurbutts, Dows, and Fellows; and slightly beyond this settlement, the Slades, Millers, Topliffes, and Storrses settled the area to be long known as the North Neighborhood.

The great virgin forests were cleared and burned—each year opening up more of the wilderness to the establishment of post-colonial Yankee civilization. Often, the smoke from the burning lands would be so dense and black as to obscure the sun from view by mid-day; and at night in the high hills the fires would present a view described by folks as sublime and terrific.

Prior to 1884, Etna Village was commonly referred to as "Mill Neighborhood," or "Mill Village," the result of the numerous small water-powered mills that were constructed along the banks of Mink Brook. However, with the establishment of a post office and the realization that other New Hampshire towns also had a "Mill Village" within their borders, the name was changed, at the suggestion of Miss Laura A. Camp, to Etna, taken from an Aetna Insurance calendar hanging on the post office wall. The "A" was dropped so that folks would not think the name misspelled! It was here in Etna Village that the annual town meeting was held, the town clerk could be found, the selectmen met, and the town's highway equipment was kept.

Hanover Center, close to (in fact, being in) the geographical center of the town, owes its existence as much to the first meetinghouse being located there as for any other reason. Always a small, quiet settlement, it is the very epitome of the hillside hamlet that, although once long ago boasting of a post office and a store, for so many years since time has passed by.

As villages became established within the town of Hanover, including the settlement that grew up around fledgling Dartmouth College soon after it arrived in August 1770, the outlying land continued to be cleared for agriculture by rural families, and an agrarian culture took hold and lightly prospered—not unlike elsewhere in northern New England. In fact, it often appeared that there existed two distinct cultures within the town, side by side: the village at the college and all the rest of the town.

And so Hanover remained, into the twentieth century, a rural community with the exception of a college within the southeast corner of its boundaries. The pastoral, agrarian character found illustrated within the pages of this book is in many ways typical of the Upper Connecticut River Valley as it existed not too many generations ago. Yet to those of us who knew some of these people and their families, it was a special time and place, worthy of recollection and tribute.

One

Heading Out into the Country

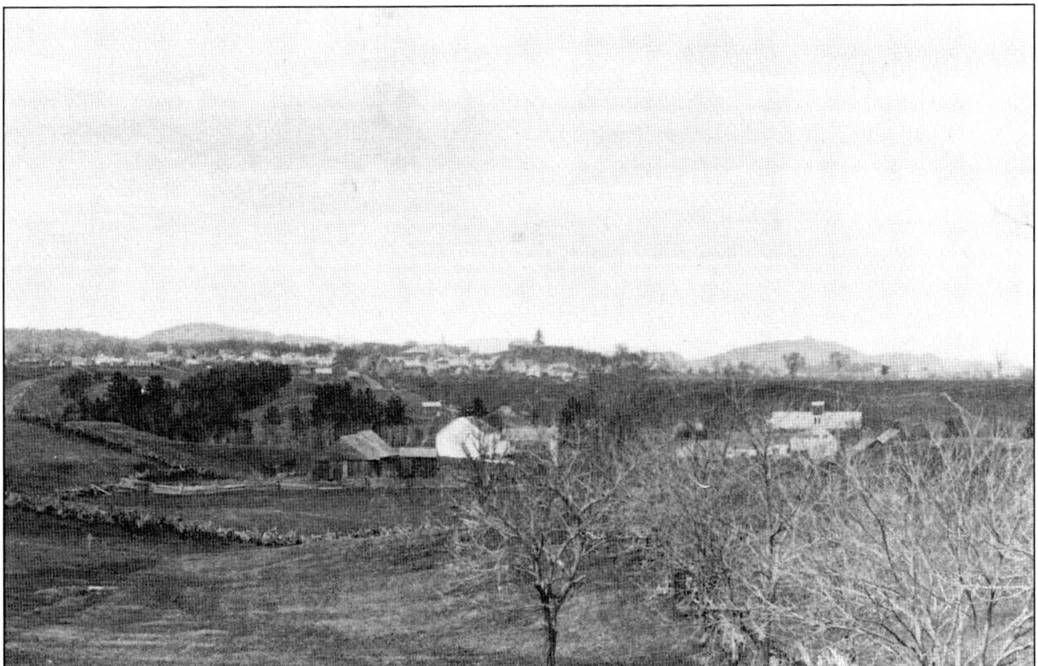

The village of Hanover is seen in the distance of this early photograph taken in 1871 looking north from the West Lebanon Road. Note the primitive stump fence along the road, remaining from colonial times when the land was first cleared. In the mid-ground are Monroe Pike's 90-acre farm, and Joseph Tilden's 117-acre spread. Today this is the Wyeth Road/Dunster Drive neighborhood. In the far right can be seen the large barn of the Benton farm situated adjacent to Mink Brook.

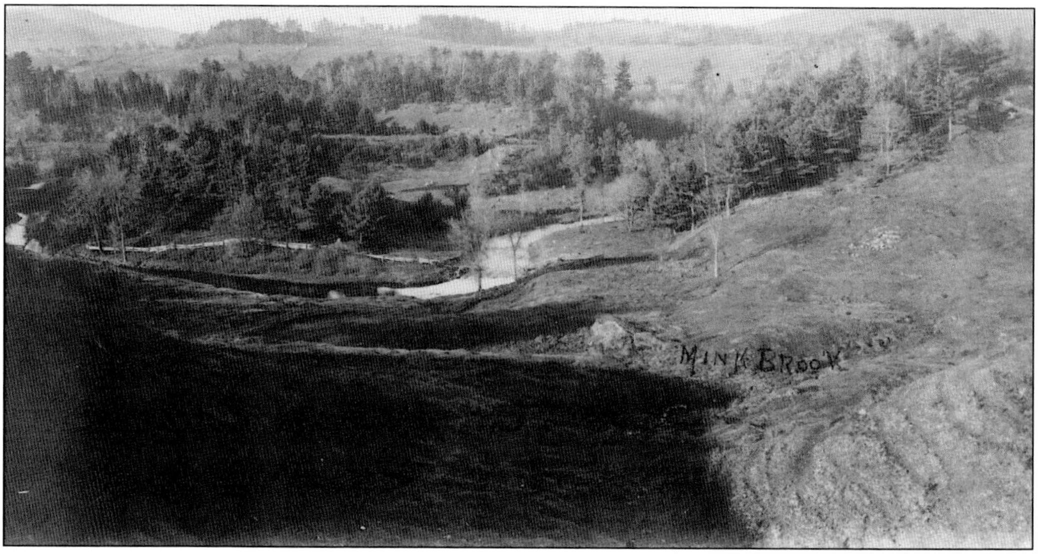

This is a later nineteenth-century view of Mink Brook looking from Pleasant Street. To the left is now located the Pine Knoll Cemetery; and just beyond the bluff to the right is the present Hanover Waste Water Treatment Plant. Since 1950, and the completion of Wilder Dam on the Connecticut River, all of the meadows on both sides of the brook have been flooded and are now under water.

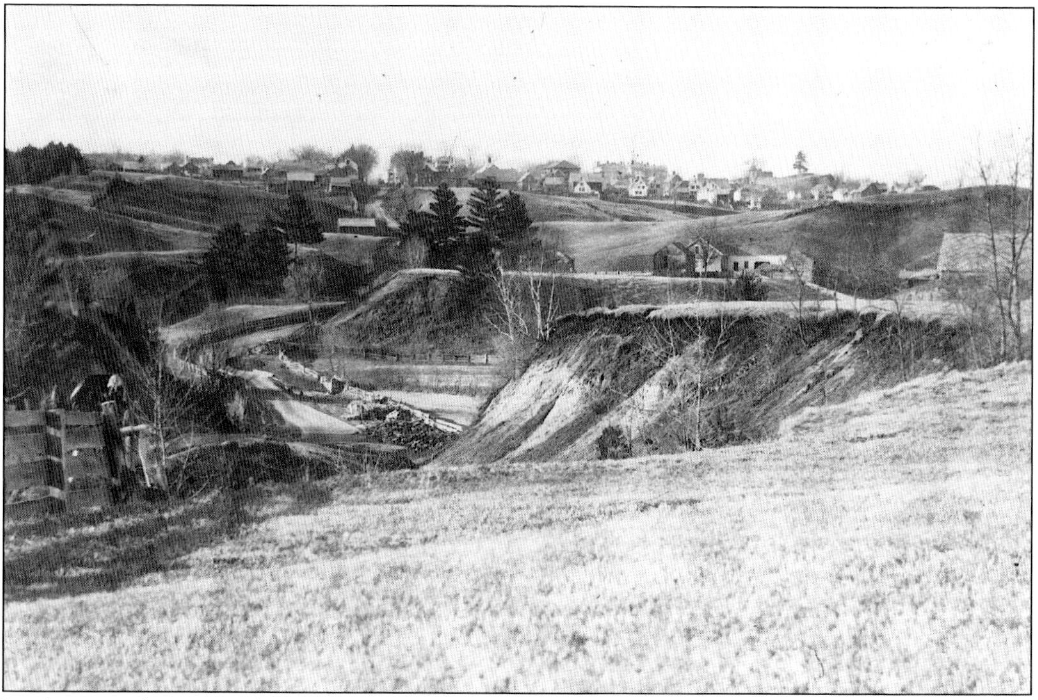

Looking north in 1868 from the present-day Mourlyn Road area, this view shows West Lebanon Road winding its way across the meadows along Mink Brook. To the left is the Charles Benton farm—the brick farmhouse is still standing today at 104 South Main Street. In the distance is the village and Dartmouth College.

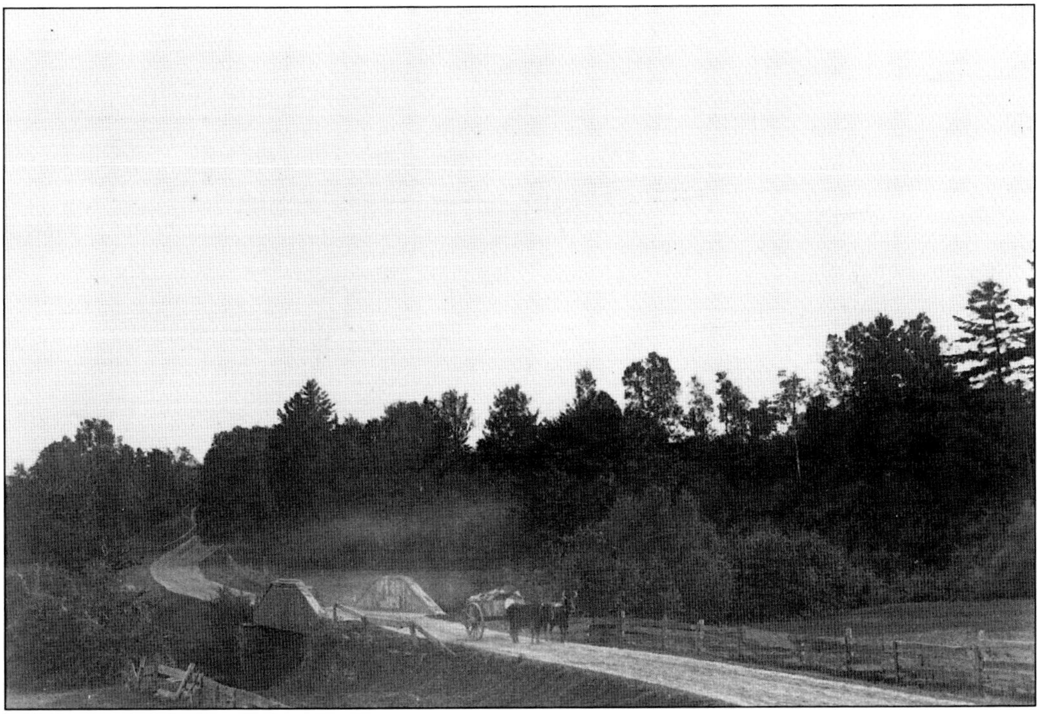

This is a view taken in the early fall of 1888 looking south along the West Lebanon Road. In the foreground are the fields of Charles Benton's farm and the wooden bridge across Mink Brook. The present-day Pine Knoll Cemetery occupies the right-hand bluff; and the Mourlyn Road neighborhood is to the left.

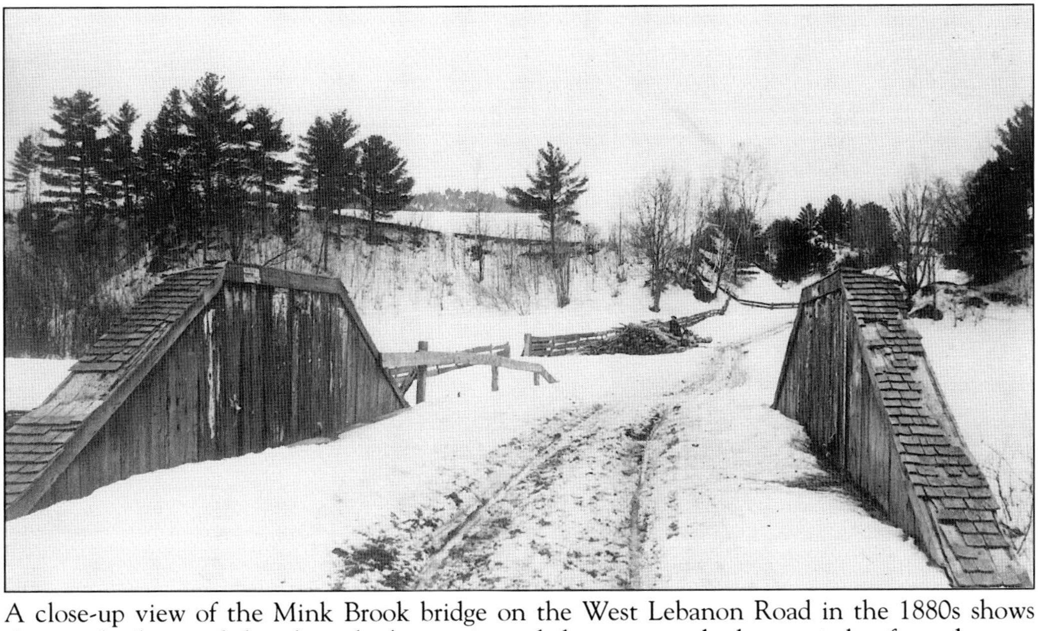

A close-up view of the Mink Brook bridge on the West Lebanon Road in the 1880s shows the wood siding and shingles, which were intended to protect the heavy timber-framed queen post truss bridge structure—typical of the era preceding structural steel and the advent of the automobile age.

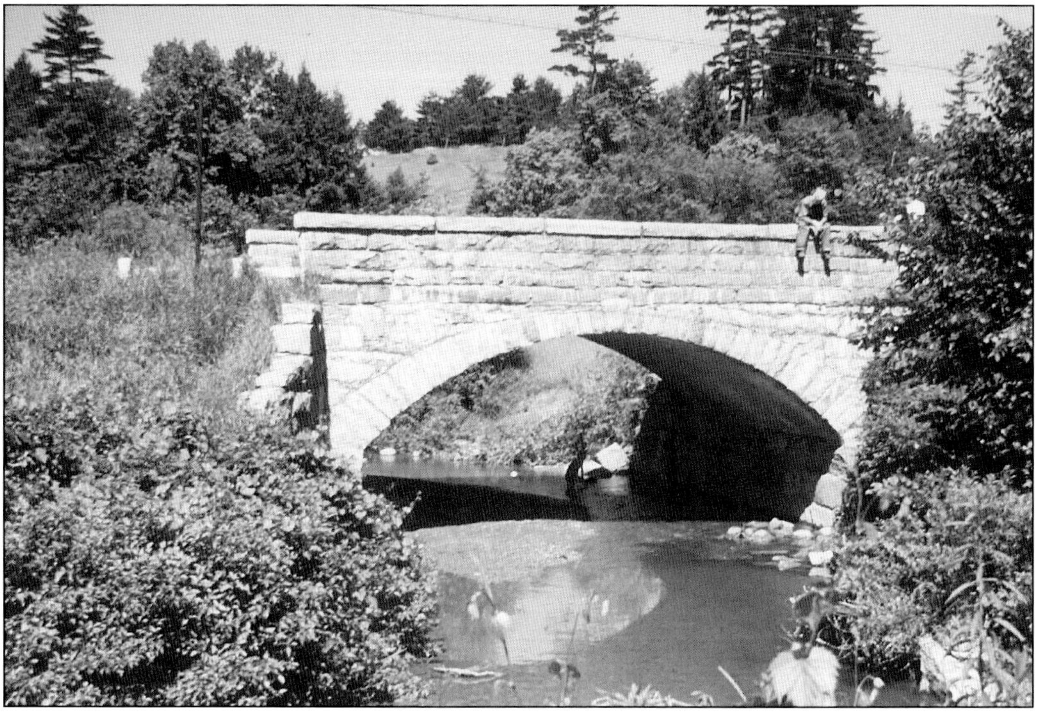

During the summer of 1914, a new stone bridge was constructed across Mink Brook on the West Lebanon Road (see page 40, Volume 1 of this series). However, a mere 26 years later, it was again replaced—this time when the highway was relocated. This view looking west was taken just prior to the bridge's demolition in 1940.

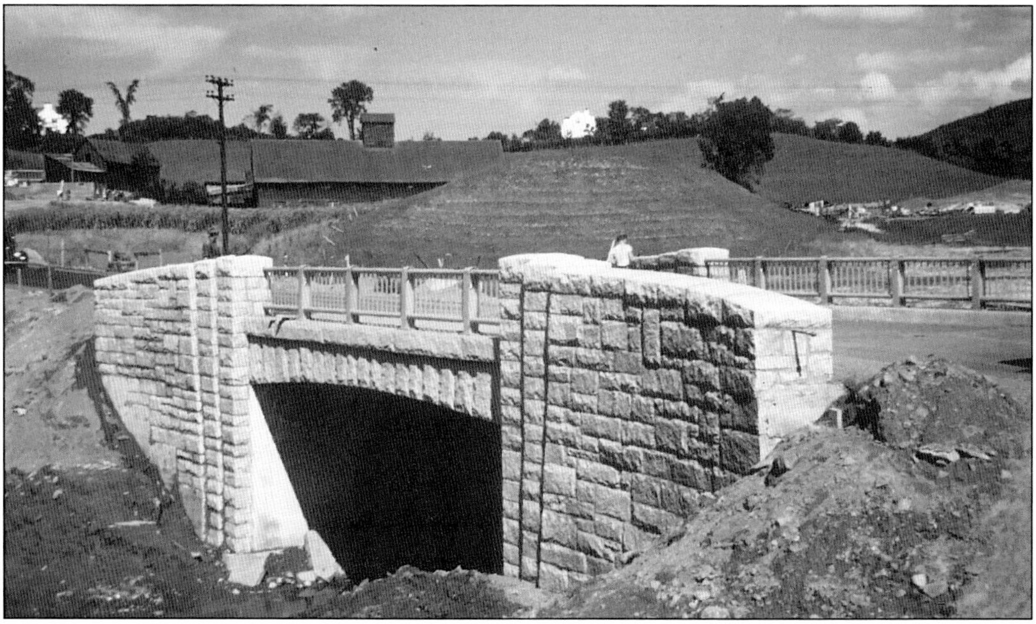

The new Mink Brook bridge appears here just after completion in 1940. With a new bridge and a relocated road, the stream location was also altered and straightened out. In the distance is the Benton farm, by then owned by the Charles Stone family.

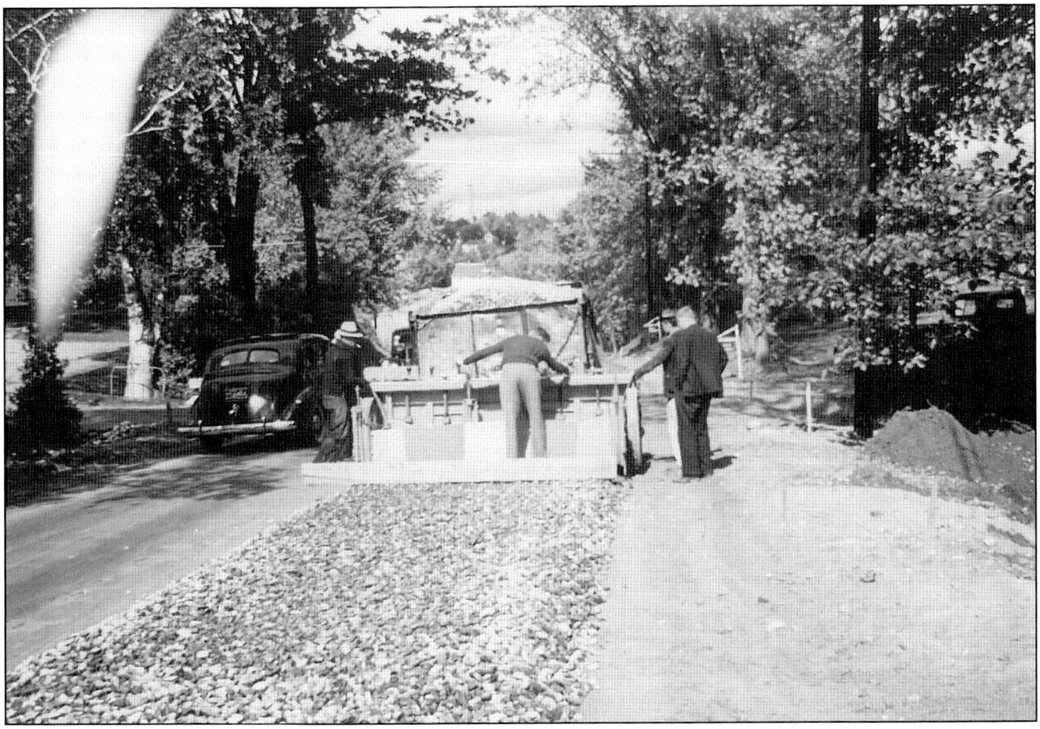

In this photograph, showing modern road building in 1940 just prior to World War II, crushed stone is being spread on the rebuilt West Lebanon Road opposite the entrance to the Wyeth Road neighborhood to the left. Once the stone had been laid down, a thick layer of tar was then applied.

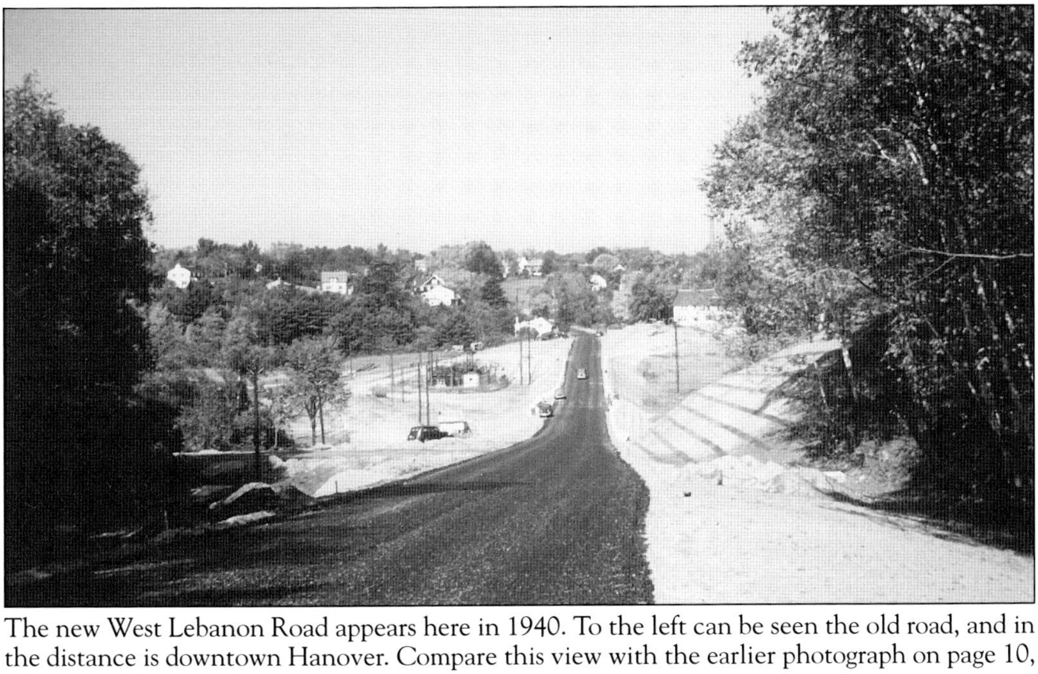

The new West Lebanon Road appears here in 1940. To the left can be seen the old road, and in the distance is downtown Hanover. Compare this view with the earlier photograph on page 10, taken in 1868 from almost the same location.

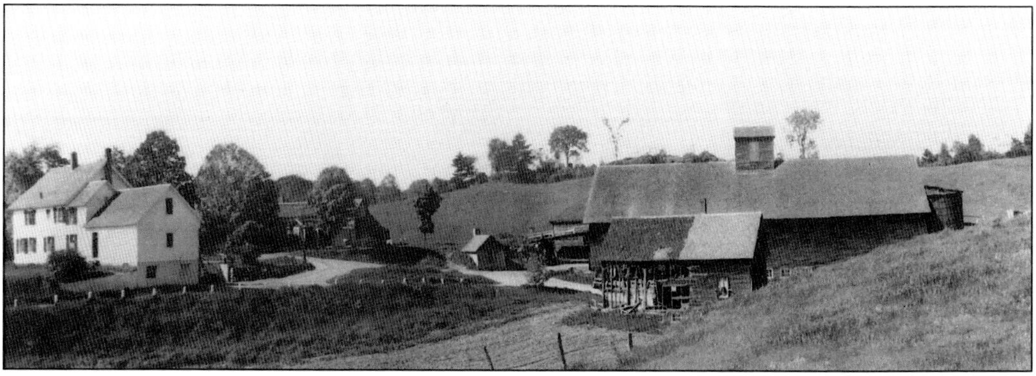

The Charles Stone farm in 1948 is seen here just prior to the large four-story barn being taken down. Charles Benton originally constructed the four-story, 135-by-45-foot barn in 1852. The white farmhouse had been moved in 1940, when the West Lebanon Road was relocated, and it is still standing at 104 South Main Street.

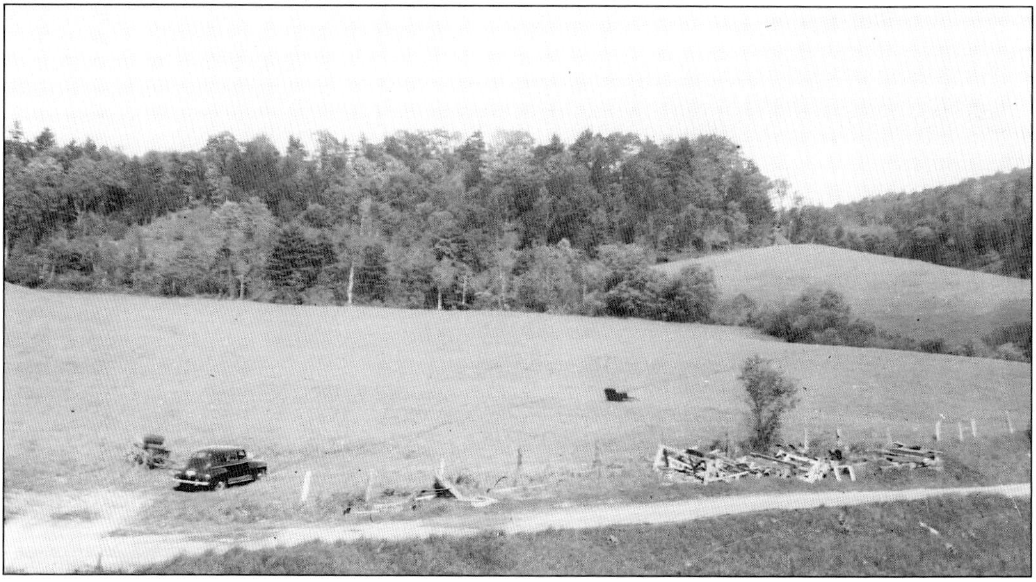

The Mitchell Lane neighborhood now occupies these fields shown in this 1948 view taken looking east from beside the Stone farm barn. The old sleigh was left from the auction of all the farm equipment when the property was sold that year for development.

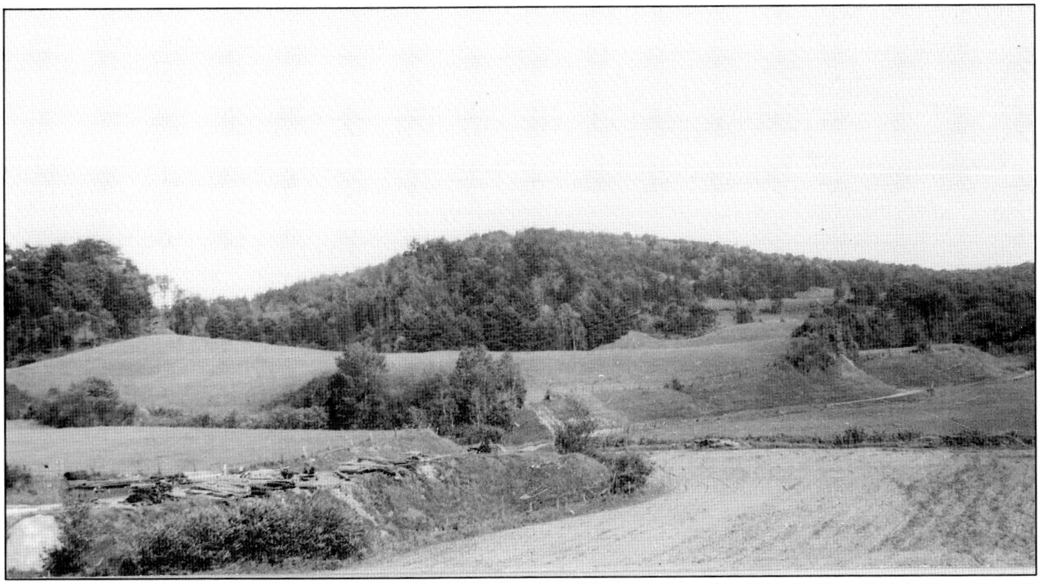

This is another view taken from the same location looking up the Mink Brook Valley. Brook Road now runs through the meadows in the foreground. At one time under the Benton family's ownership, this farm had 324 contiguous acres, 175 of which were in Hanover; and they grazed more then 225 head of Merino sheep.

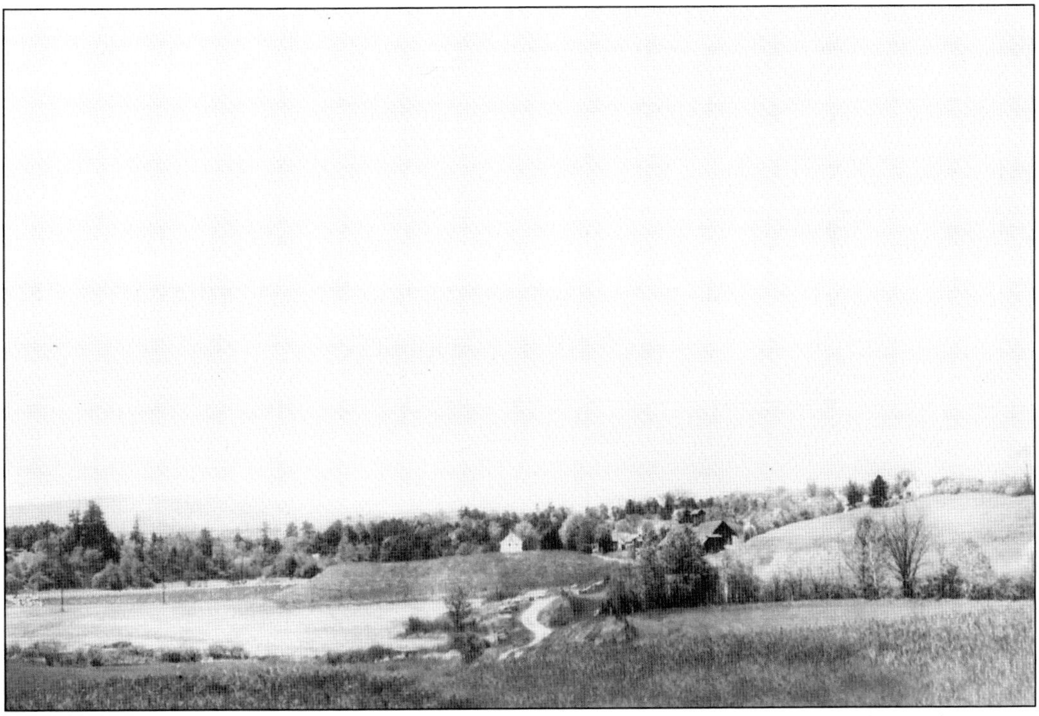

Looking west in 1948 from the bluff of present-day 10 Brook Road, this view shows the Stone farm buildings in the distance. To the left are the meadows along Mink Brook and the West Lebanon Road cutting across them.

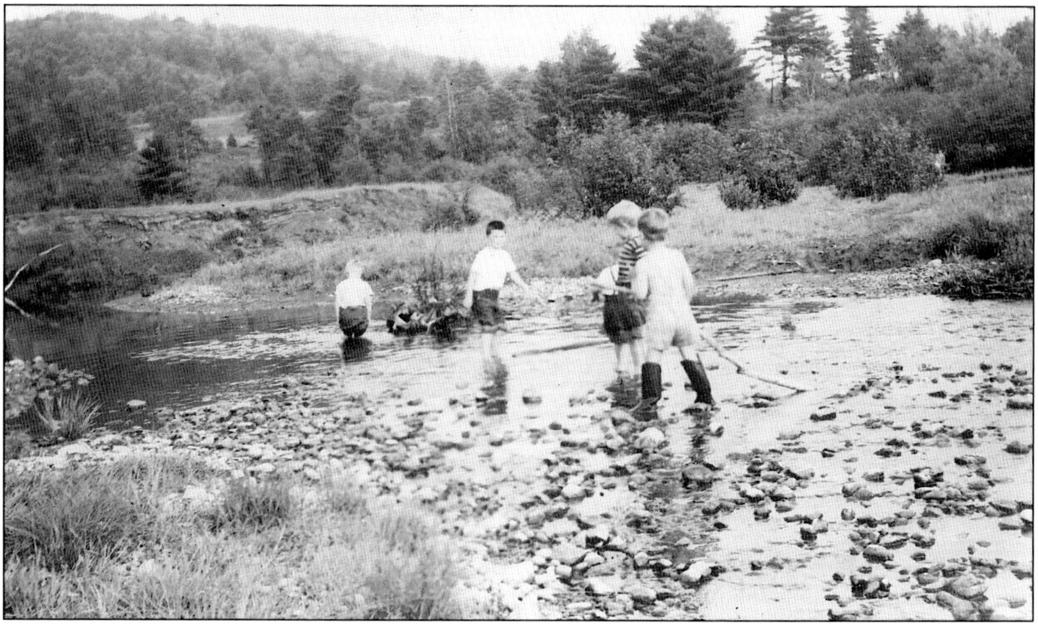

Children of the Barrett and Ransmeier families are playing in Mink Brook during a summer picnic in 1948 at the Stone Farm. To the right of this view, years before, was once located a water-powered mill structure, built in the early days of the town's settlement. Today the earthen dikes are still visible in the meadows along the south side of the brook.

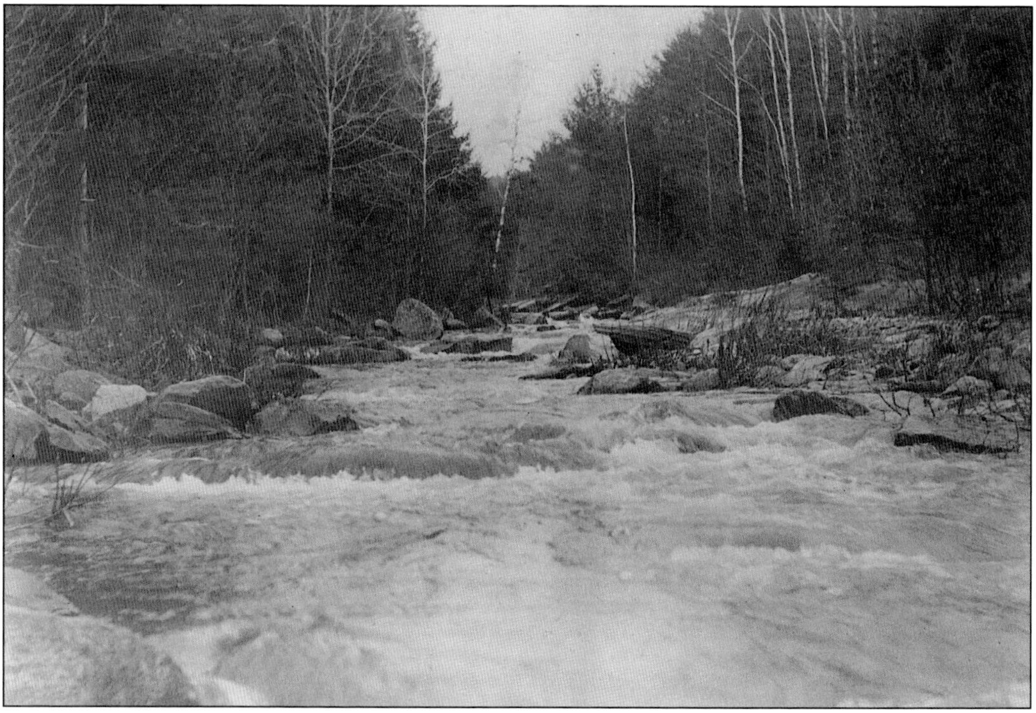

This view of Mink Brook shown just downstream of the present-day Tanzi Preserve was photographed in the 1880s. Due to conservation efforts of the Barrett and Ransmeier families, this view and the two following have changed little in more than 100 years.

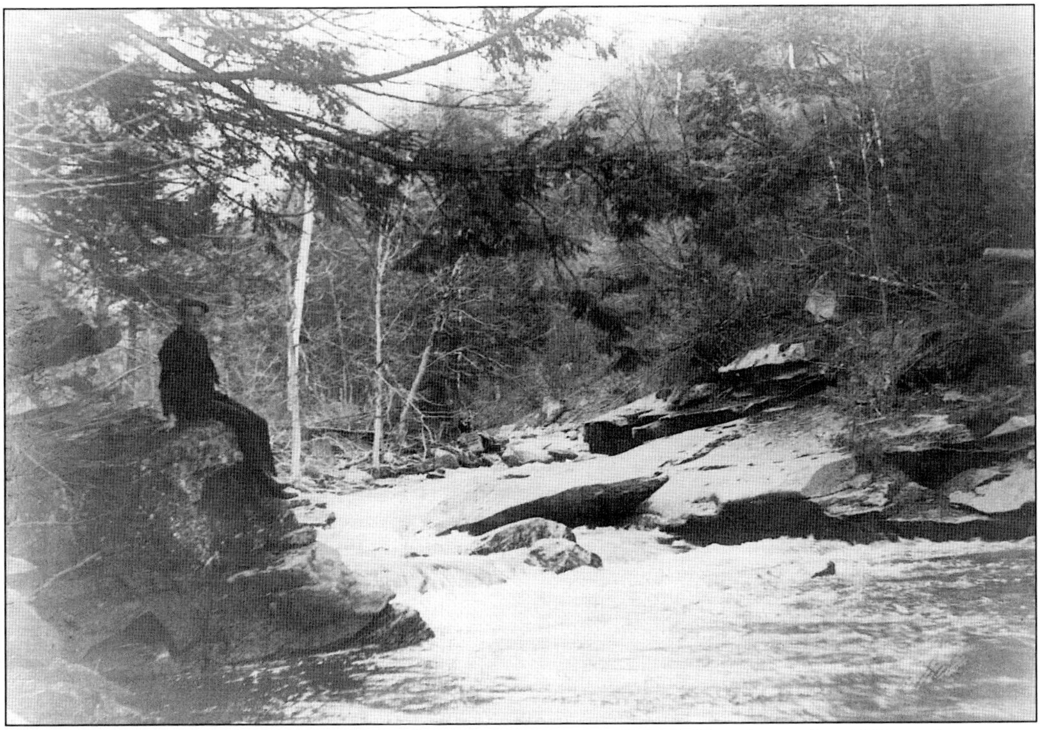

This is a companion photograph to the previous view—Mink Brook in the 1880s adjacent to the Tanzi Preserve Area. Wrote Hanover historian Frederick Chase in 1891 of Mink Brook, "It was in early days a large and handsome stream, well stocked with trout and with mink, as its name implies."

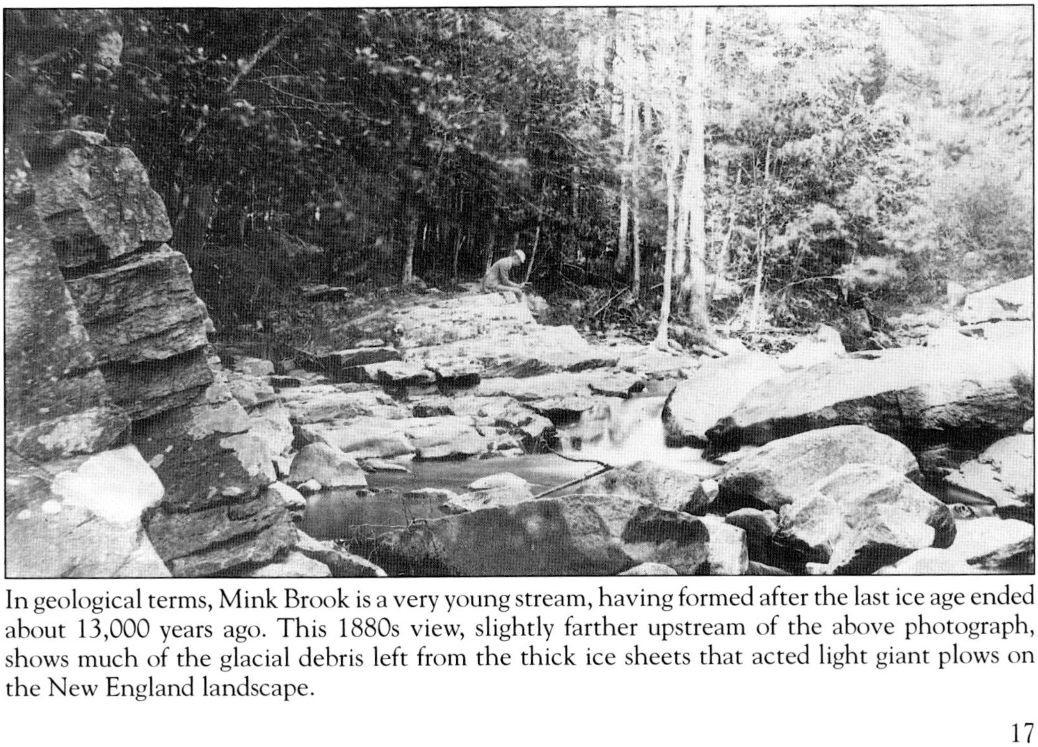

In geological terms, Mink Brook is a very young stream, having formed after the last ice age ended about 13,000 years ago. This 1880s view, slightly farther upstream of the above photograph, shows much of the glacial debris left from the thick ice sheets that acted light giant plows on the New England landscape.

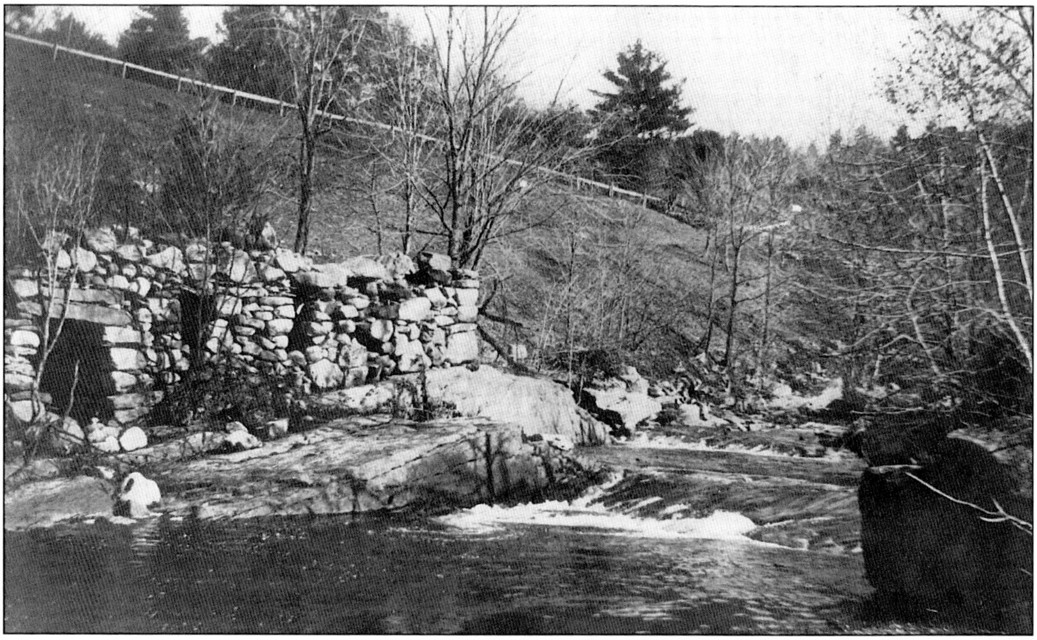

This early-twentieth-century view shows foundations that still remain from Dartmouth College's first saw and gristmills, built in 1771 and 1772, on Mink Brook just below Lebanon Street/Route 120. The wood guard rails along the road are visible above the brook.

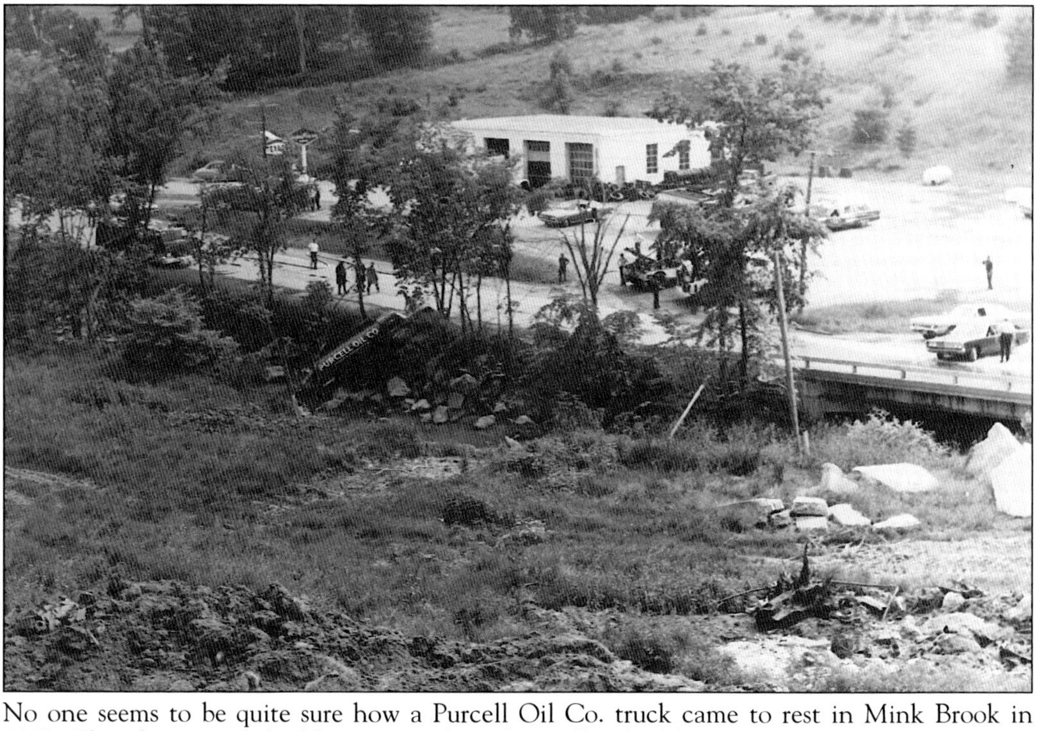

No one seems to be quite sure how a Purcell Oil Co. truck came to rest in Mink Brook in 1969. The white garage building is now (1998) an office building at 10 Buck Road, and a new highway has been constructed about where the photographer of this view was standing. In fact, clearing has already started in the foreground for the new road.

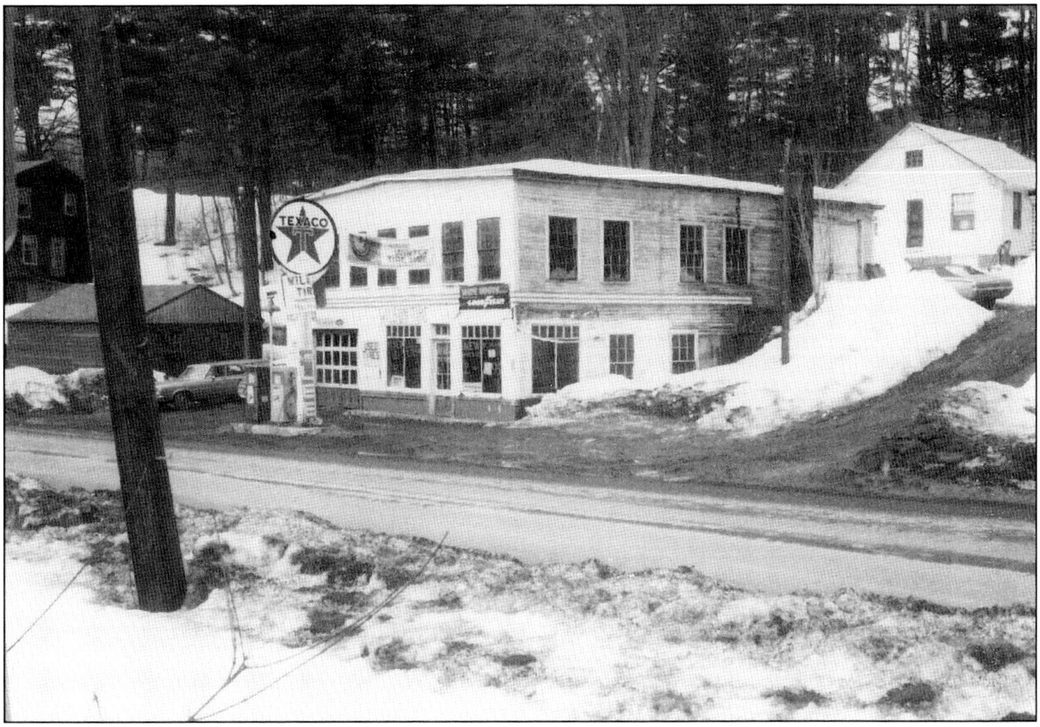

Prior to 1970, when much of Route 120 and its intersection with the Greensboro Road was rebuilt and relocated, there existed a small settlement of commercial and residential buildings located in the hollow where the two roads dangerously came together. For many years, this building was home to Ware's Garage.

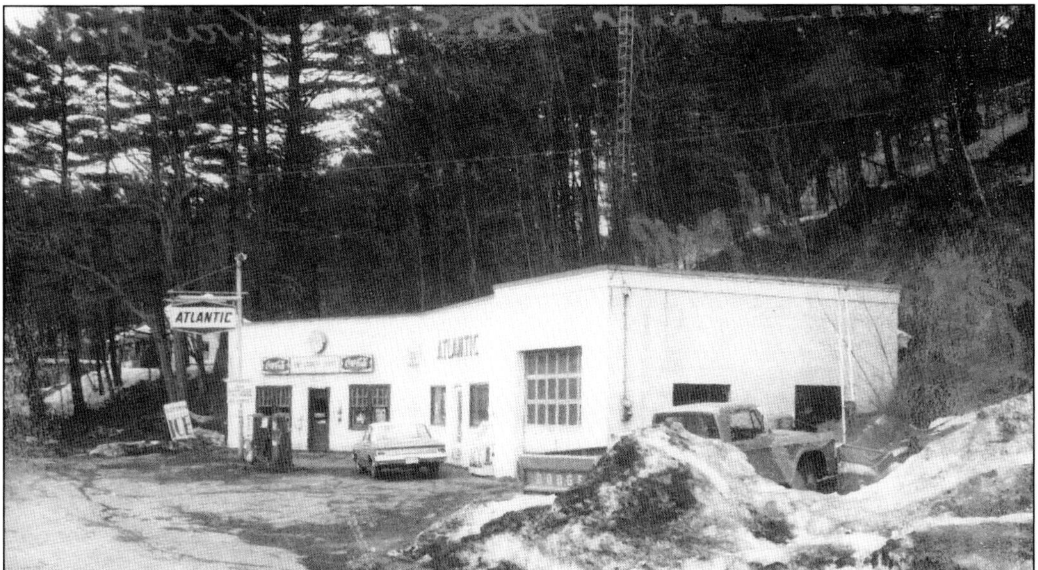

To the east of Ware's Garage was Jim Peavey's Corner Store, situated right at the intersection of Route 120 and the Greensboro Road. Today, the highway exists about 50 feet above the site of these two buildings; and a deadly section of road was eliminated.

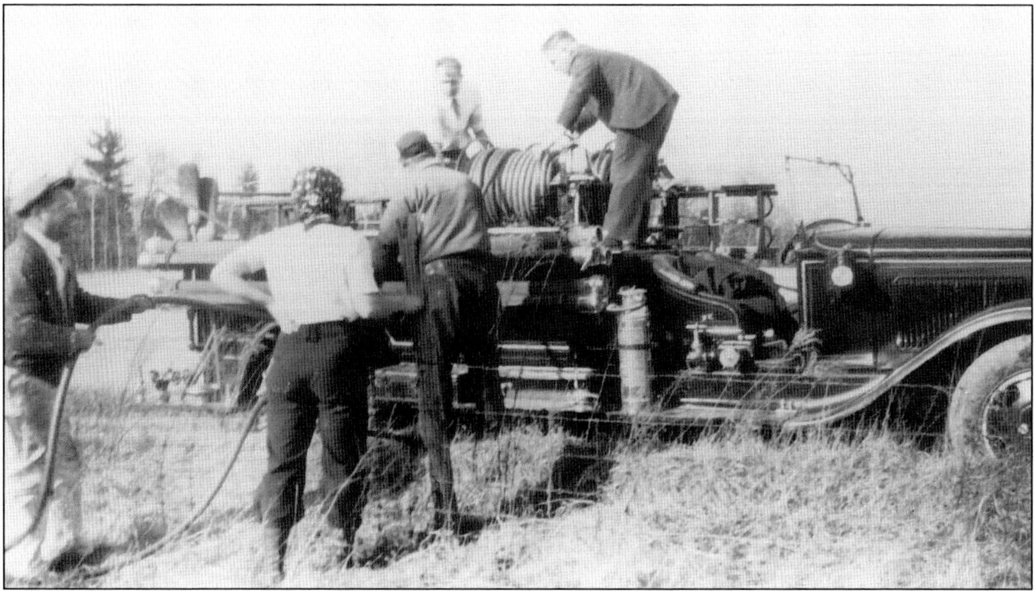

Through the 1950s and 1960s, the town dump was located out off from Route 120 in the so-called Gile Tract, near the site of the present-day Medical Center. From time-to-time, the mostly volunteer fire department had to be called out to extinguish out-of-control fires burning the trash. Here we see a crew with Hanover's 1930 Model A Ford firetruck.

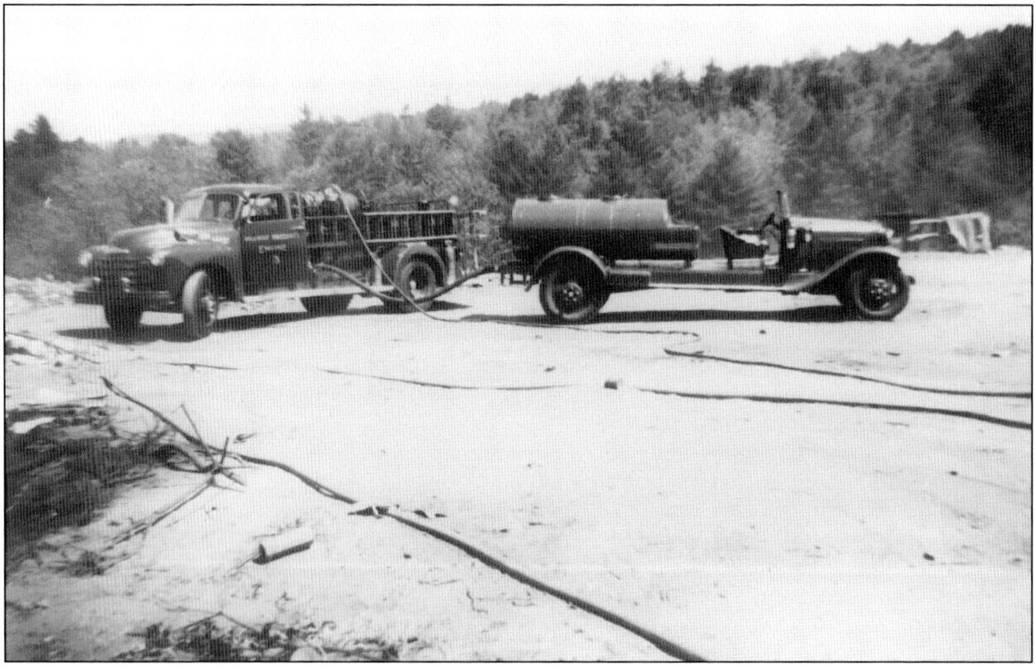

This is another view of the fire equipment taking care of a problem at the town dump, probably in the early 1960s. By then the 1930 Model A lived there pretty much on a permanent basis during the summer months. The village precinct's 1949 Chevrolet is assisting in this operation.

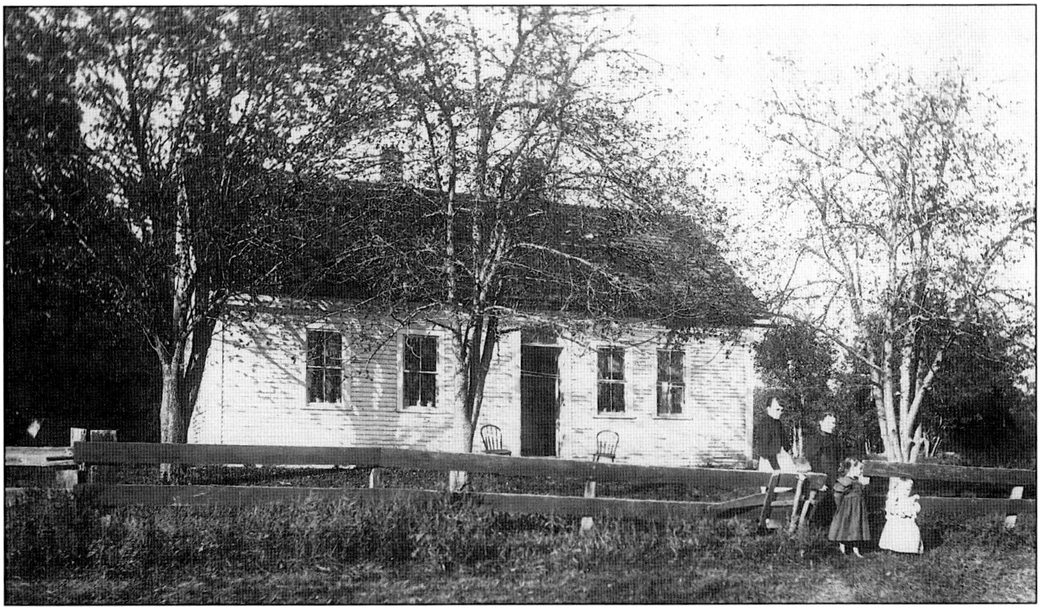

The date and builder of this early home is unknown; however, since 1941 it has been the residence of Ray and Velda Dickinson at 22 Greensboro Road. The names of the persons shown in this later nineteenth-century view are not known, although they might well have been the family who resided at the property when the photograph was taken.

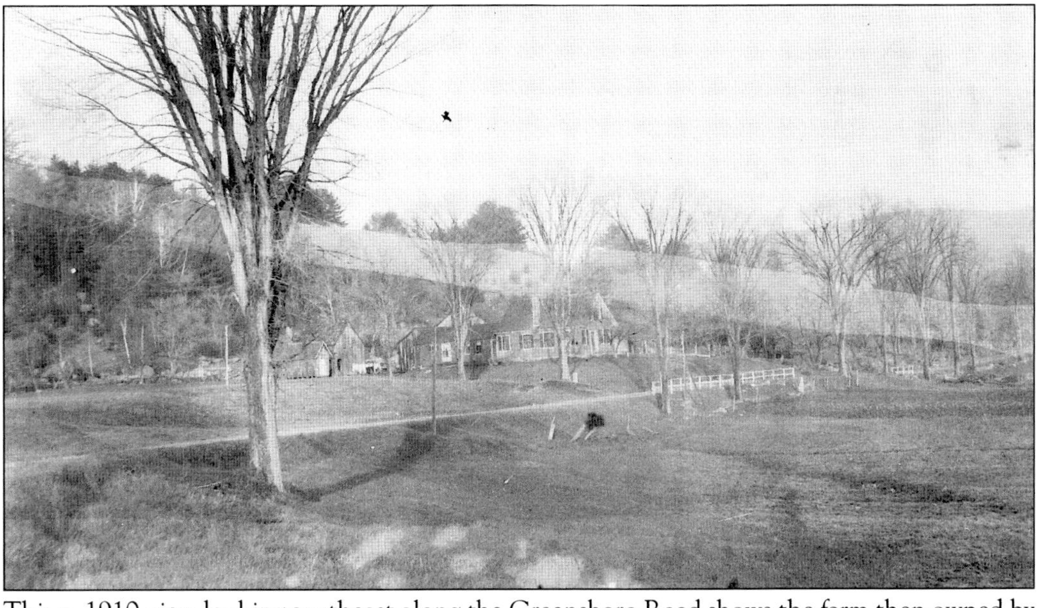

This *c.* 1910 view looking southeast along the Greensboro Road shows the farm then owned by John A. LaBombard. Today the brick farmhouse still stands at 110 Greensboro Road, and the meadows across the road from the house are still kept mowed and open to Mink Brook.

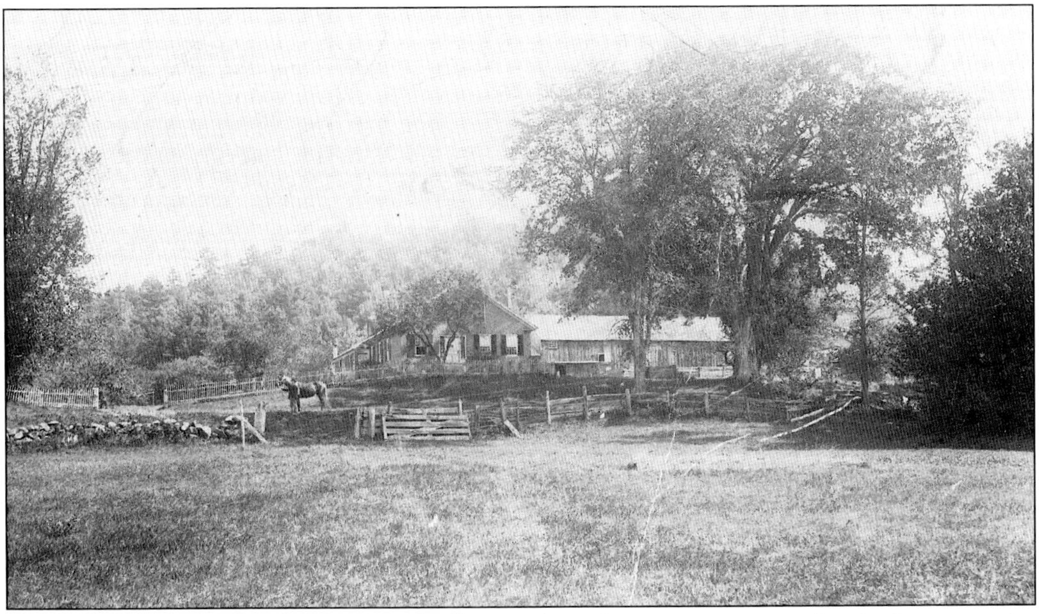

An earlier photograph of the LaBombard farm than the previous view, this looks across the meadows and Greensboro Road northerly toward the farmhouse and some of the outbuildings. To the right of this view was situated the main barn of this complex that at one time consisted of 380 acres of agricultural and woodlot land.

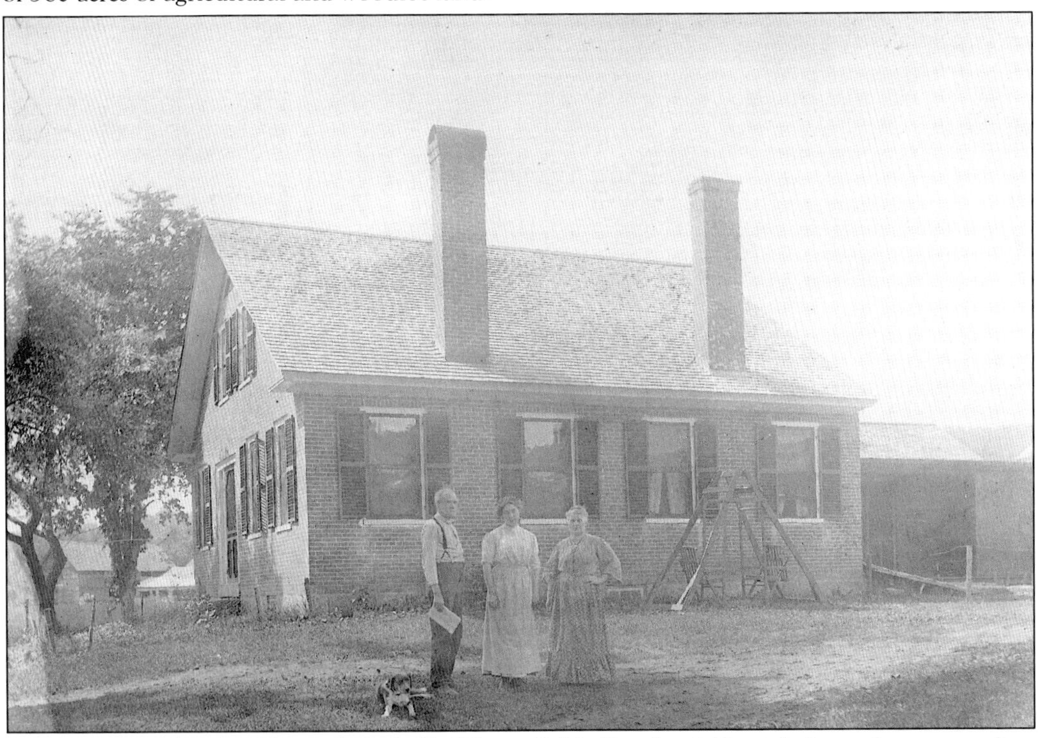

John A. LaBombard and his wife, Isabelle (Tourville) LaBombard (far right), are shown standing beside their brick farmhouse. The woman standing in the middle is Mrs. Samual LaBombard. To the far left can be seen the main barn beyond.

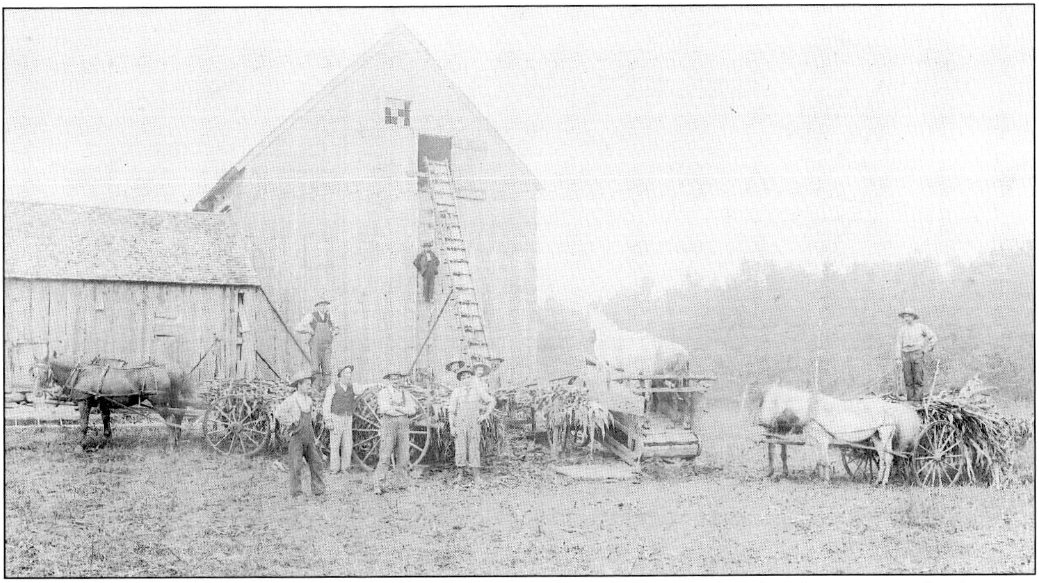

Two horses are providing motive power to the conveyor being used to load corn into the barn at the LaBombard farm. John and Isabelle LaBombard raised seven sons and one daughter on this farm that they owned and worked from about 1895 until 1933—shortly after John's death in the depths of the Great Depression.

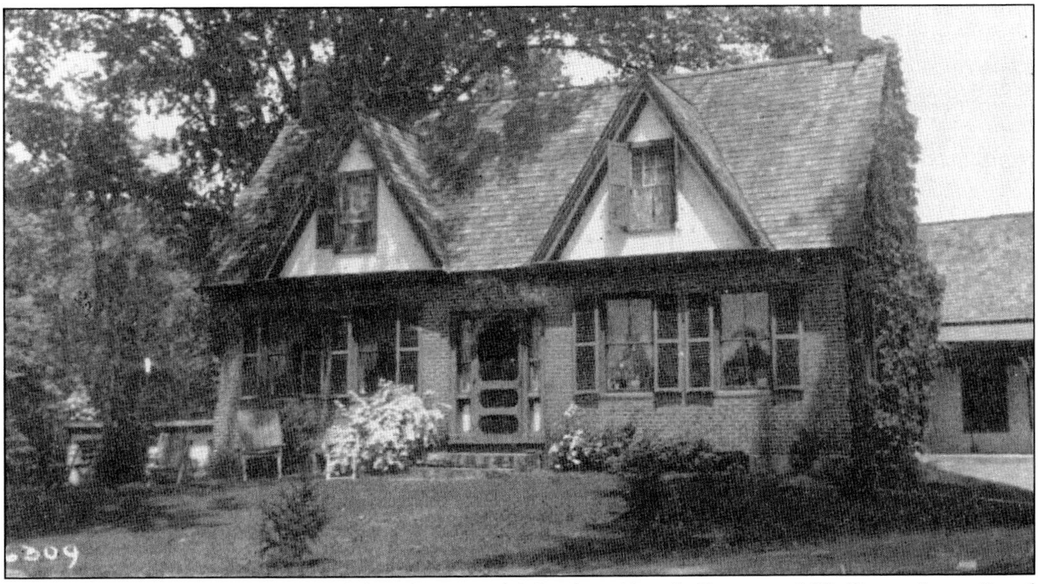

Two generations of the Merrill family owned Meadow Brook Farm at 150 Greensboro Road before selling it to Schyler and Marion Berry in the 1950s. This postcard view shows the farmhouse *c.* 1940, when Lester and Marion Merrill took in overnight guests. Today much of the land is part of the Berrill Farms condominium complex.

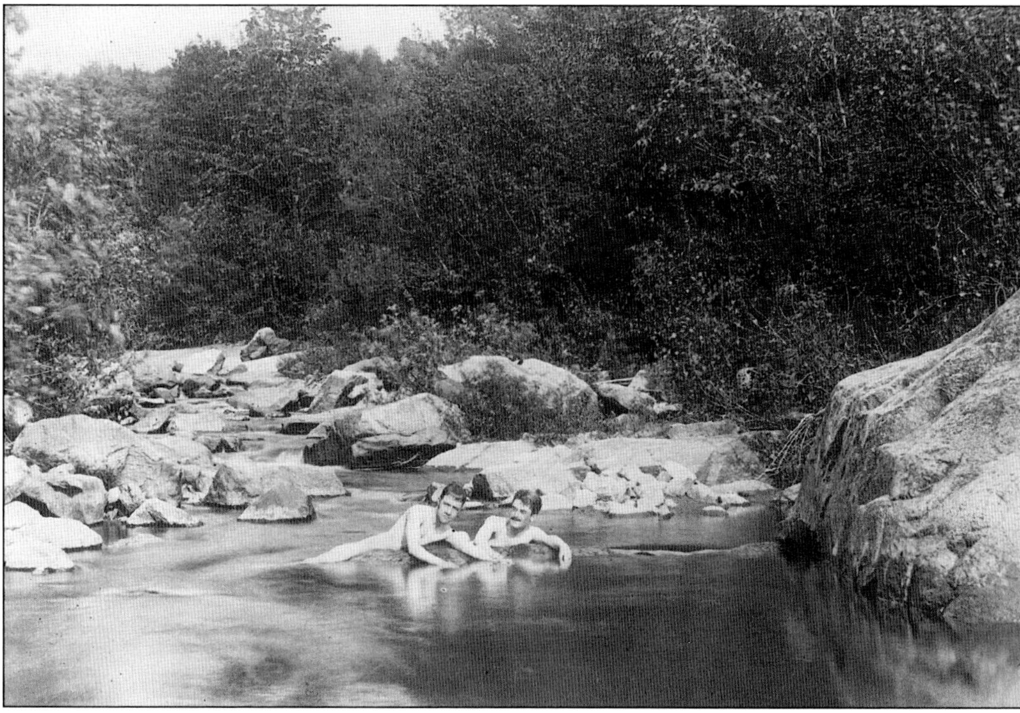

An 1880s view shows several young Dartmouth men swimming in one of the many pools made by Mink Brook as it winds through the meadows along the Greensboro Road. This photograph is thought to have been taken just upstream from the location near present-day Hollenbeck Lane of a Dartmouth College sawmill constructed in the early 1780s to supply building material for the first Dartmouth Hall.

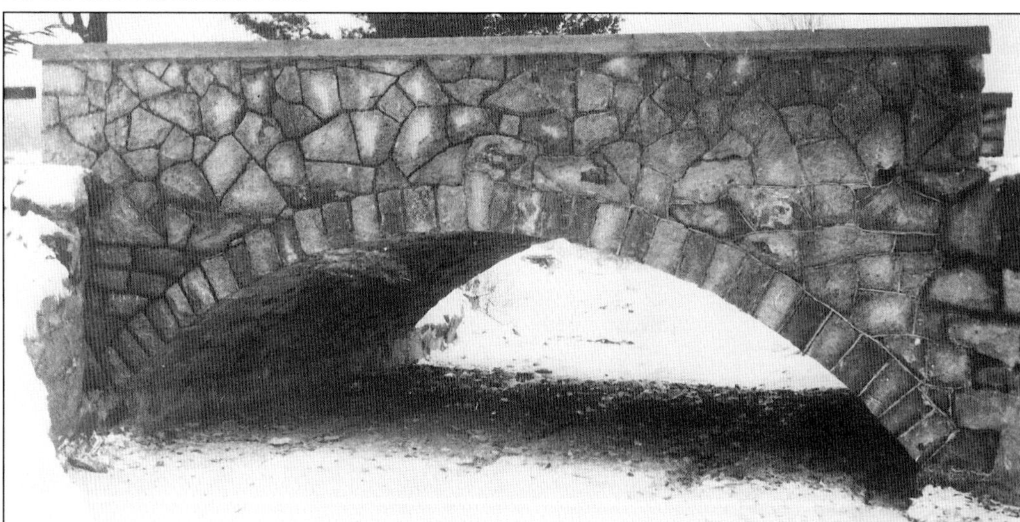

The so-called Great Hollow Road stone bridge over Mink Brook was constructed in 1914 by the Town of Hanover, after receiving prices from contractors that were beyond the available budget. At the time of the bridge's completion, Great Hollow and Greensboro Roads were the primary southern route into Hanover from the outside world. In 1996, this author placed the bridge on the National Register of Historic Places.

Two

Etna Village

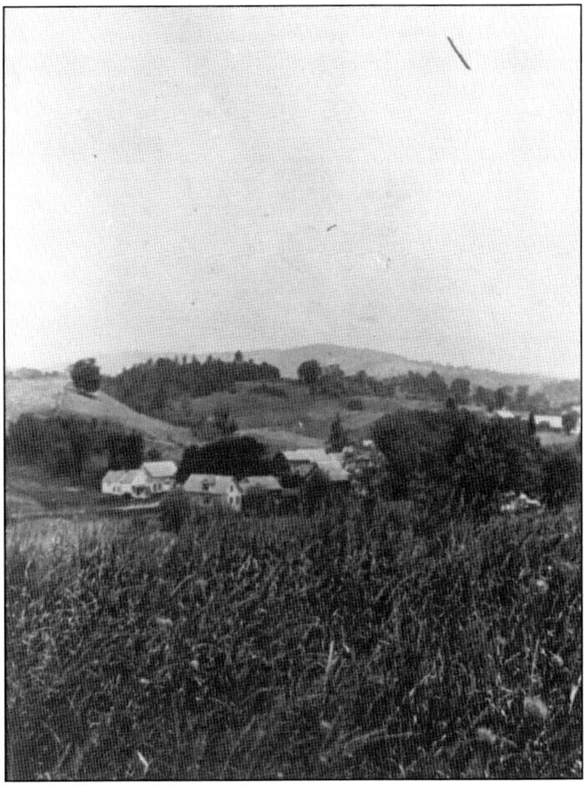

This photograph, taken in 1936 from up on Etna Highlands Road, looks north across the Mink Brook valley, and down onto the center of Etna Village. The two houses shown to the left of this view still stand at 98 and 97 Etna Road.

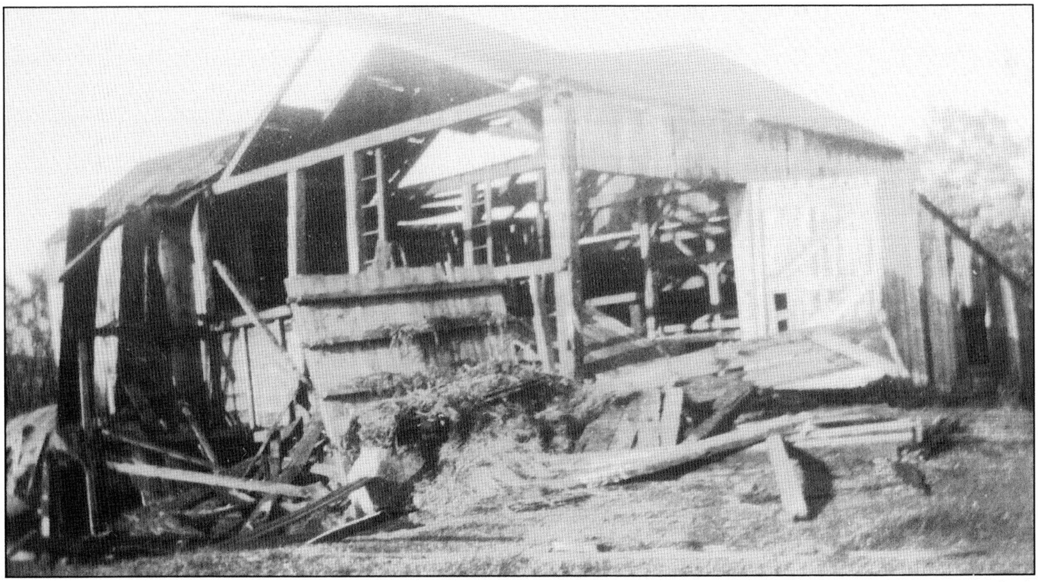

On September 22, 1938, the Upper Valley was visited by a hurricane that, in its wake, left behind a path of destruction of downed trees and made a mess out of Mary Cutting's barn, located at "Cuttings Corner"—the intersection of Greensboro and Etna Roads.

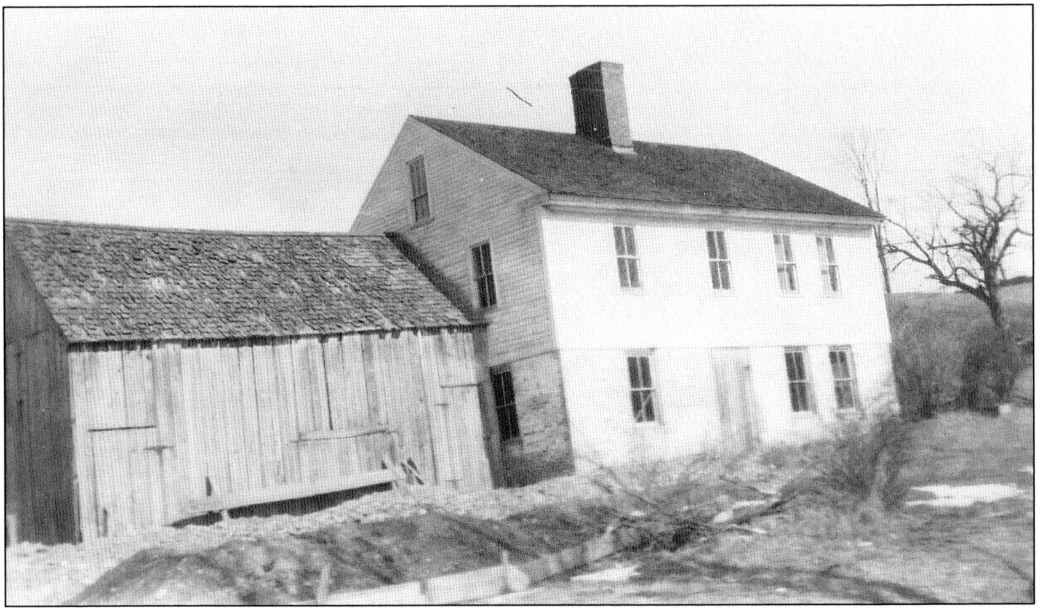

Very little appears to be known now about this curious early farmhouse with its brick lower story. A Mrs. Warren lived at the premises in 1892, and in 1915, young Walter Harrison Trumbull bought the property from the Sanborns for $1,600 as a site for his new house. A year later the old building was torn down, and today the Trumbull-House Bed and Breakfast occupies the site at 40 Etna Road.

Walter Harrison Trumbull was only several months old when his father, Harrison Trumbull, moved from Canaan to Etna Village in 1889. At age 20, Walter became a self-employed carpenter, establishing the contracting business in 1914 that would late become Trumbull-Nelson Construction Company, located in downtown Hanover. For a brief time, from 1916 to 1918, "Harry," or "Trump," as he was affectionately known by his workmen, also owned and operated the general store in Etna Village with his brother Myron. Mr. Trumbull passed away in 1977 at age 89. He was perhaps age ten when this photograph was taken.

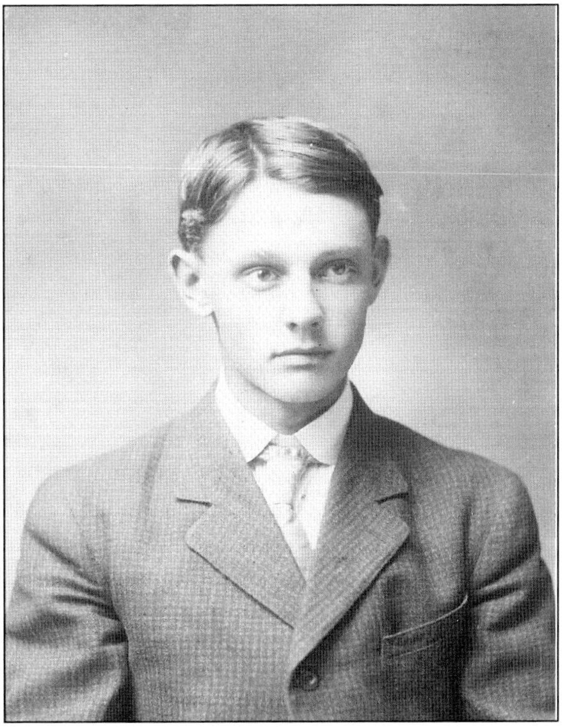

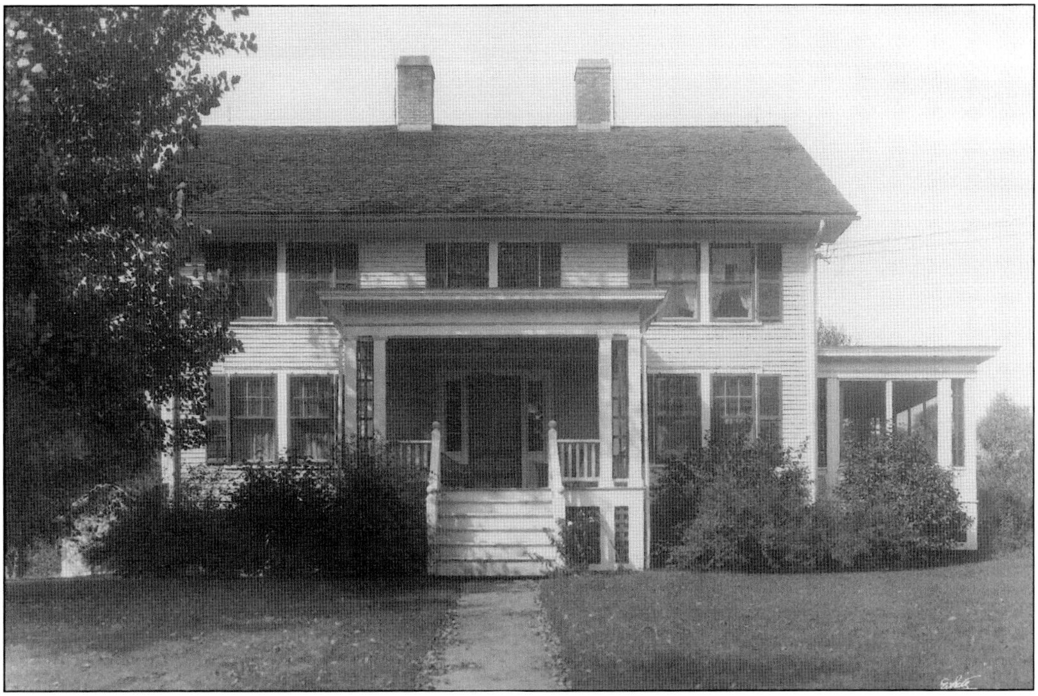

Mr. Trumbull began construction of his new home in 1917; however, because of material shortages due to World War I, construction was not completed until 1921. For many years this was the most substantial and best kept house in the village—the residence of a very successful building contractor. This professional photograph was taken in 1937.

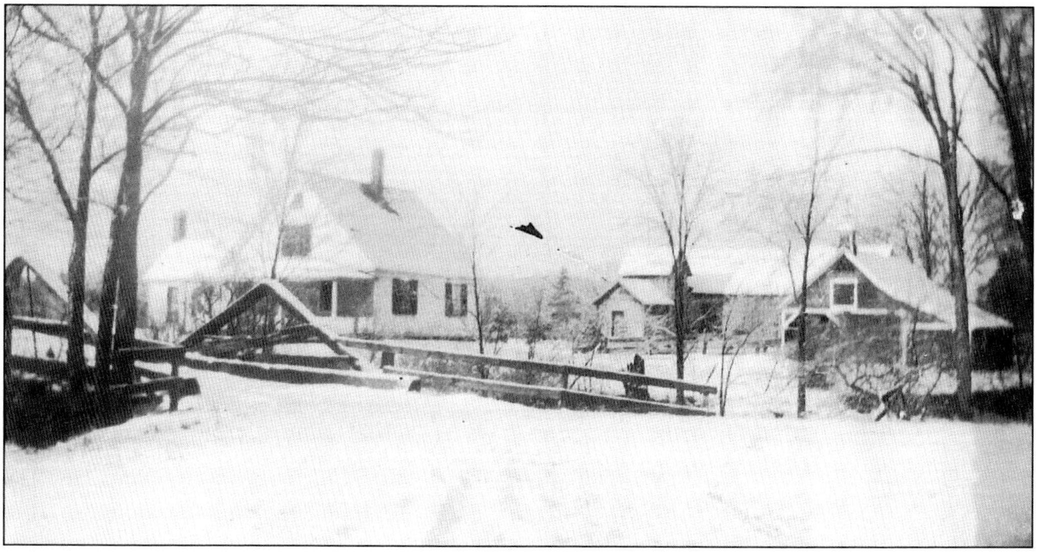

This early-twentieth-century view shows the wooden king post truss bridge at the base of Stevens Road and the Stevens farm beyond. The farmhouse is one of the oldest known buildings in the Etna area, originally built by Isaac Bridgman in the early 1770s, and it incorporated some of the original logs from Bridgman's first log cabin of 1768.

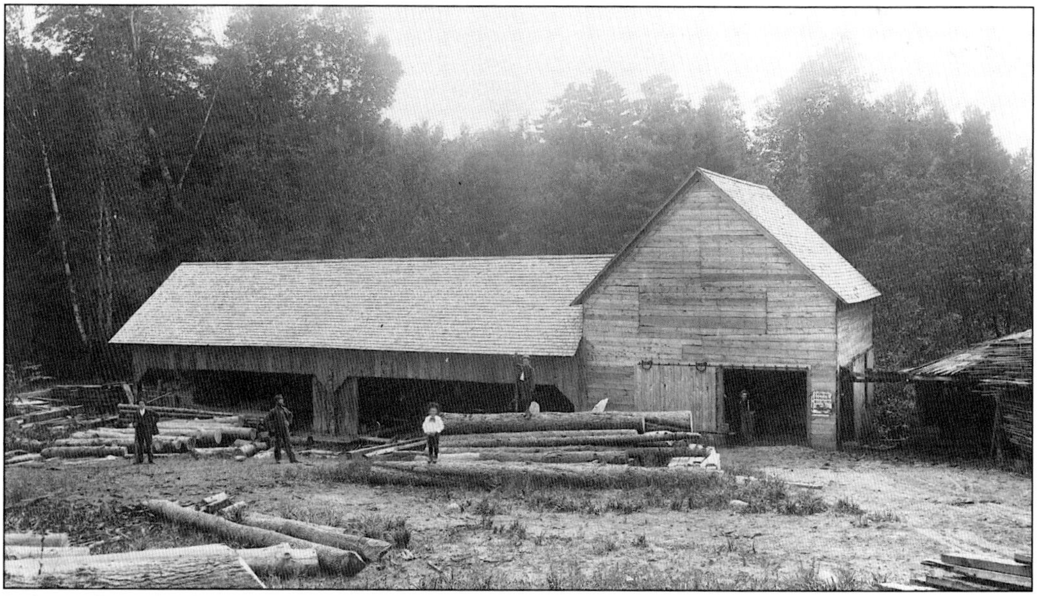

Judging from the dress and appearance of the persons standing in the photograph and the general overall good condition of the building, this view was probably taken shortly after John Gould and Joseph F. Smalley first erected this sawmill on Mink Brook in 1871. Later the operation belonged to Etna resident Will Hart, and it was for many years a thriving business. Today only the foundations remain along the brook, opposite the Baughman residence at 60 Etna Road.

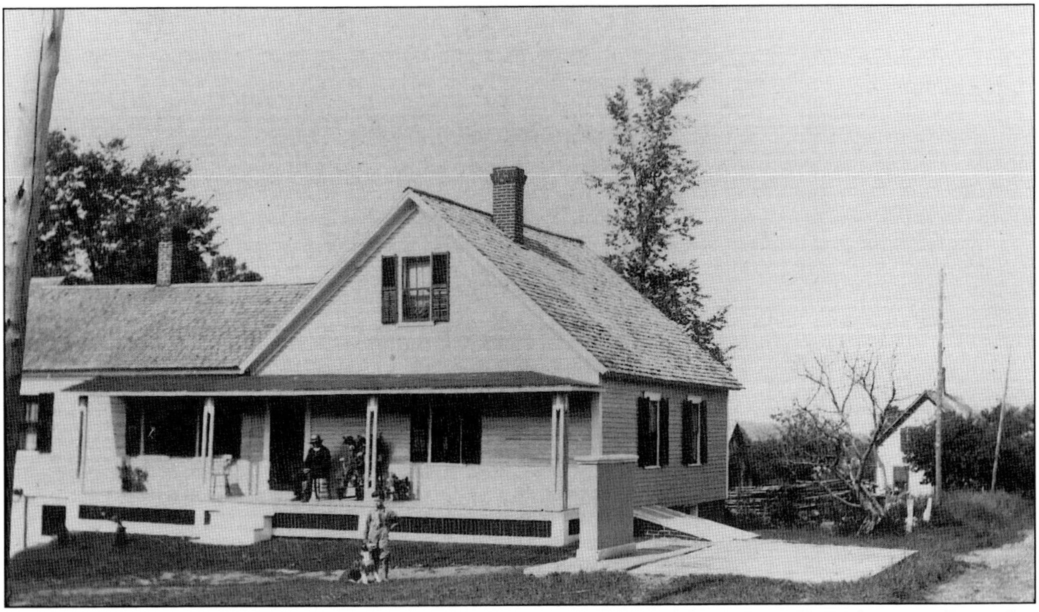

This c. 1910 postcard view shows the "Mill House," occupied by one miller after another who tended the nearby old gristmill. Note the scales located beside Etna Road for weighing mill product. For many years the property belonged to Alvin Poland, and today it is the home of his daughter Eunice and her husband, Don Ballam, at 75 Etna Road. This is believed to be a very early building.

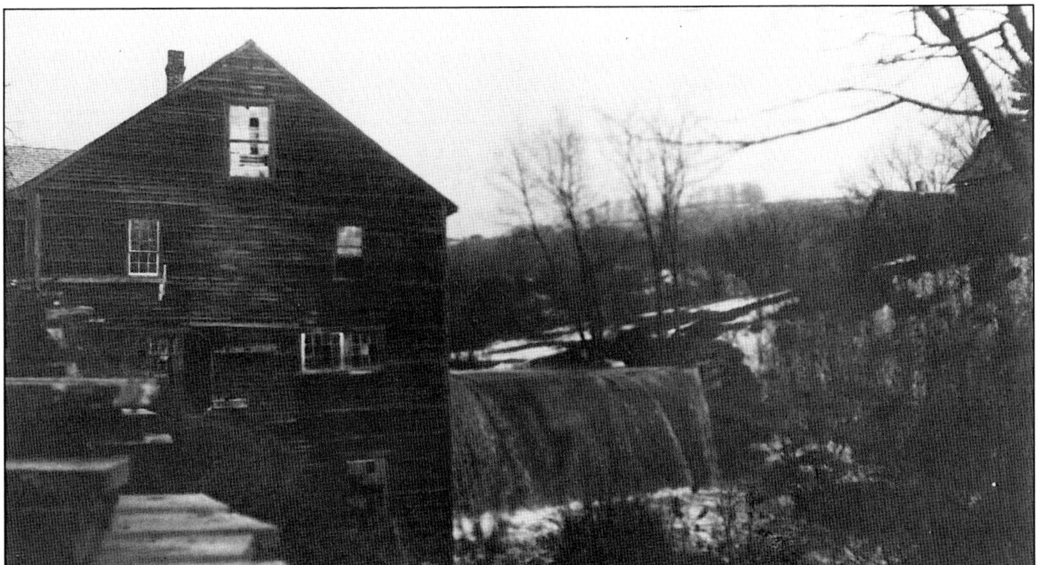

This c. 1905 postcard view shows the second gristmill to be built at this site on Mink Brook in Etna, erected in 1828 by John Williams. It replaced an earlier facility constructed in 1769 that was the first gristmill in operation in the entire town of Hanover. In later years the building was used as a ladder factory before being torn down in the early 1940s.

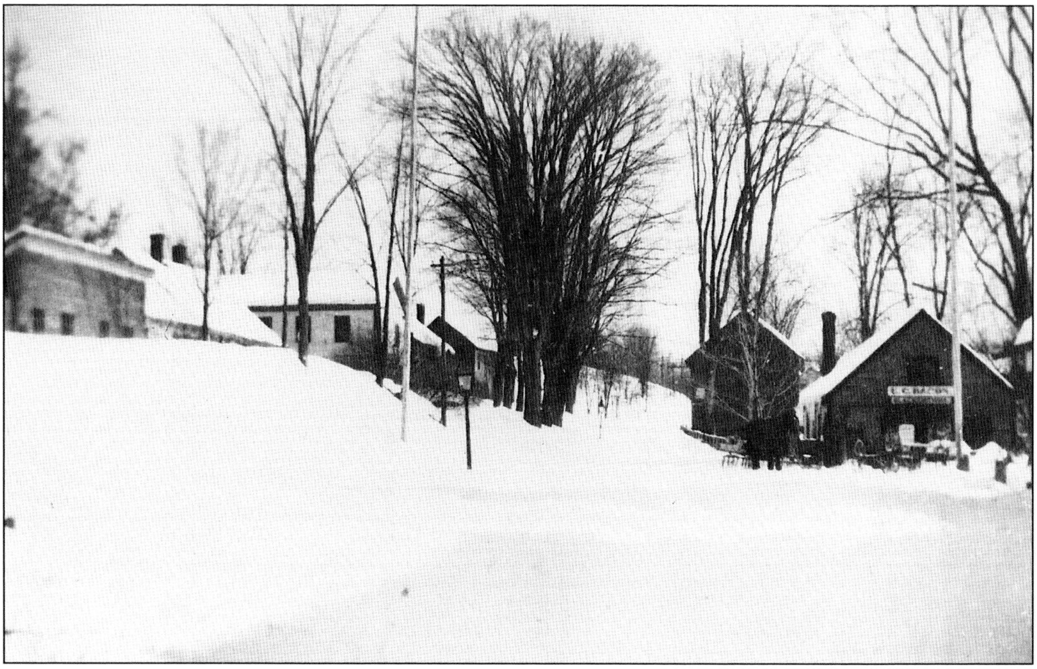

This is a wintry view *c.* 1900 looking up Etna Road, through the village, from about in front of the present-day Etna Store. Prior to 1884, this area of Hanover was commonly referred to as "Mill Village," or "Mill Neighborhood," the result of the numerous small and varied mills then clustered along that section of Mink Brook. To the right is L.C. Bacon's blacksmith shop at the northeast corner of Etna Road and School House Lane.

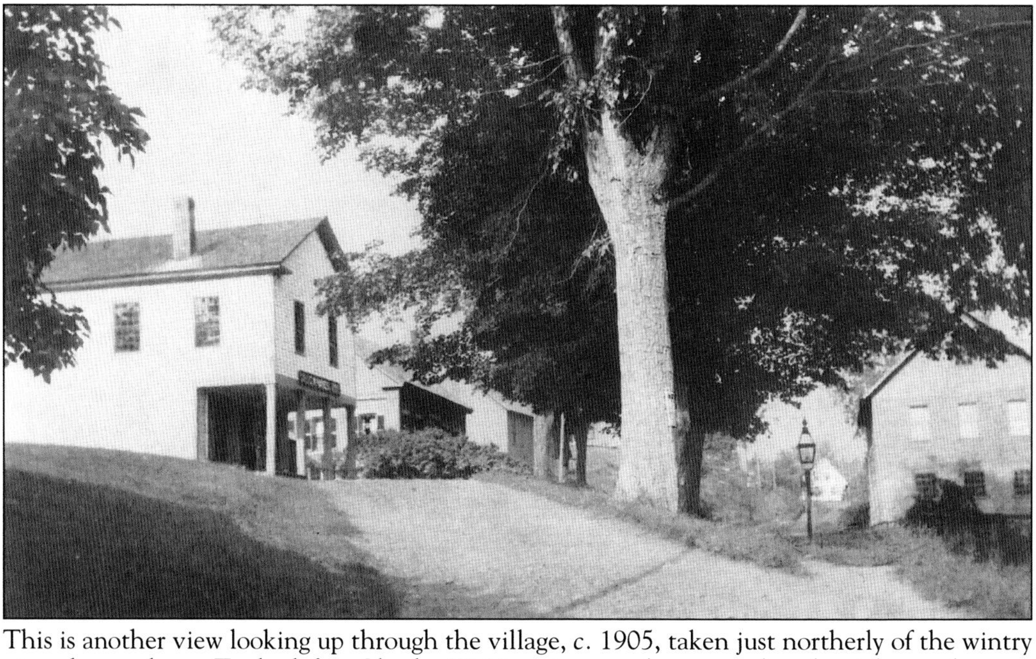

This is another view looking up through the village, *c.* 1905, taken just northerly of the wintry view shown above. To the left is Charles W. Hayes's general store, and to the right can be seen the Derby Manufacturing Company's main building.

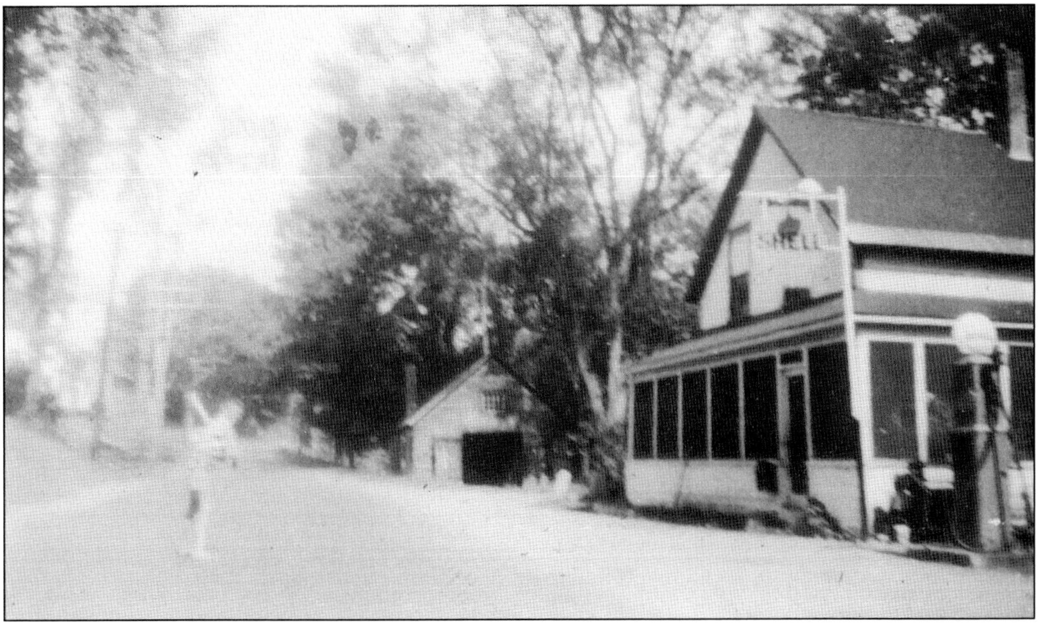

By 1939, when this view was taken, the road passing down through the village area had been widened and somewhat straightened out—necessary to accommodate the automobile. To the right is Cliff and Lena Elder's Etna Store, also home to the Village Post Office.

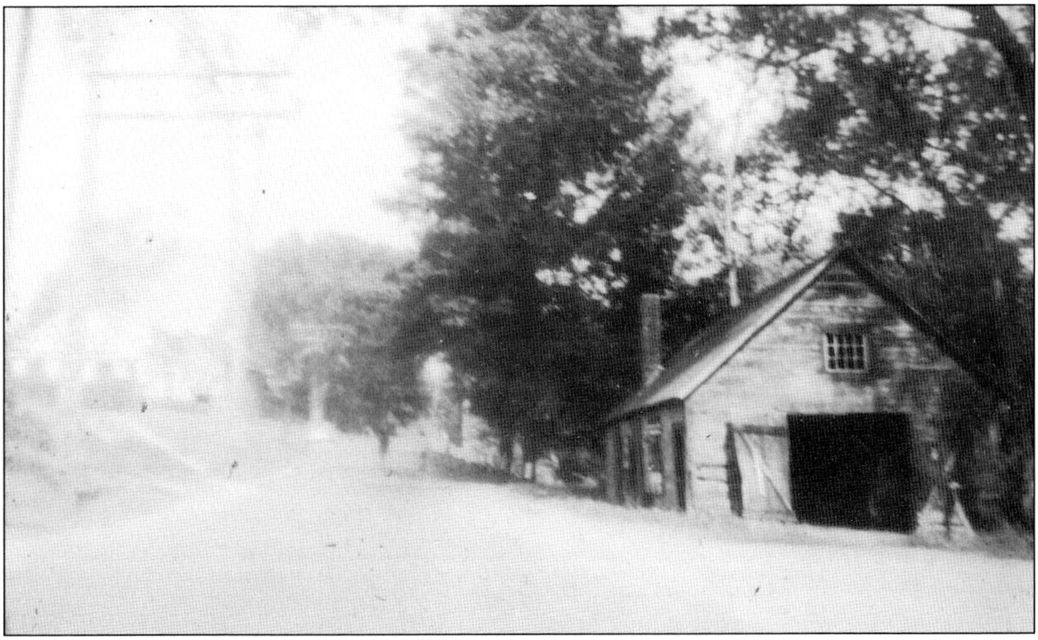

This is another 1939 view looking north up through the village. By this time the blacksmith shop, shown to the right, was just an old garage building that in 1948 was demolished. Compare this photograph with the similar view on page 30 taken only about 40 years earlier.

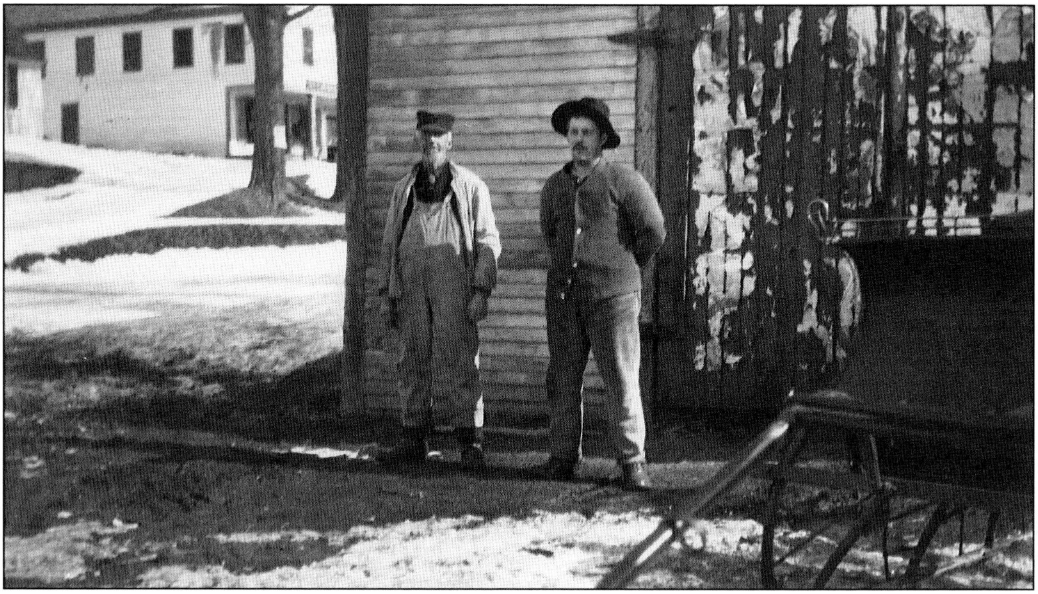

Shown standing in front of L.C. Bacon's blacksmith shop are Doug and Fred Paul, two brothers who are believed to have worked on the premises. To the far left of this *c.* 1900 view can be seen Charles W. Hayes's general store, located across Etna Road up on a slight rise.

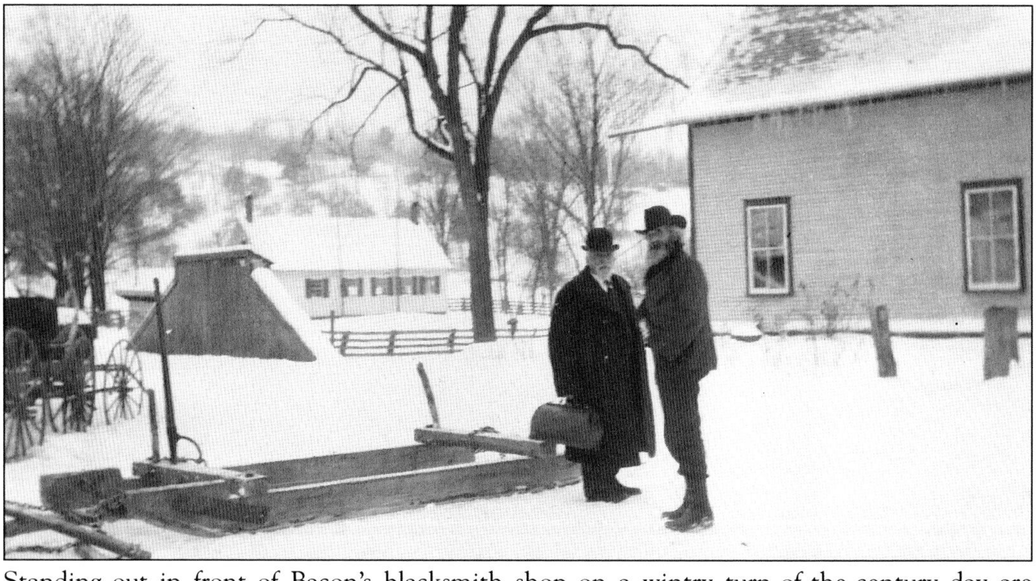

Standing out in front of Bacon's blacksmith shop on a wintry turn-of-the-century day are John D. Bridgman (left) and Horace F. "Deacon" Hoyt Jr.—both longtime Etna residents from old Hanover families. Mr. Bridgman was an attorney and breeder of Hambletonian horses and Spanish Merino sheep. "Deacon" Hoyt was a farmer, district court clerk, local newspaper correspondent, and deacon of the local Baptist church.

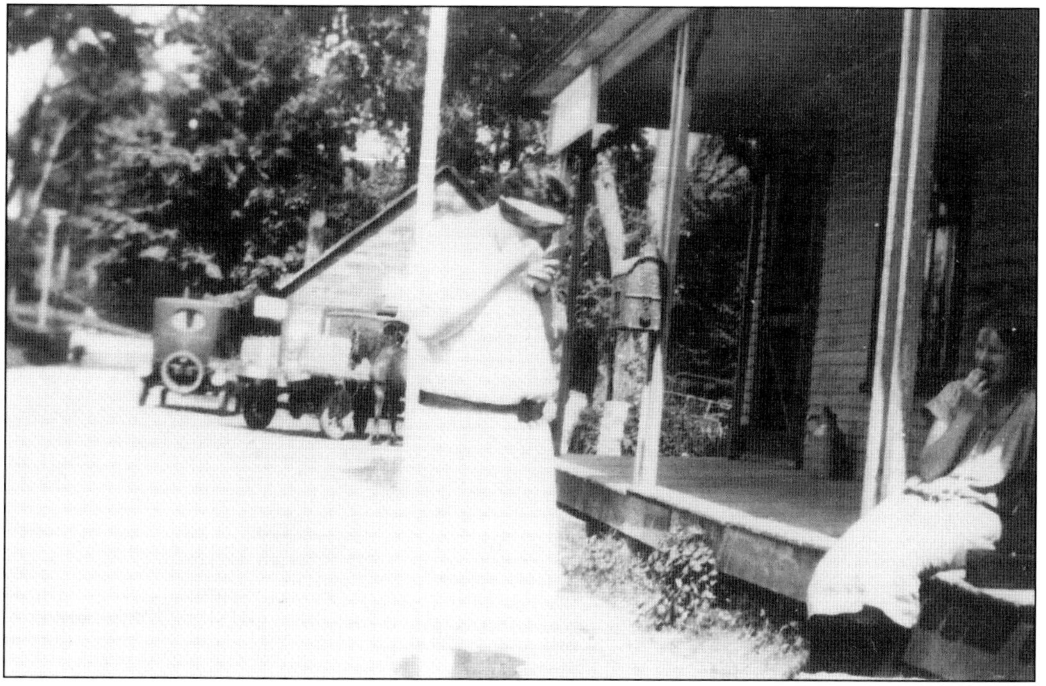

Two young Etna ladies are dressed up and appear ready to venture forth from the village for a night out on the town in this latter-1920s view. Pearl Camp is sitting on the front porch of the Etna Post Office, while Lena Elder is powdering her nose. In the background is Bacon's blacksmith shop.

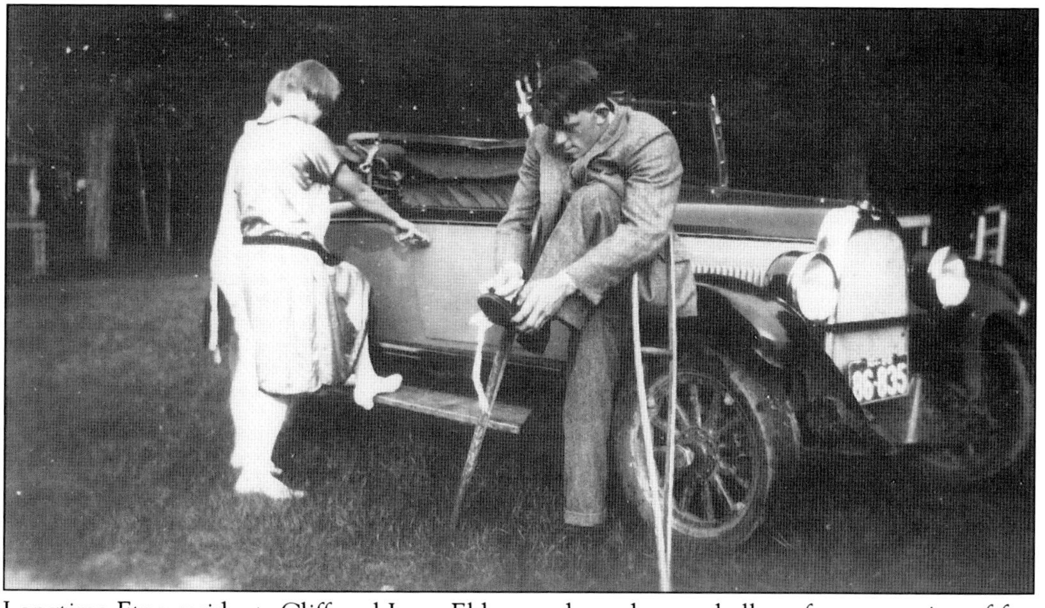

Longtime Etna residents Cliff and Lena Elder are dressed up and all set for an evening of fun in this 1928 photograph, about the time that they were married. Cliff, who had polio as a youngster, is polishing his shoes while leaning on their new Whippet Roadster, a car made by Willys-Overland. Lena later was the village postmaster, spanning the years 1951 to 1971, and she and Cliff had the Etna Store from 1930 to 1967.

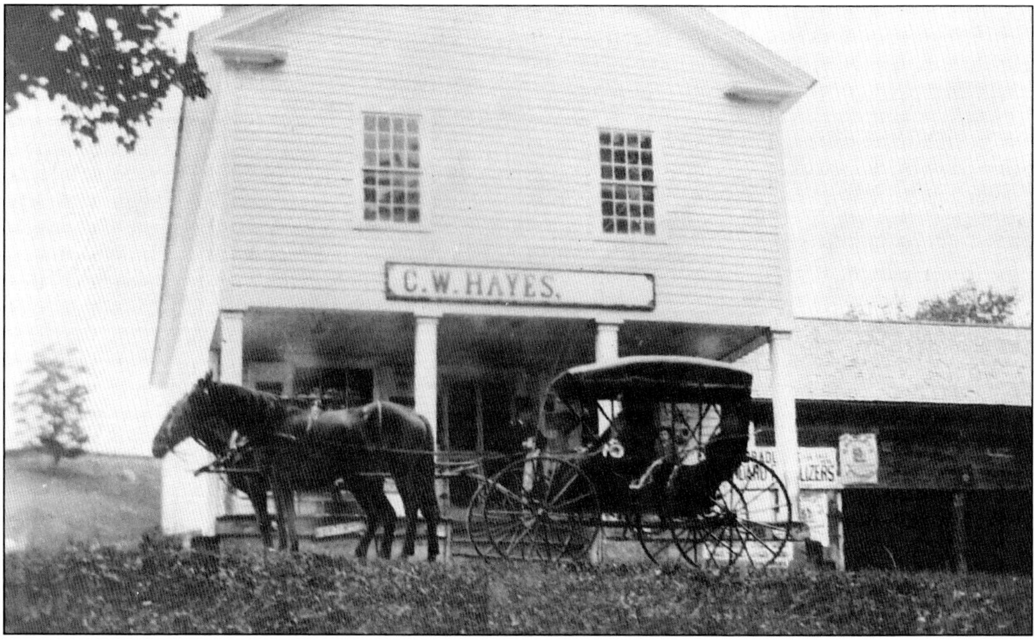

In this *c.* 1890 view, Charles W. Hayes's general store stands on the west side of the Etna Road, just north of the present residence of Matthew and Elizabeth Marshall, at 104 Etna Road. The building was originally constructed in 1833 by Ashel Packard as a store with a second-floor meeting hall made available for community use. In fact, starting in 1844, until the building burned many years later, this was the location of Hanover's annual town meeting.

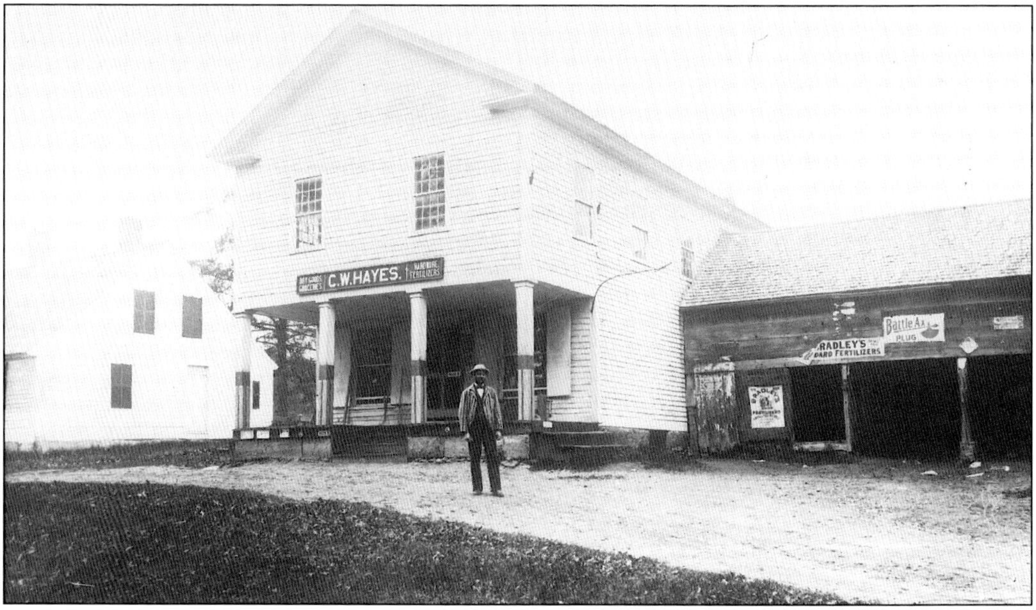

This is another view *c.* 1900 of Hayes's general store. To the left can be seen the present-day Marshall residence. In addition to continuously operating as the village's general store and town meeting location, for a brief period of time in the 1840s, the premises was also a hotel operated by Horace and Walter Buck—the only hotel the village ever had. The name of the dapperly dressed gentleman in the foreground is no longer known.

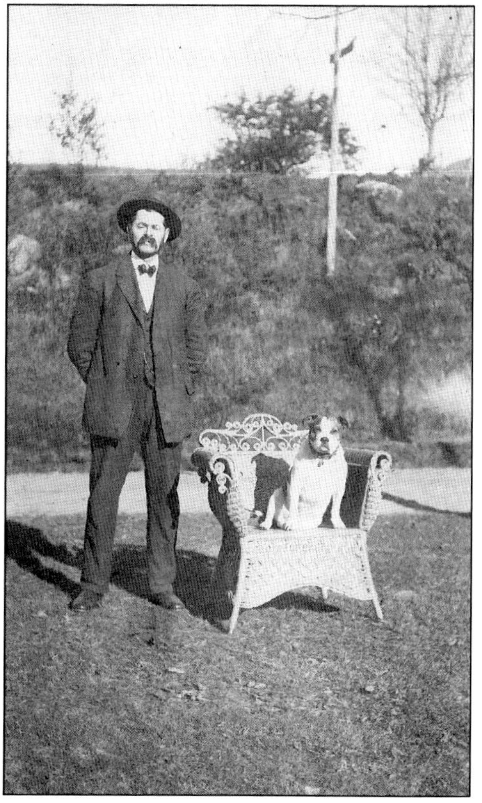

This is a c. 1905 postcard view of storekeeper Charles W. Hayes, who, from 1883 thru 1914, owned and operated the general store. Childs' 1886 *Grafton County Gazetteer* lists Mr. Hayes as "Librarian of Etna Library, Dealer in Groceries, Provisions, Dry Goods, Crockery, Boots, Shoes, Etc." The name of his dog we no longer know.

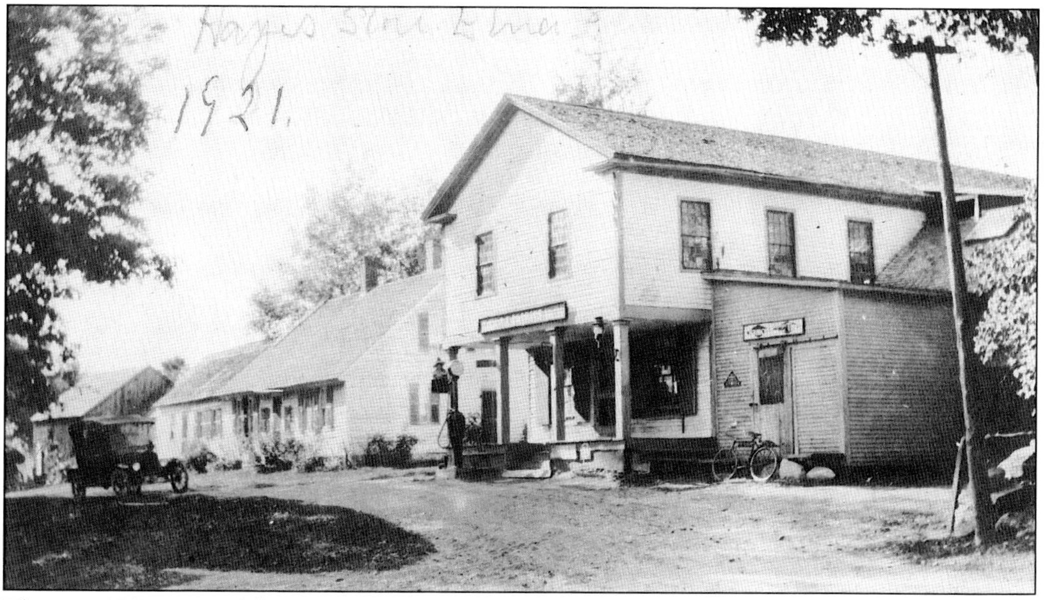

This is a 1921 view of the store, now owned by R.E. Barrows, who purchased it that year. A gas pump has been added, and a Model T Ford "Flivver," or "Tin Lizzie," can be seen resting in the shade of a nearby tree. Beyond the store is Town Clerk George M. Bridgman's home and office, today the Marshall residence.

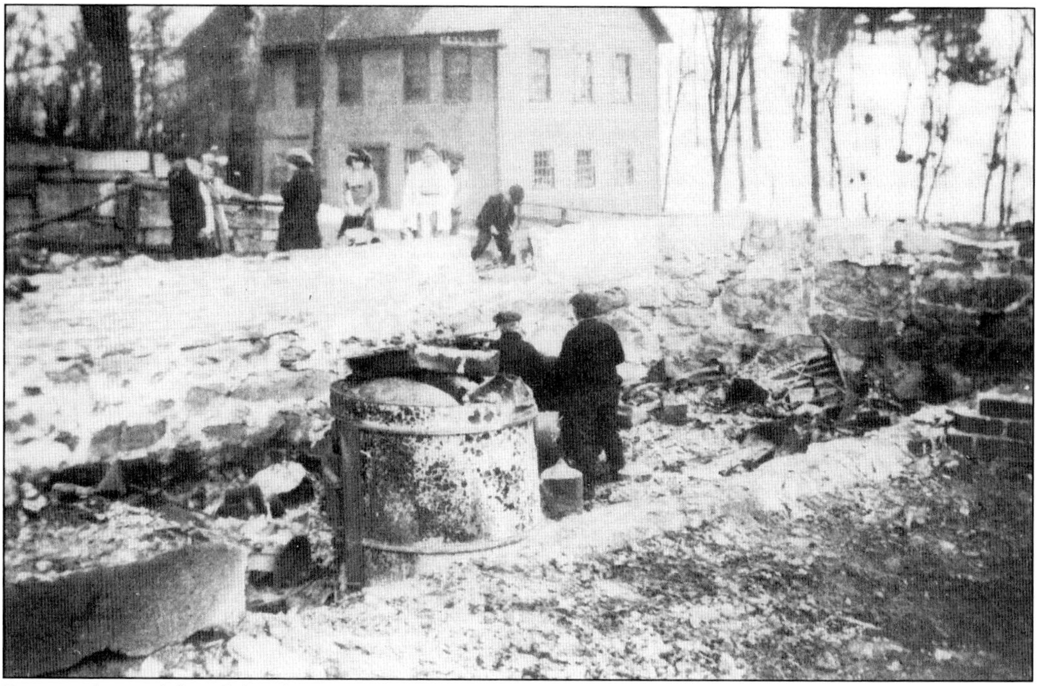

During the middle of the day, on April 3, 1922, R.E. Barrows's store completely burned—caused by a defective furnace in the basement. This view, looking easterly across the newly exposed cellar hole, shows the suspect furnace. Beyond, on the Mink Brook side of the Etna Road, is the Derby Manufacturing Company's main mill building

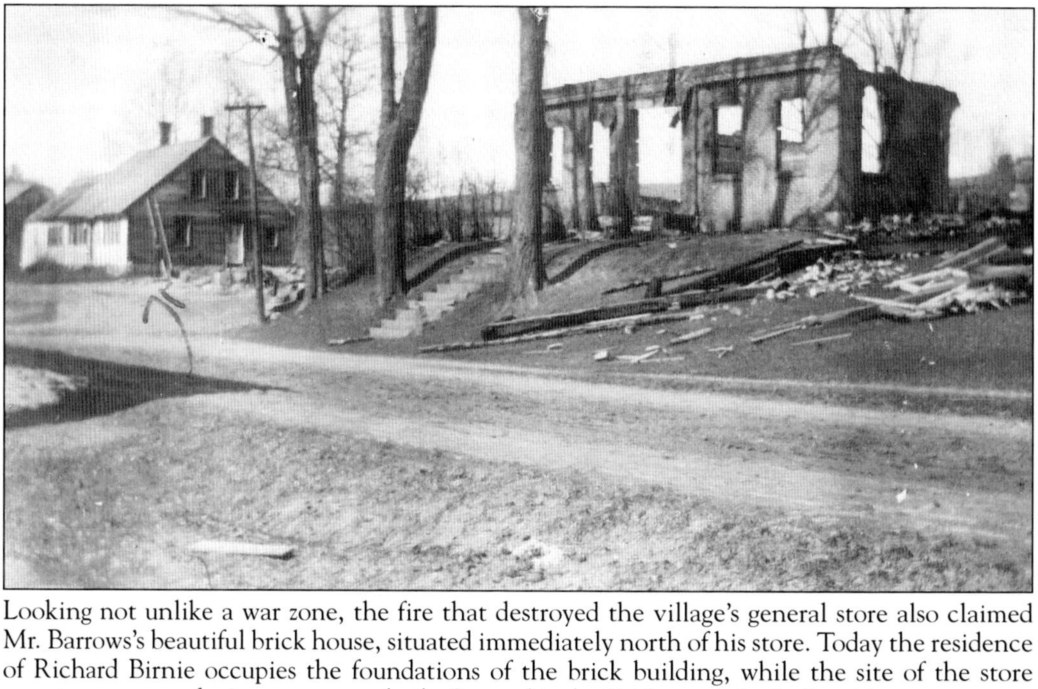

Looking not unlike a war zone, the fire that destroyed the village's general store also claimed Mr. Barrows's beautiful brick house, situated immediately north of his store. Today the residence of Richard Birnie occupies the foundations of the brick building, while the site of the store remains vacant—for it was never rebuilt. Beyond is the Bridgman/Marshall residence.

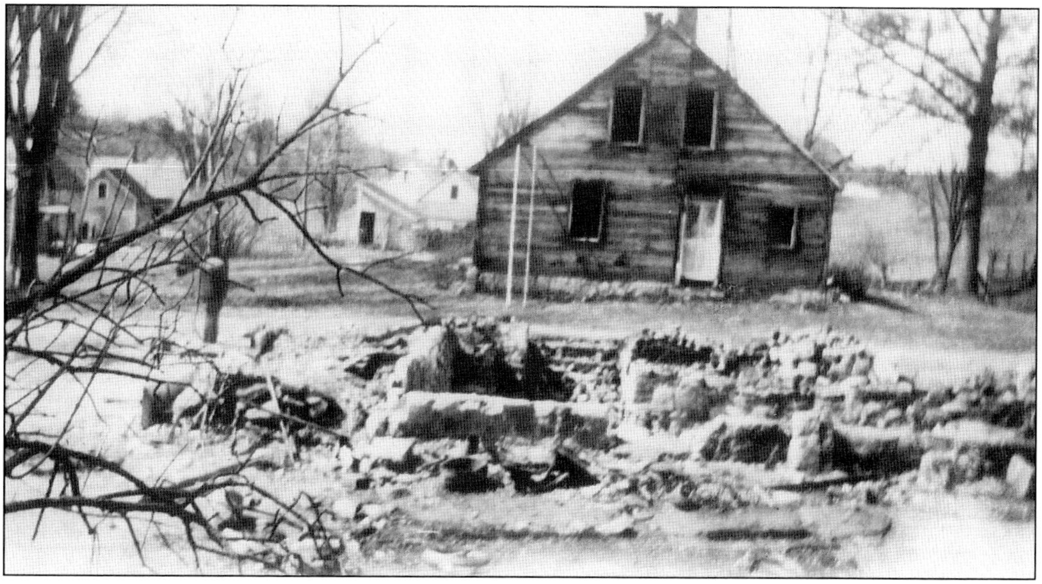

One last view looking southerly of the aftermath of the general store fire shows only the store's foundations in the foreground and the scorched end of George M. Bridgman's residence. It was only with determined effort by village residents that this building escaped the fast-moving flames on that early spring day.

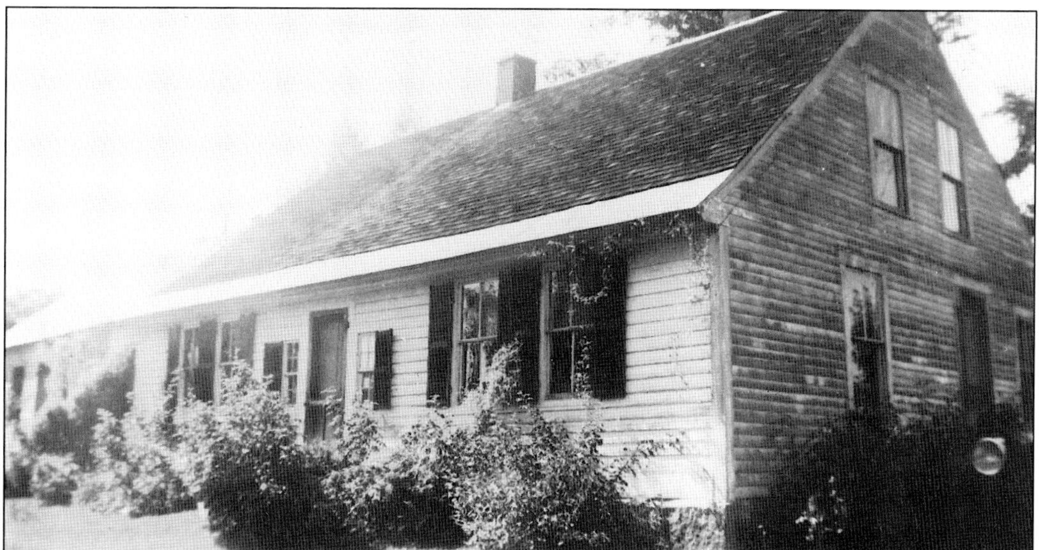

This house still stands in the center of the village, and today it is the home of Matthew and Elizabeth Marshall at 104 Etna Road. The original date of construction is not known, nor is the name of the builder; however, it is an early structure and is thought to be a composite of several buildings put together. This view was taken in the 1930s, and the charred gable end wall, damaged in the general store fire, is still apparent.

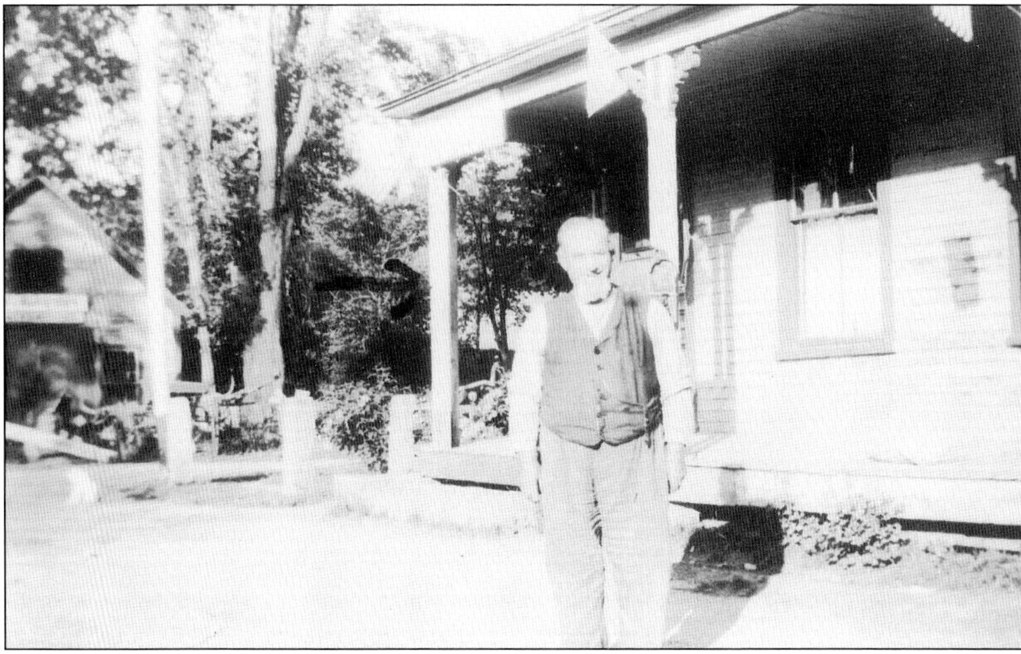

Longtime village postmaster Willie Spencer is seen standing in front of the Etna Post Office in this late-1920s view, about the time of his retirement. Willie was postmaster from 1891 to 1928, and when this photograph was taken, the post office was located in the present-day Etna Store building. In the background is L.C. Bacon's blacksmith shop.

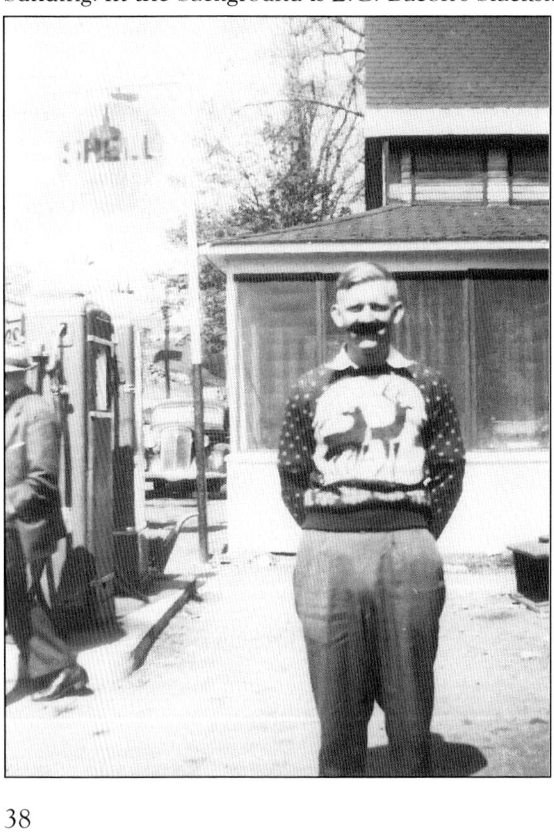

Etna native Stanley Elder is posed in front of his parents Etna Store in this 1952 view. In later years, Stan was the village's postmaster, serving a total of 20 years, from 1971 until his retirement in 1991. His mother, too, was postmaster, also serving 20 years, from 1951 thru 1971. The gentleman in the left background is Fred Stevens.

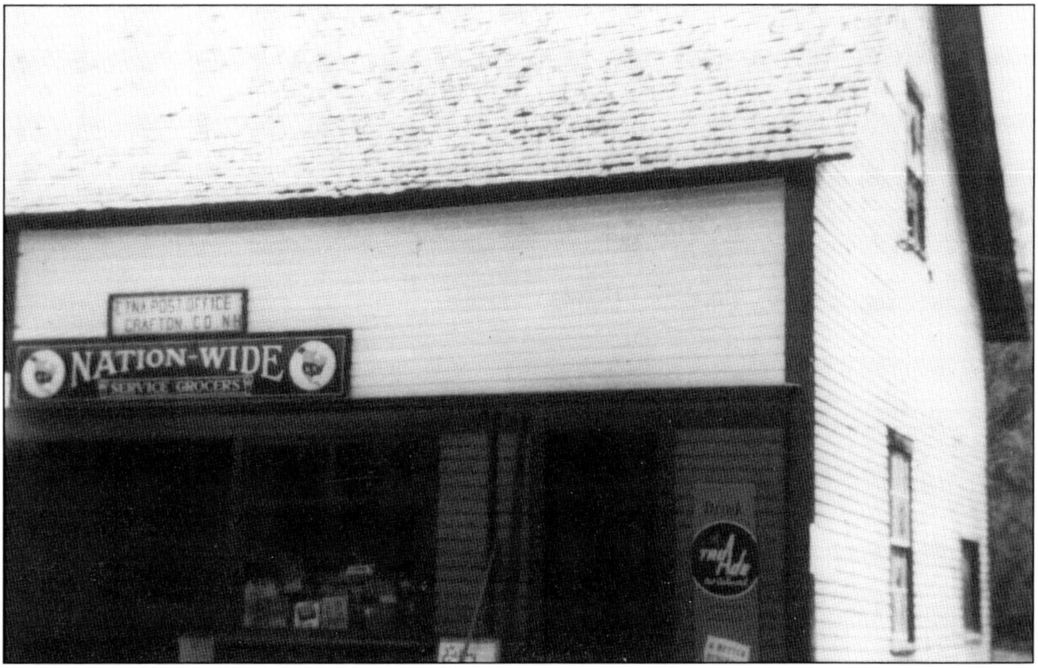

In 1930, Cliff and Lena Elder opened the Etna Store on the front porch of the building that also housed the post office. Through the years that followed, they built the business up and expanded it into the attached barn area of the property, as seen here *c.* 1940. Ethel Hewes was postmaster during the years 1928–1951, and the Elders operated the business until selling it in 1967.

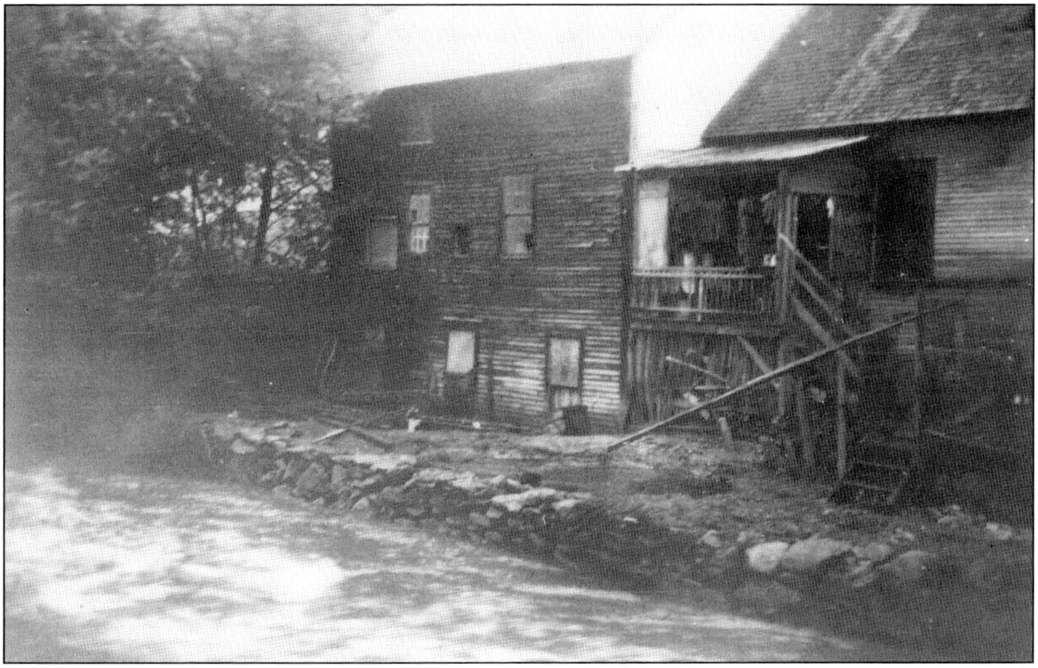

This is the backside of the Etna Store, *c.* 1930, shortly before getting a rebuilt porch overlooking Mink Brook. The property looks little different 65 or so years later.

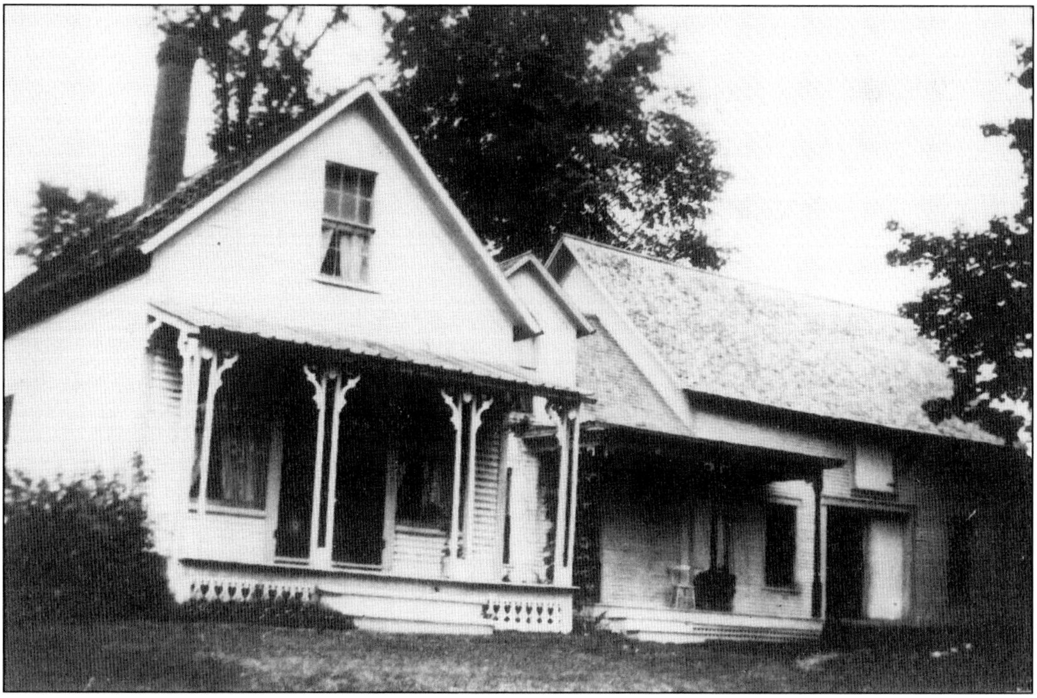

Thomas Praddex constructed this residence at 98 Etna Road in 1891, today the home of Janice Wright. Remarkably little of this house has changed over the years, including the simple Victorian front porch.

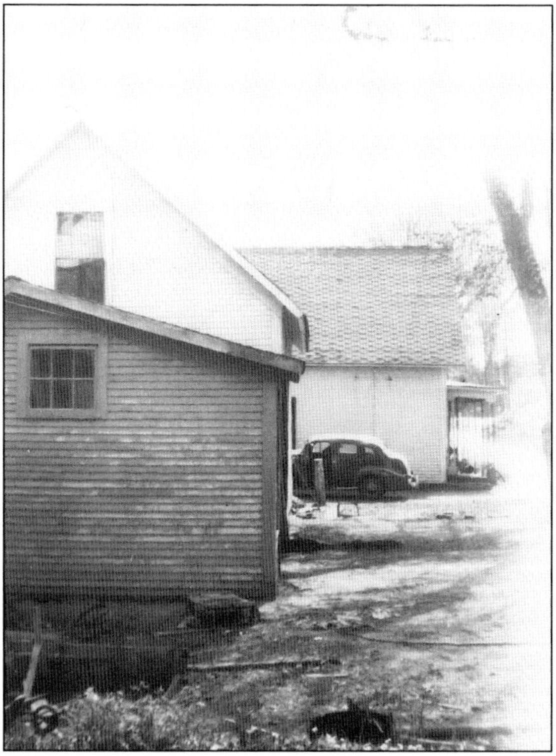

What is now the main house of this complex of buildings at 97 Etna Road originally began life as a grocery store, constructed in 1884 by Horace L. Huntington and operated by E.H. Wright. In later years Cliff and Lena Elder owned the property, and since about 1970, the post office has occupied space in the barn. This view was taken *c.* 1940.

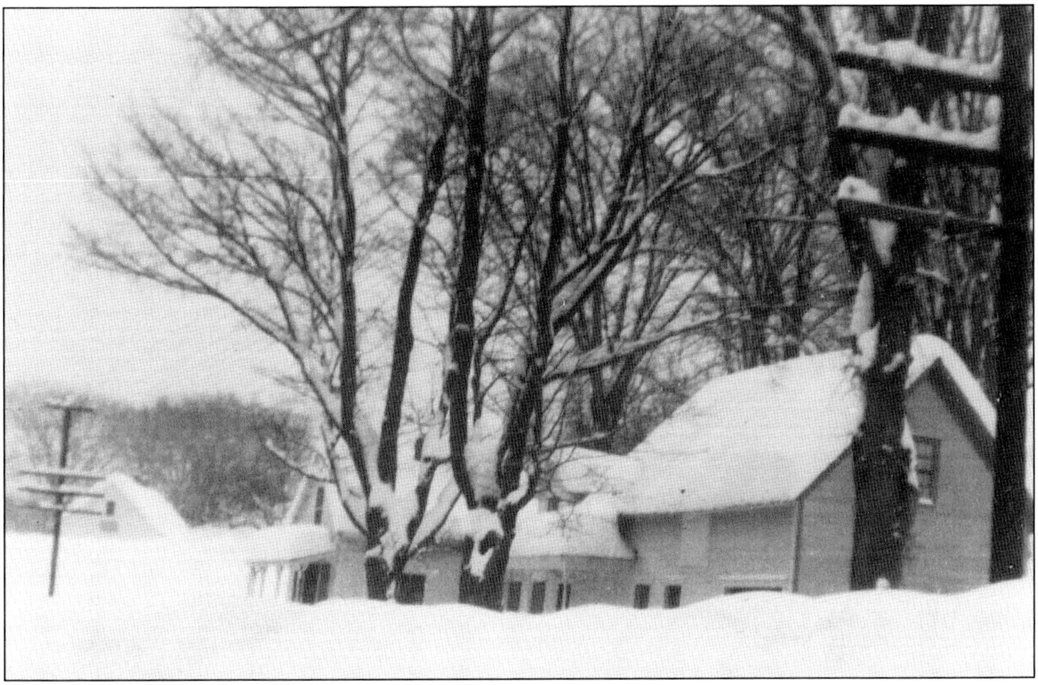

Does it snow now-a-days like it used to in years past? Perhaps that is a question best left for meteorologists to ponder; however, this 1950s–1960s view shows a substantial amount of snow in the village. In the background is the Wright residence at 98 Etna Road.

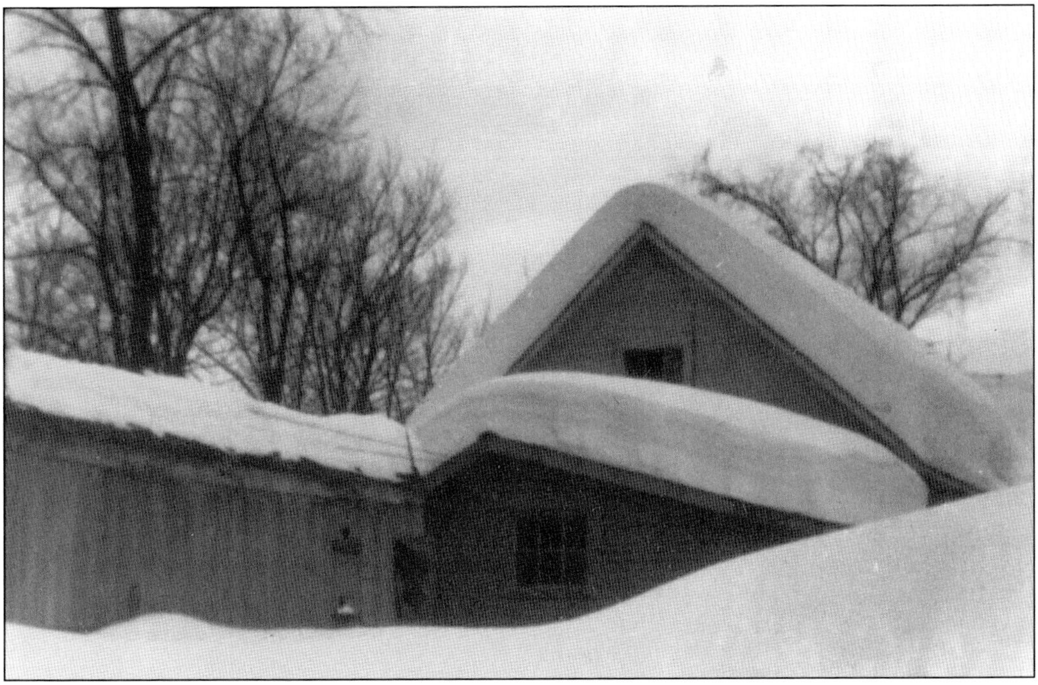

This is another view of the same snowfall seen above, looking from in front of the Etna Store. The building behind the drift is the present post office at 97 Etna Road, owned by Willa N. Barrett.

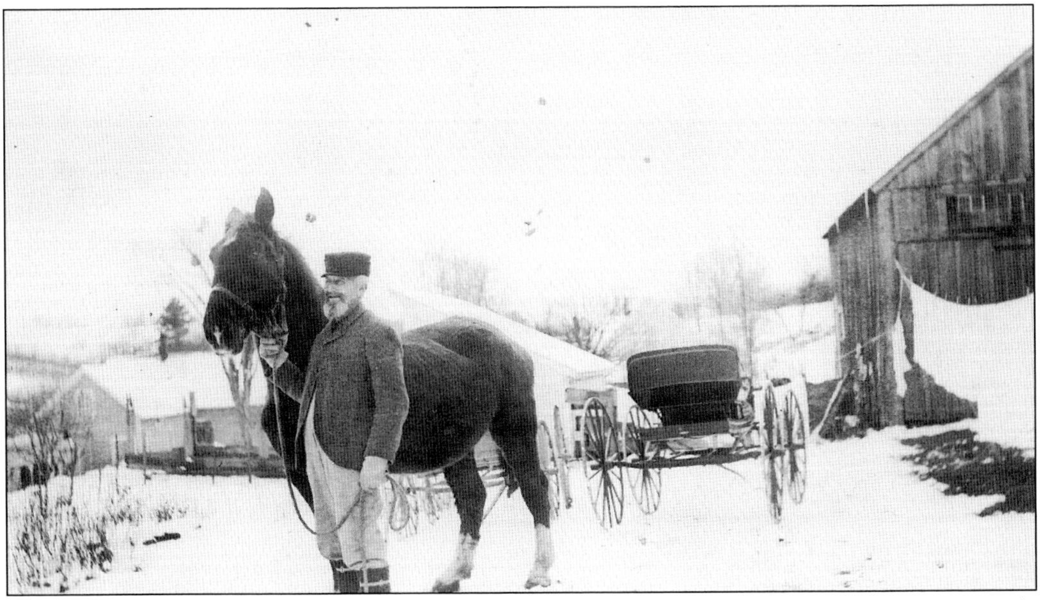

Hanover's longest serving town clerk (1884–1934), George M. Bridgman, is seen getting ready to hitch up his horse Draco in this 1906 winter scene, taken in front of Bridgman's house, now the Marshall residence at 104 Etna Road. In the left background is the present home of Willa N. Barrett at 97 Etna Road.

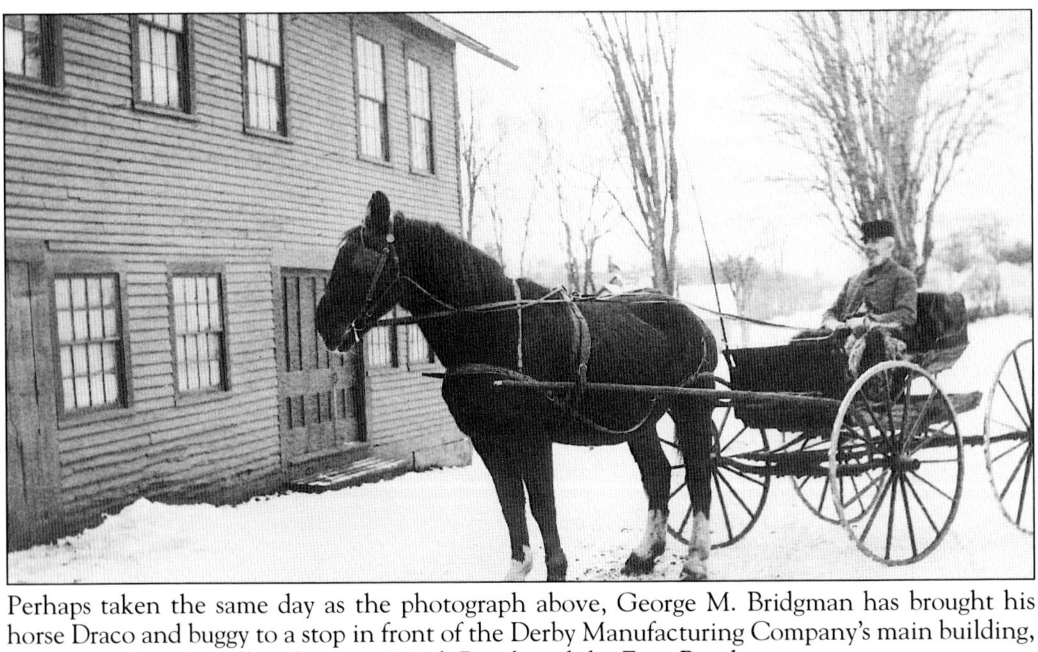

Perhaps taken the same day as the photograph above, George M. Bridgman has brought his horse Draco and buggy to a stop in front of the Derby Manufacturing Company's main building, situated within the village between Mink Brook and the Etna Road.

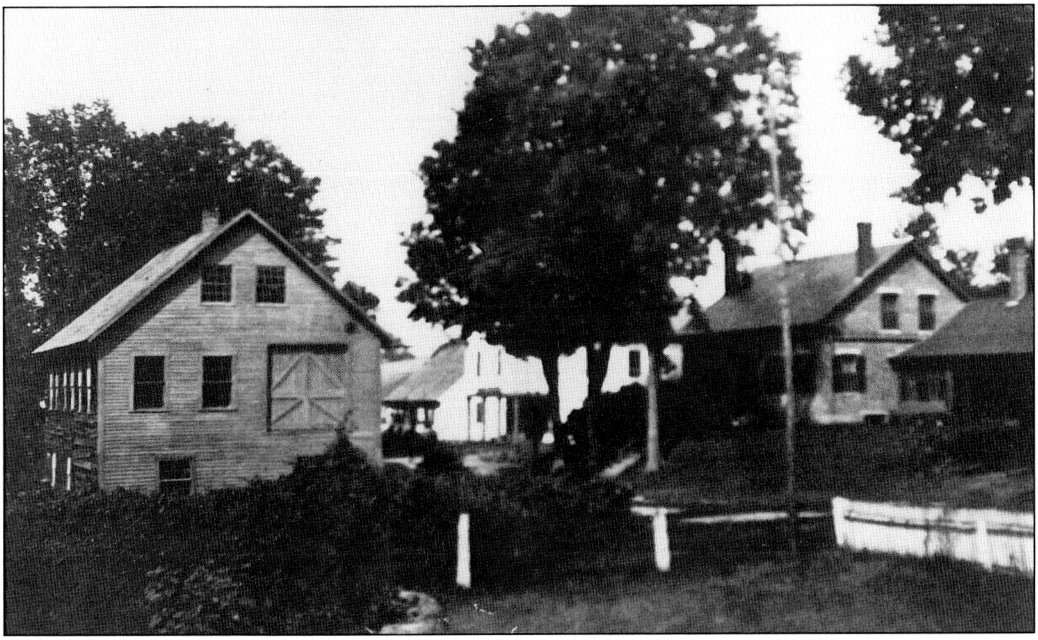

A Mr. D.C. Whipple first constructed this mill building; however, it was Walter N. Derby, who in 1881 constructed a dam on Mink Brook so as to provide the building with waterpower and founded the Derby Manufacturing Company. The best known of a wide variety of wooden products made by Mr. Derby was the patented "Etna Extension Ladder," sold throughout the Northeast including Canada. This view was taken *c.* 1908, about the time Walter N. Derby was mortally afflicted with tuberculosis at age 45.

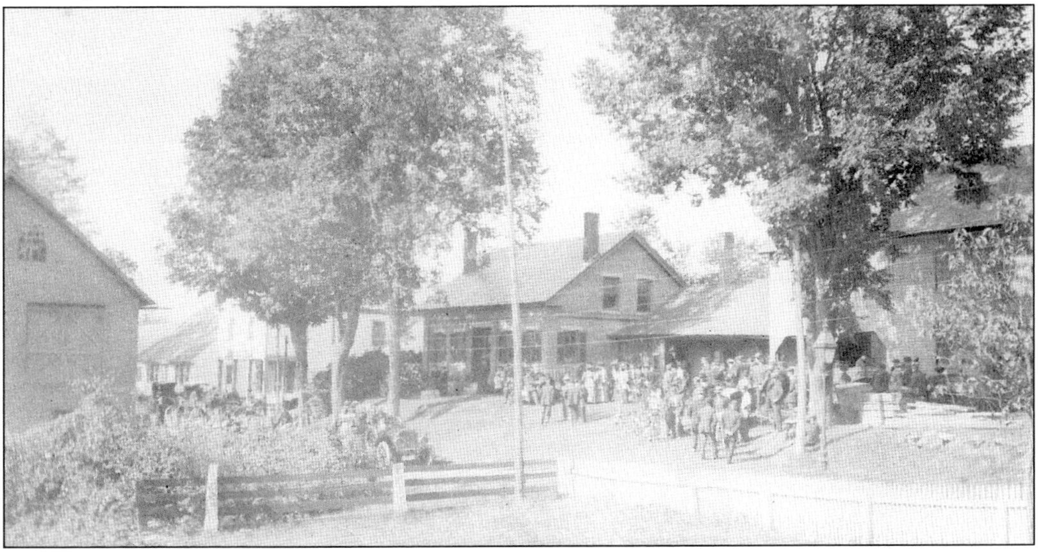

A similar view to the photograph above appears to show an auction in progress at the brick house that once stood at 116 Etna Road. Beyond, between the brick house and the Derby Manufacturing Company building, can be seen Charles W. Hayes's general store. Judging from the early automobile shown, this view too is *c.* 1908. Childs' 1886 *Grafton County Gazetteer* lists the Derby Manufacturing Company as "Manuf. of Derby's fire escape and extension ladders, step ladders and eave troughs."

This view looks south down the Main Street of Etna Village c. 1890. To the left is the Derby Manufacturing Company, and to the right is the brick house that burned in the 1922 general store fire. Beyond can be seen the backside of the blacksmith shop and the side of the general store.

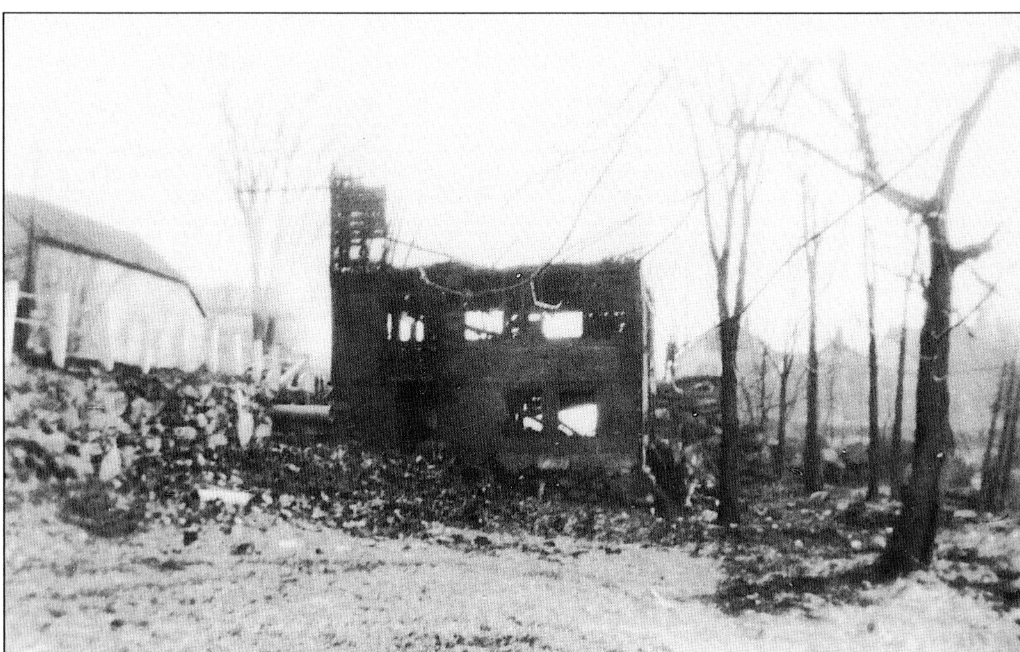

After R.E. Barrow's general store burned in April 1922, the operation soon opened back up for business in the old Derby Manufacturing Company building, by then vacant, across the road from the previous site. However, in 1929, this building too burned, as seen in this photograph taken looking from behind the blacksmith shop. To the left is the main road, and the barn of R.E. Barrow's house at 116 Etna Road is beyond.

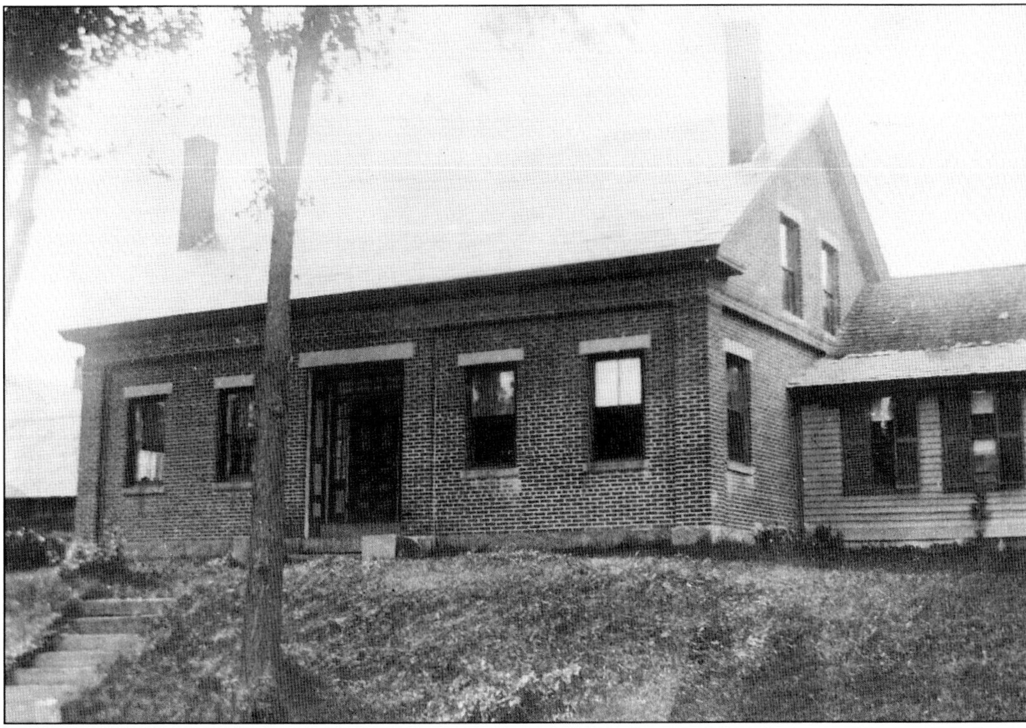

The builder and date of construction of the R.E. Barrow's house is not known; however, judging by the fine Greek Revival exterior detailing and chimneys, one would think it perhaps of the later 1830s. Certain aspects of the home are quite similar to other brick buildings to survive in Hanover—most notably Dartmouth's Reed Hall.

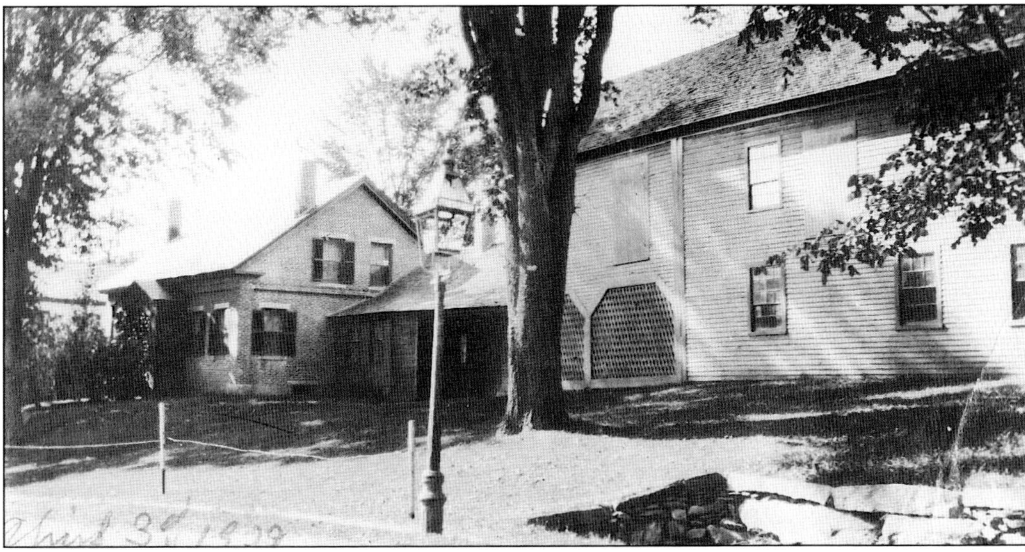

Here is one last view of the Barrow's home, taken shortly before it burned in 1922. The barn, although it survived the fire, was taken down years later—the foundations though are still visible today. Note the early kerosene street light, typical of those installed along Etna's Main Street—a gift from the Village Improvement Society shortly after that group's formation in 1903.

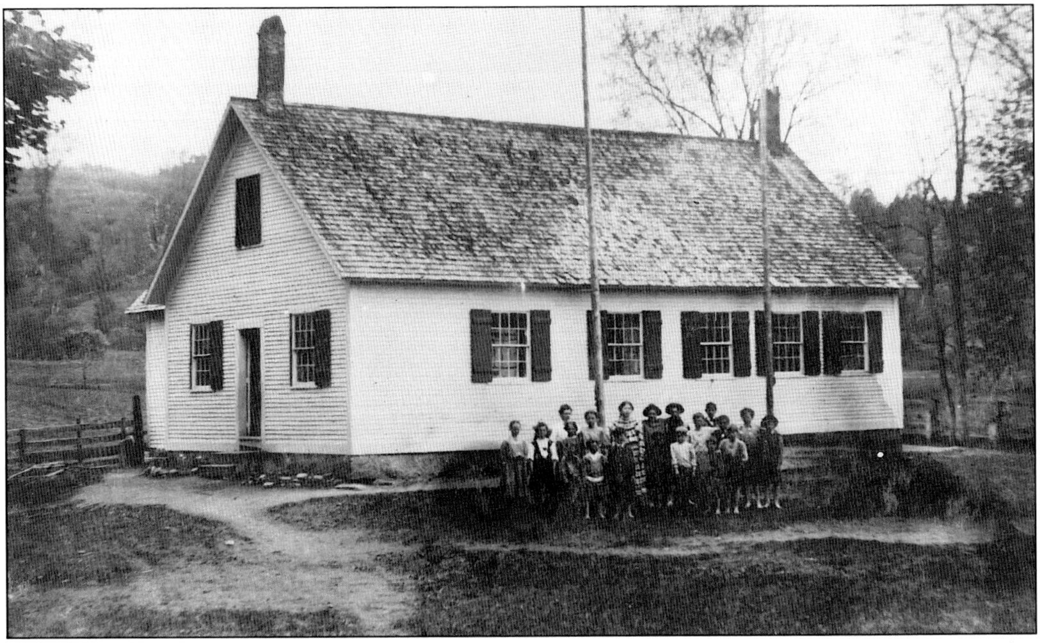

In 1852, after much controversy, this schoolhouse building was erected in Mill Village, also known as Hanover School District Number 5, and later to be called Etna Village. This postcard view is thought to have been taken in 1908.

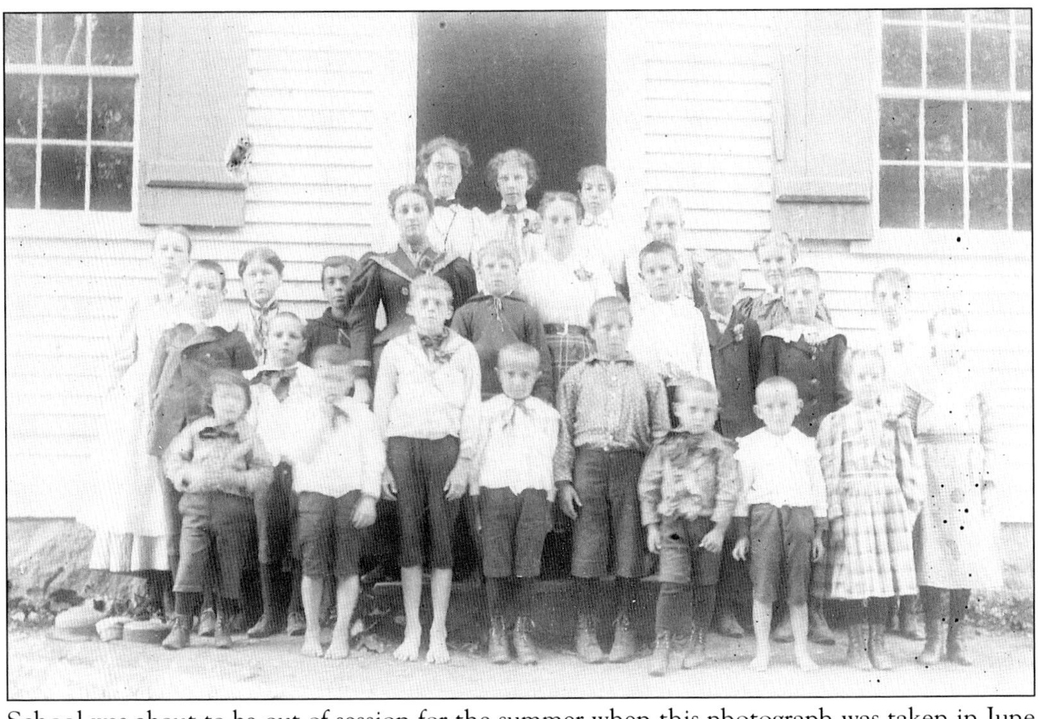

School was about to be out of session for the summer when this photograph was taken in June 1898. It appears that there were two teachers employed to educate this interesting looking crew of village youth!

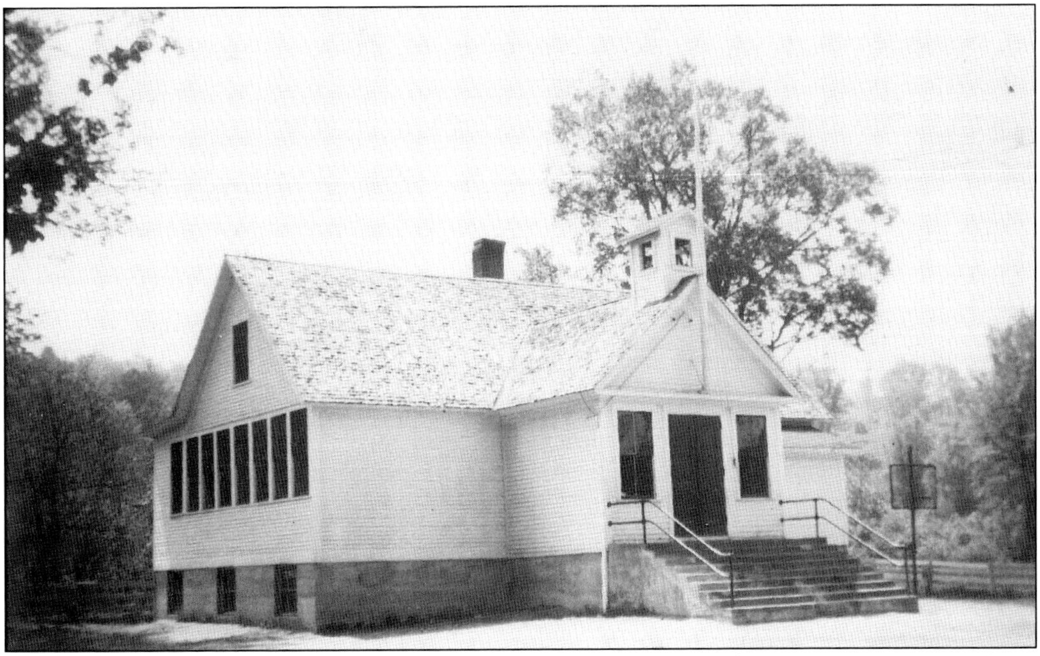

By 1931, the Hanover School District thought it time to spend $4,500 on the aging village schoolhouse, and they extensively remodeled the facility to make two modern classrooms instead of one, provide indoor plumbing, and furnish a full basement area suitable for recreation. Finally, in June 1958, the doors closed for the last time, and the village's elementary-age children started attending school in downtown Hanover.

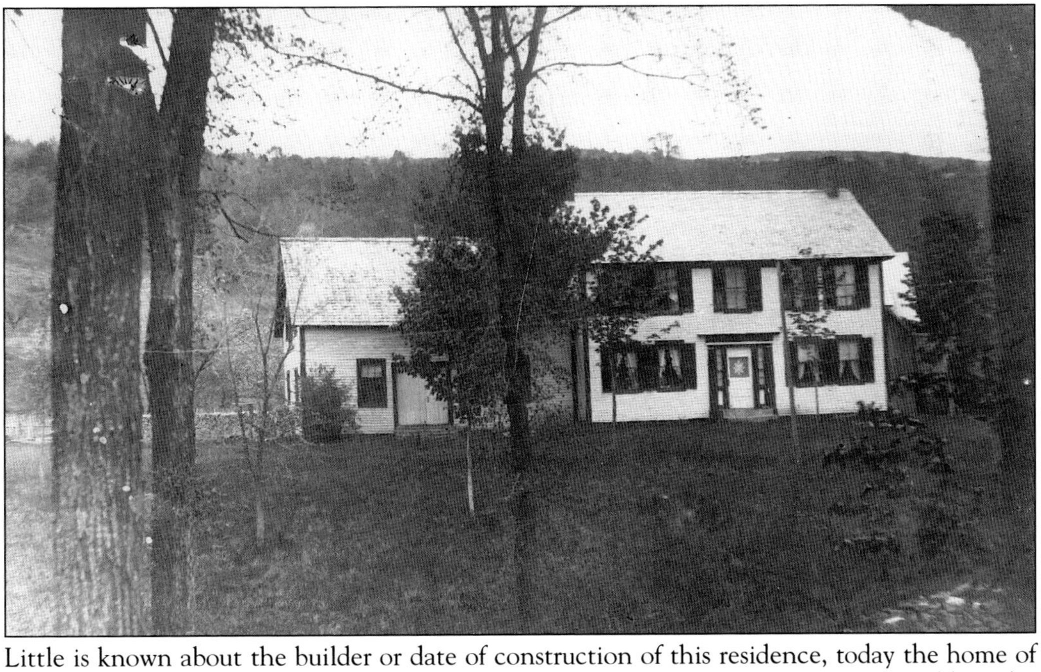

Little is known about the builder or date of construction of this residence, today the home of Mrs. Elenita C. Chickering at 2 School House Lane. The house appears to be of possible early-nineteenth-century origins. During the 1920s, it was the residence of Mrs. Gilman Wright.

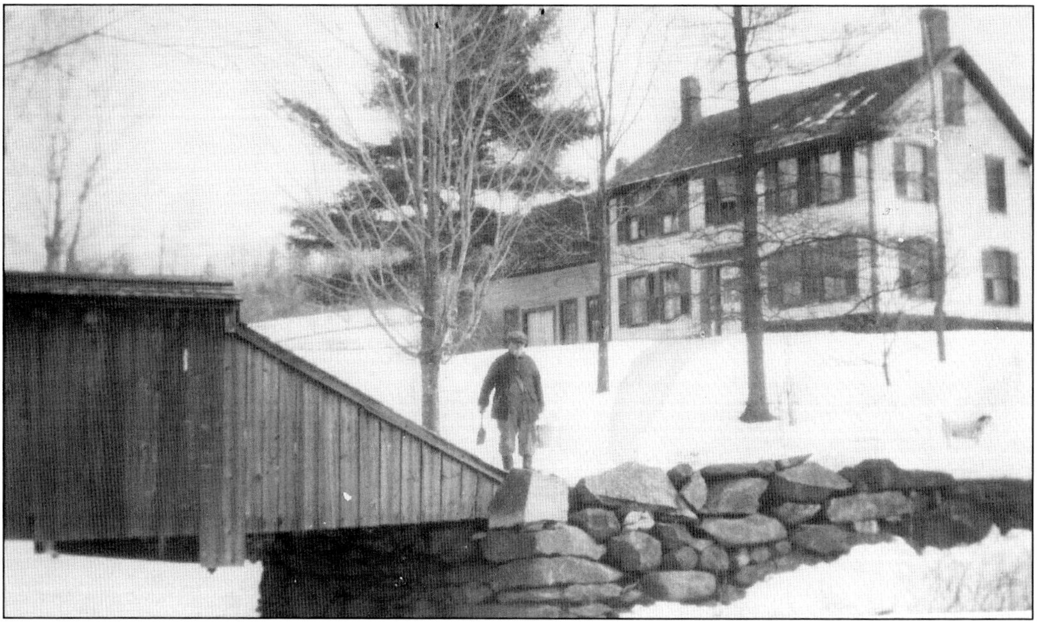

Retired village postmaster Willie Spencer is shown standing on the east end of the School House Lane bridge in this early-1930s photograph. In his retirement years, Willie was the janitor at the Etna School House. In the background is the present day Chickering residence at 2 School House Lane.

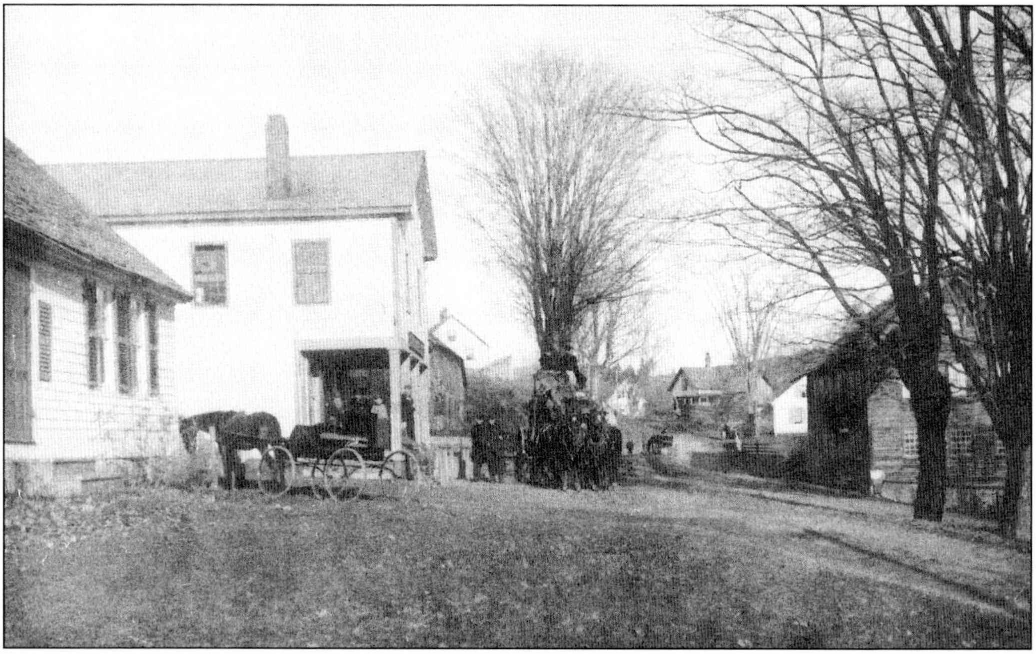

It is town meeting day in this early-twentieth-century view showing folks arriving at Charles W. Hayes General store, with the meeting room upstairs on the second floor. On other occasions, this space was also known as a good dance hall. Horse-drawn stages were used to bring citizens from "the village at the College" out to the town meeting in Etna, much to the excitement of the village's youngsters.

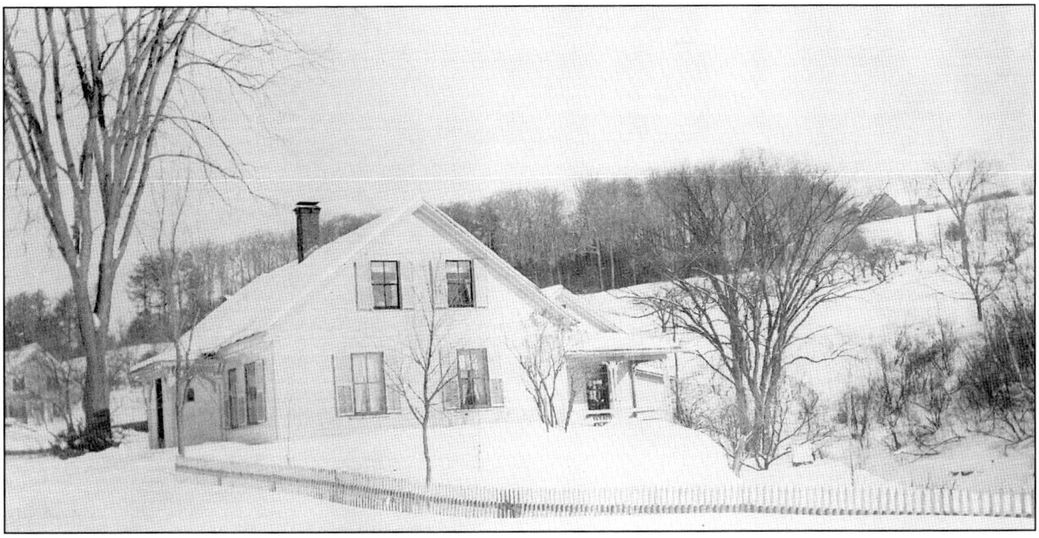

Here is a wintry turn-of-the-century view of general store owner Charles W. Hayes's home, today the Stacy residence at 123 Etna Road. This fine "Cape"-type home is one of the village's earliest surviving buildings, thought to have been erected in 1799.

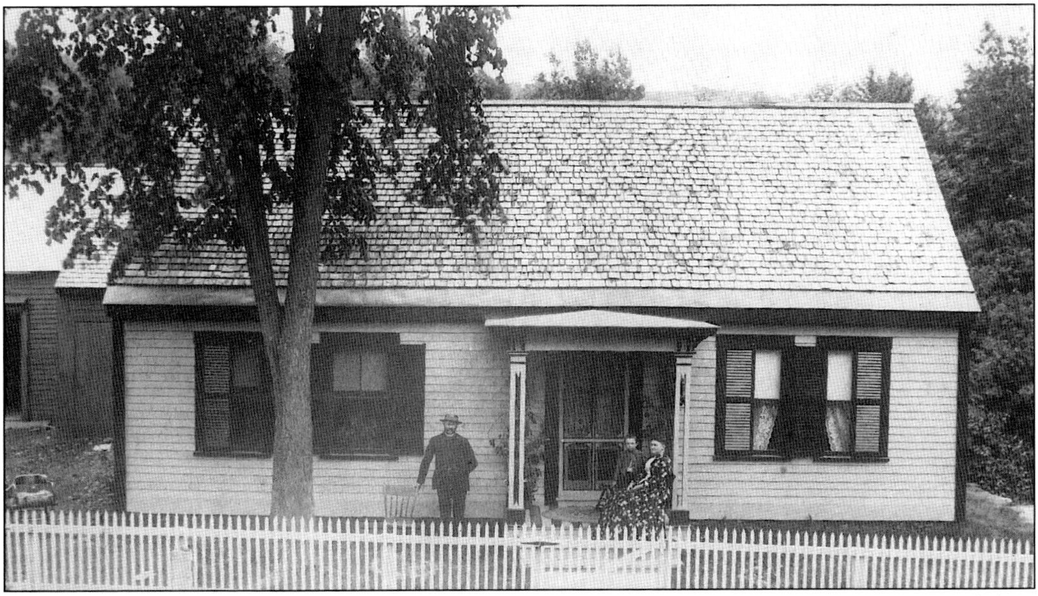

Charles W. Hayes and his family pose in front of their tidy village home, *c.* 1890. A remodeling about the time of this photograph has undoubtedly changed several features of the house's original construction—the elimination of the big central chimney and the substitution of larger pane window sash. Also note the addition of a handy and very fashionable small Victorian front entry porch.

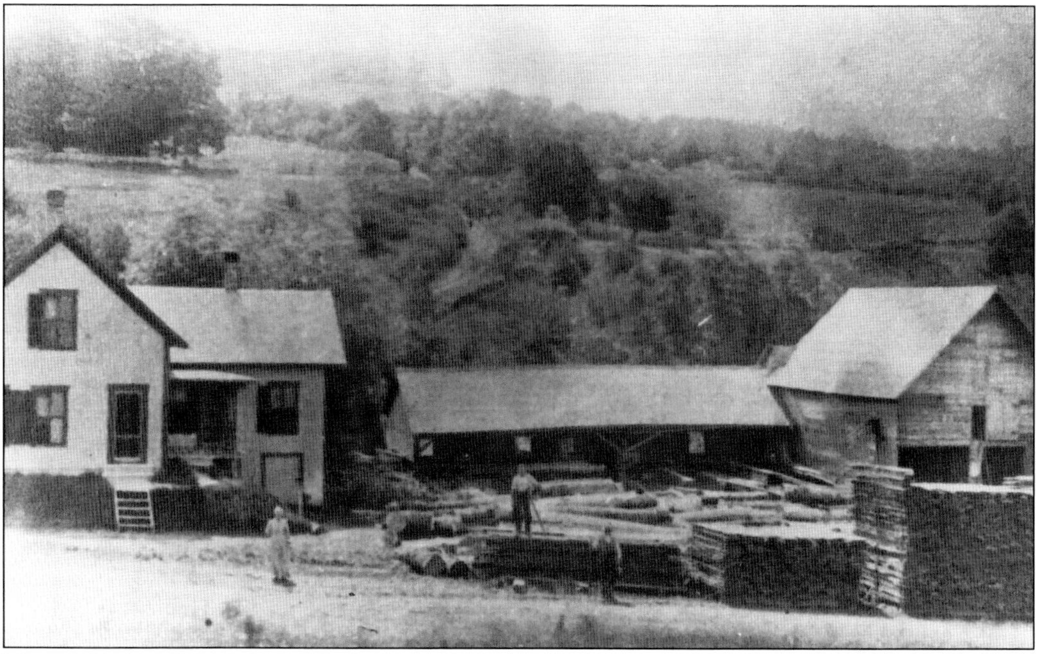

Horace L. Huntington was an enterprising individual, originally from upstate New York, who in 1882 purchased this mill site on Mink Brook for its excellent waterpower. Six years later in 1888, he constructed this residence for himself, today the home of Paul Tobias and Brenda Silver at 129 Etna Road. The mill's foundations still remain beside the brook's waterfalls.

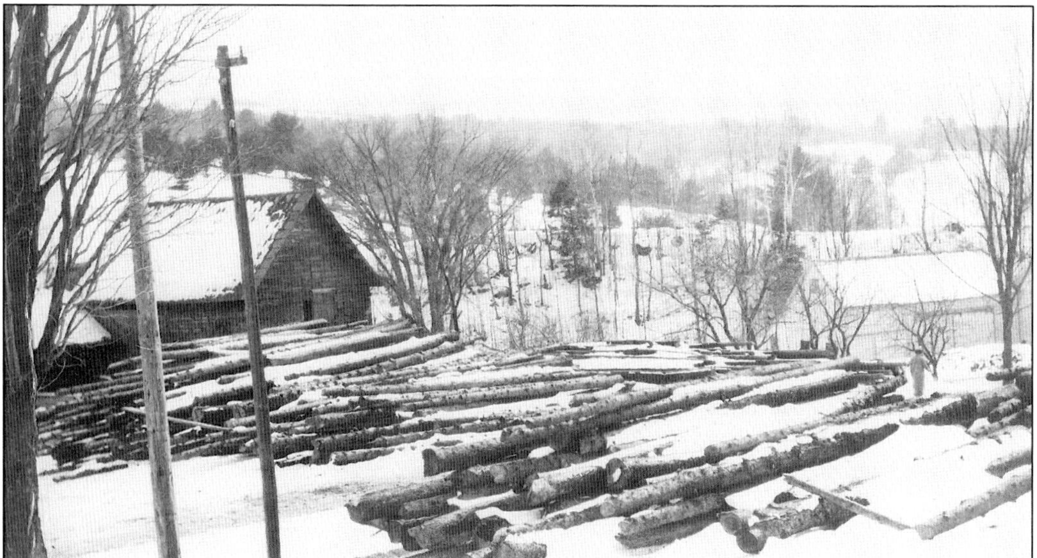

By the turn of the century, when this view was taken, Mr. Huntington had quite a sawmill operation going, storing logs on both sides of Etna Road. To the right is Charles W. Hayes's residence. In 1896, a newfangled stationary gas engine was added to supplement the seasonal waterpower. The mill was complete with not only sawing equipment, but a planer as well, and it produced more than 250,000 feet of lumber, plus equipment to press 250–300 barrels of good cider each year!

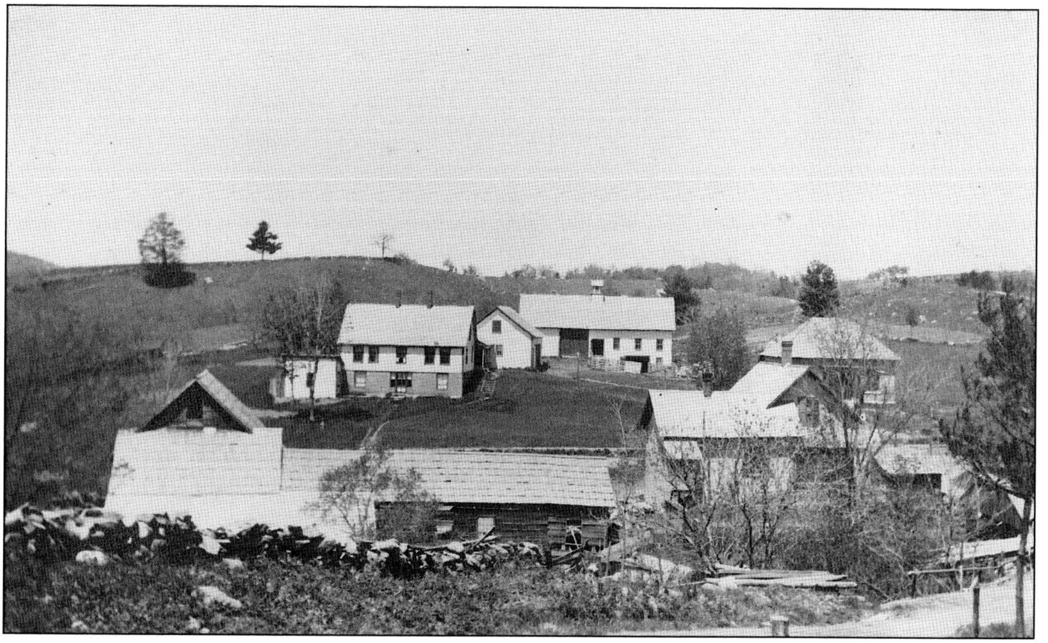

This *c.* 1910 view looks westerly from the base of the King Road Hill, across the roofs of Horace L. Huntington's residence and sawmill, to his village hillside farm. Huntington purchased the farm in 1905—then about 38 acres. Note the open hills beyond and the new town library building to the right of the photograph.

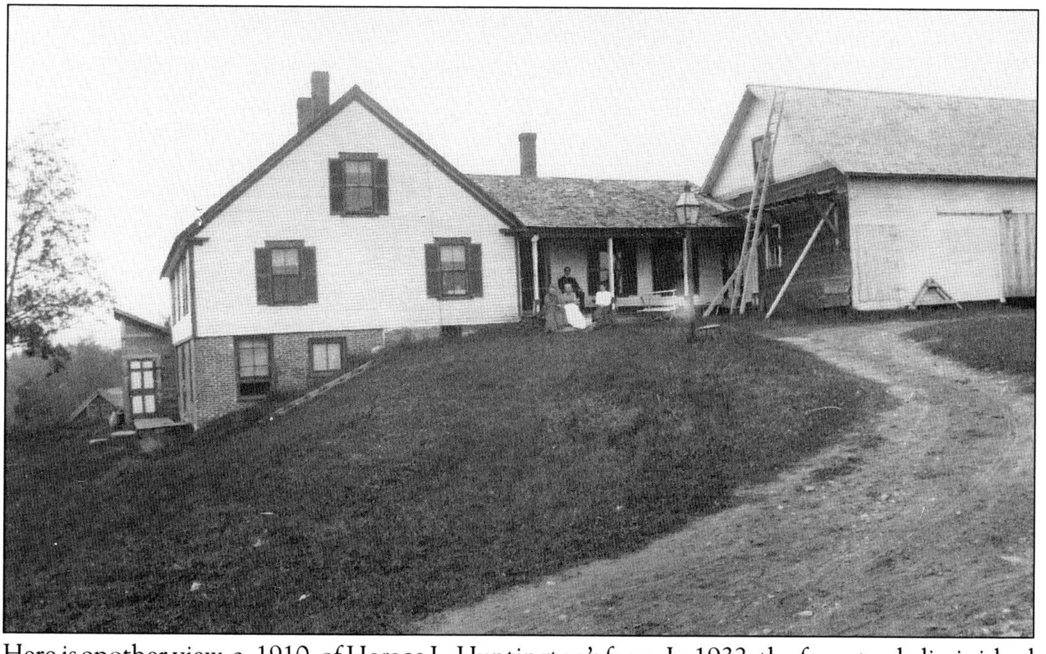

Here is another view, *c.* 1910, of Horace L. Huntington's farm. In 1932, the farmstead, diminished in size to about 11 acres, became the home of Morris and Ethel (Elder) Hayes, where they raised a family and kept a small farming operation going, while Morris worked construction as a mason. Note the early kerosene street lamp similar to those placed elsewhere in the village. Today, Ethel Hayes still resides in her house at 122 Etna Road.

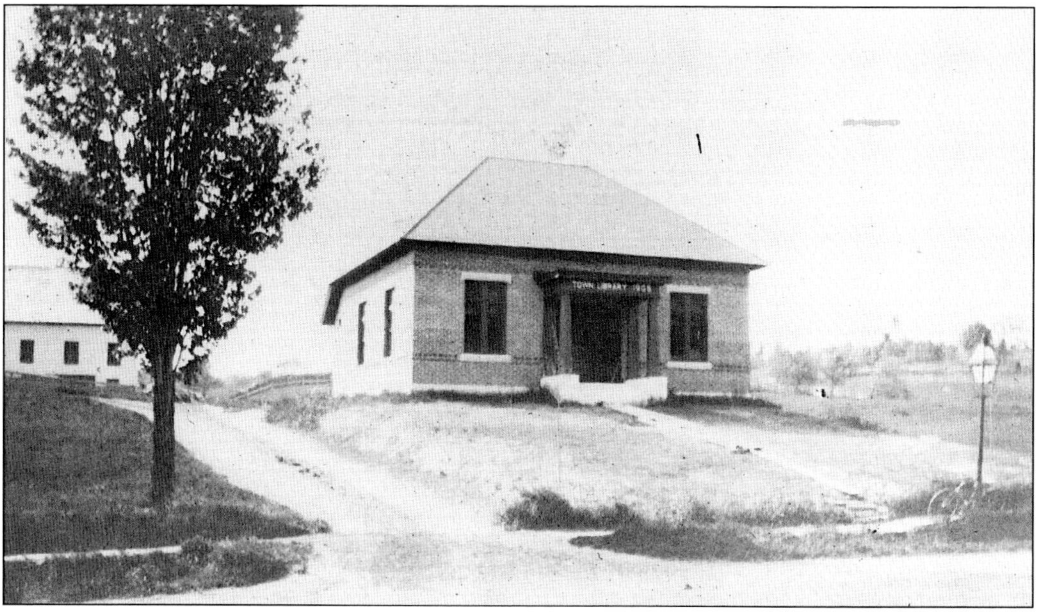

In 1903, a small corner of the Huntington/Hayes farm was purchased by the Town of Hanover for the purposes of constructing a public library. Two years later the building shown in this c. 1908 postcard view, designed by Dartmouth Engineering Professor Robert E. Fletcher, was erected for the total cost of $2,822.11. Today the library, after being nominated in 1996 by the author, is on the National Register of Historic Places.

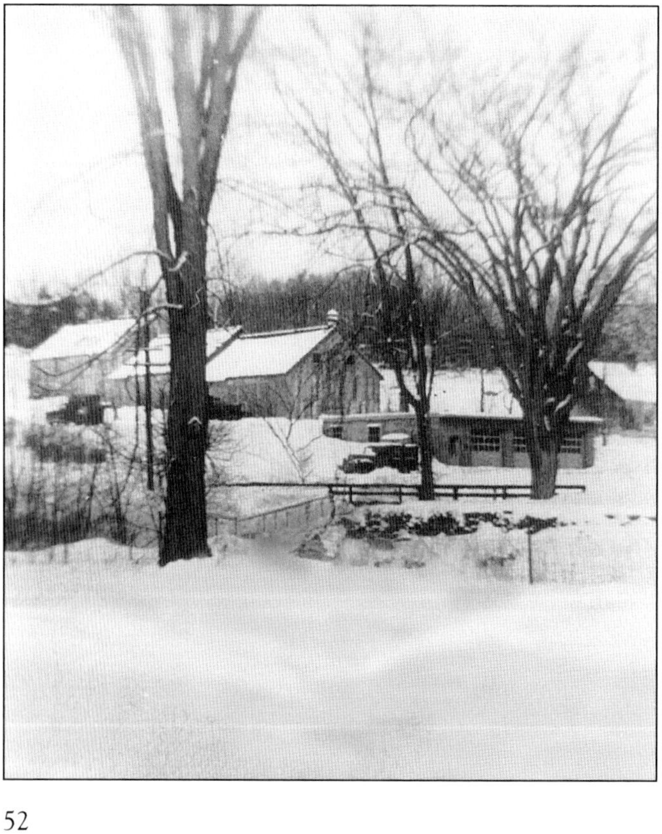

Until their destruction by fire during the middle of the day on Thursday, February 13, 1964, the town's highway maintenance equipment had for years been kept in the wooden-framed barns visible in the uphill far ground of this 1959 photograph. In front of them is the village's new fire station erected in 1952. Lost in the town highway shed fire, caused by an acetylene cutting torch, were two trucks, a payloader, and numerous tools.

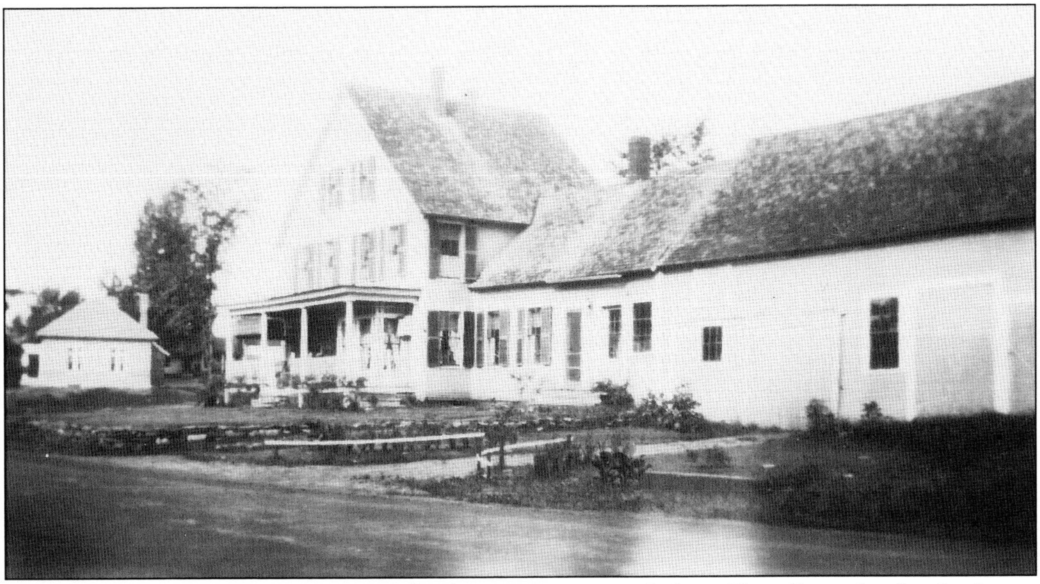

Amos Camp began construction of this home, but it was Laban Chandler, who finished it in 1873. This view shows the property as it existed in the 1920s when owned by Nellie (Hill) Blood. Note the town library building beyond. Today the residence is the home of John E. Connolly at 138 Etna Road.

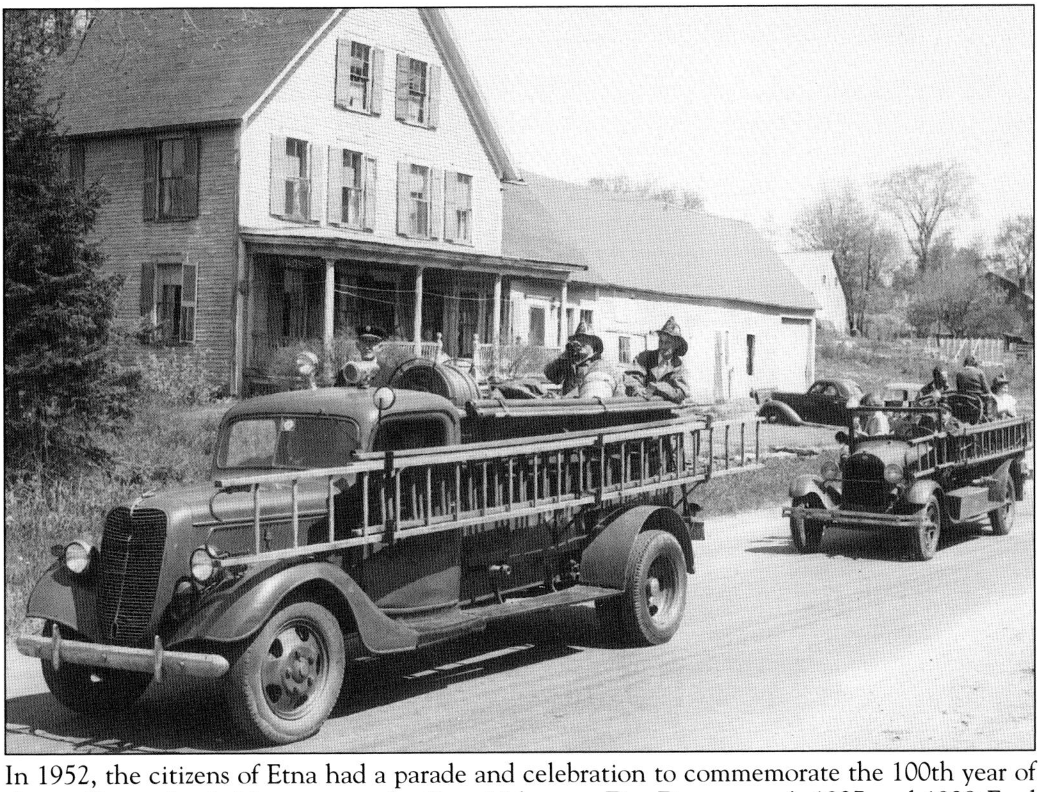

In 1952, the citizens of Etna had a parade and celebration to commemorate the 100th year of their village school. Here we see the Etna Volunteer Fire Department's 1937 and 1929 Ford trucks passing down the Main Street with a full compliment of firemen on board.

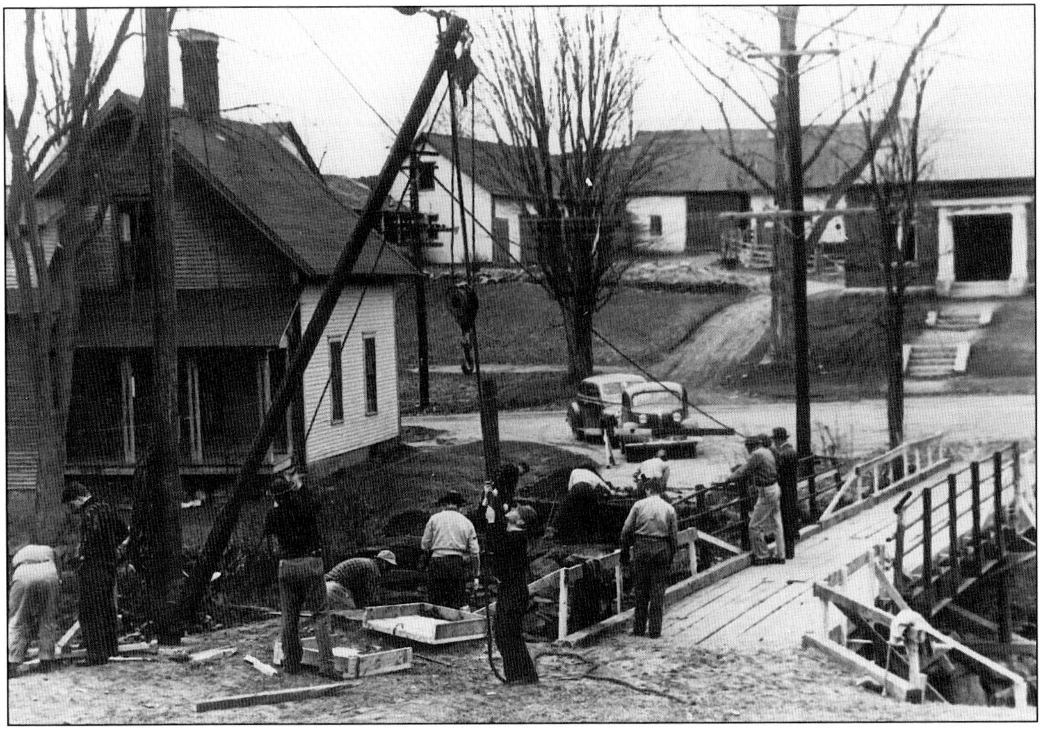

Prior to the popular use of concrete and large metal culverts, the many bridges located throughout the village area that crossed Mink Brook required much attention. Here we see the bridge at the base of King Road being replaced in 1942. The town library and Hayes farm is in the background.

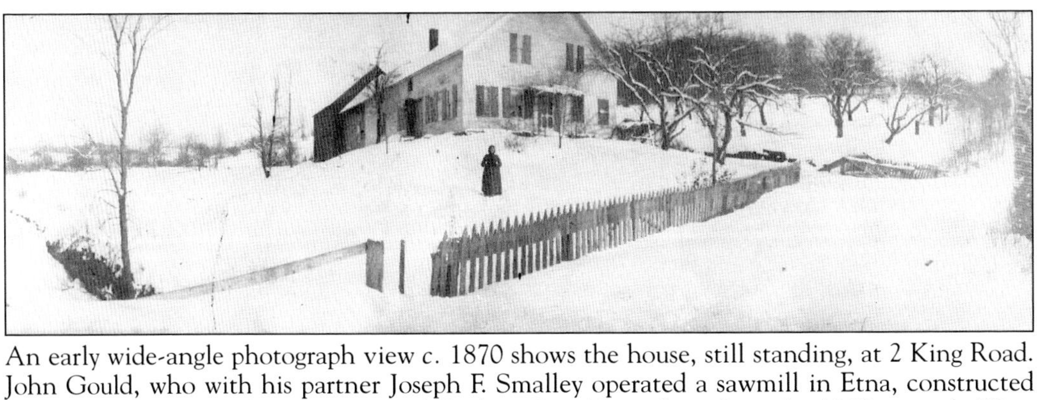

An early wide-angle photograph view c. 1870 shows the house, still standing, at 2 King Road. John Gould, who with his partner Joseph F. Smalley operated a sawmill in Etna, constructed this residence, although it is not recorded when. Possibly, it dates from the 1860s or early '70s.

At the annual 1924 Town Meeting, it was voted to appropriate $1,000 to erect a new building for the village's volunteer fire department. The final cost ended up being $1,227.36; however, the fire department had its first permanent home that served well until a new concrete and masonry facility costing $9,500 was built in 1952, located diagonally across the road.

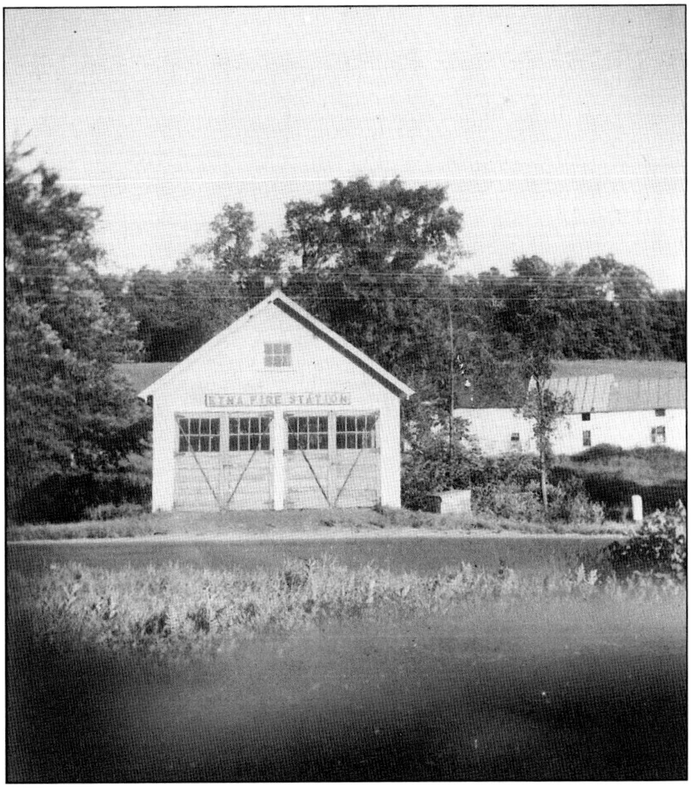

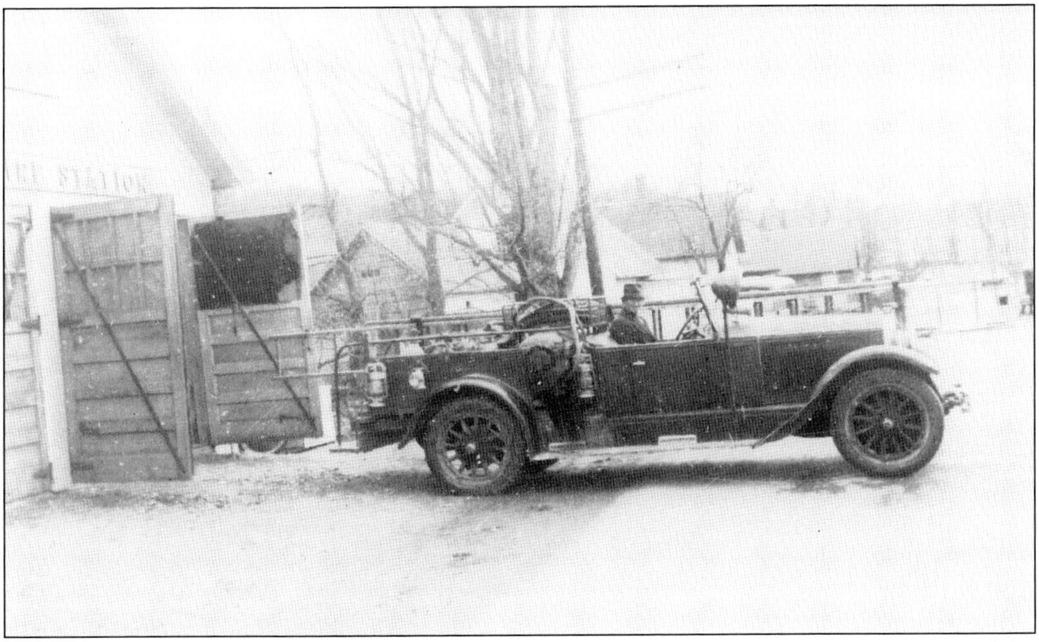

In many small rural communities like Etna, it was not uncommon in the early years of the twentieth century for the first pieces of motorized firefighting equipment to be homemade from passenger cars or light trucks. And in fact, one of Etna's first pieces of equipment was the firetruck seen here, made from a mid-1920s rugged Buick Master series touring car.

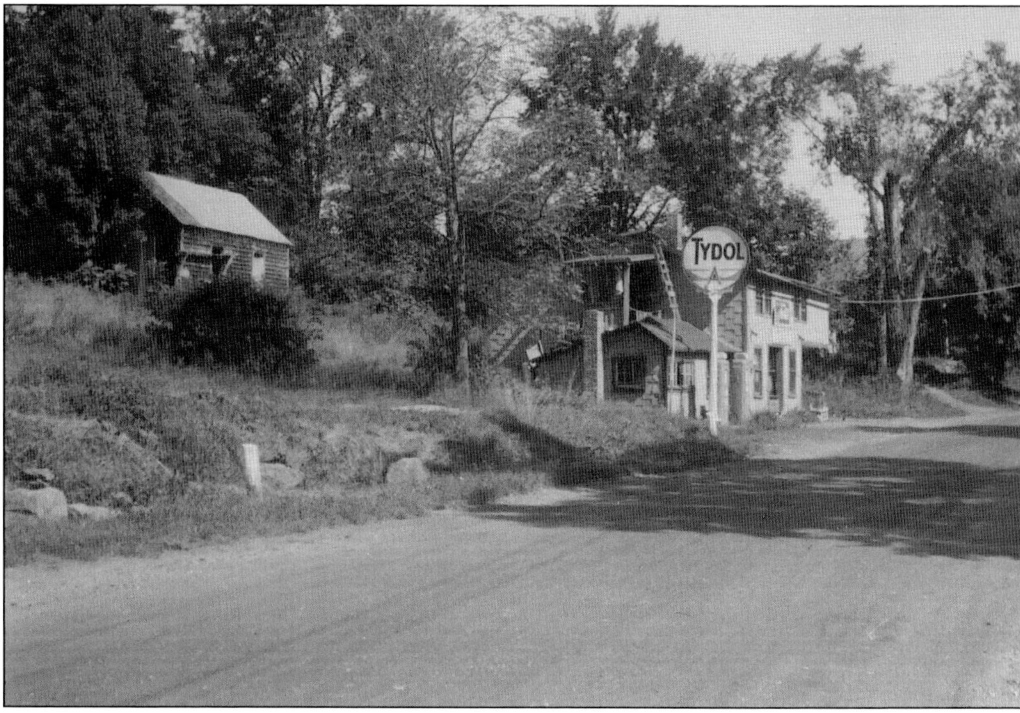

During the 1930s, Adna Camp established a small gas station along Etna Road, north of the village center, hoping to attract gas customers away from Elder's Etna Store. About 1940, Adna's son John and John's wife, Lillian, greatly enlarged the premises to include a full store as well as gasoline. This view was taken about 1959 after the whole business had ceased operation.

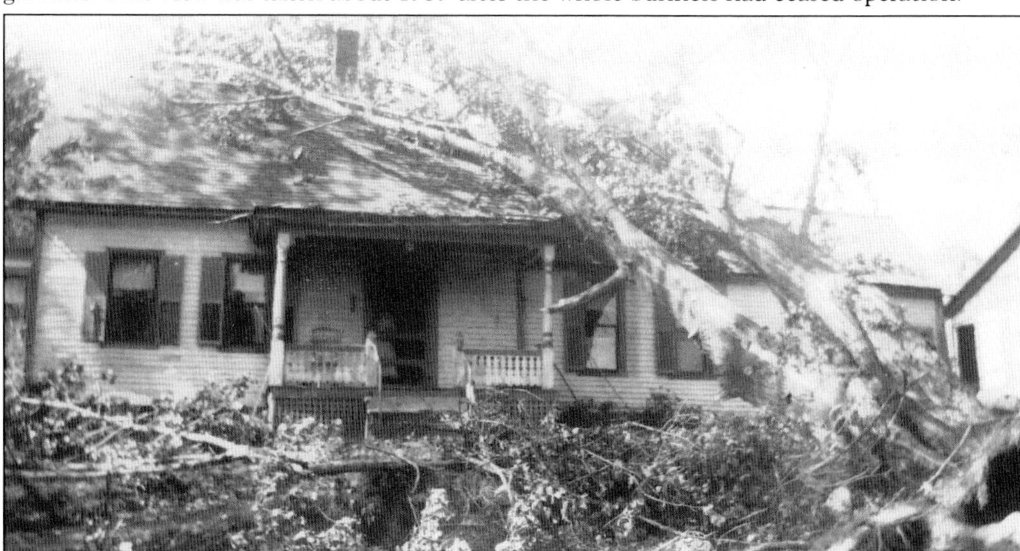

On September 22, 1938, the Connecticut River Valley was visited by a hurricane that blew as far north as the Canadian border before losing its destructive force. Much damage was done to Hanover, including the rural areas in and around Etna. This view shows a large tree toppled upon the home of Jim Spencer and his sisters. Today the house still survives at 164 Etna Road, and it is the home of Ken and Norma Pelton.

Like so many of Hanover's rural homes, very little is known of this residence, now the home of Bruce King at 149 Etna Road. It is thought that possibly the building was constructed by Horace L. Huntington in the late nineteenth century. This view shows it *c.* 1930, when owned by Charles Richardson.

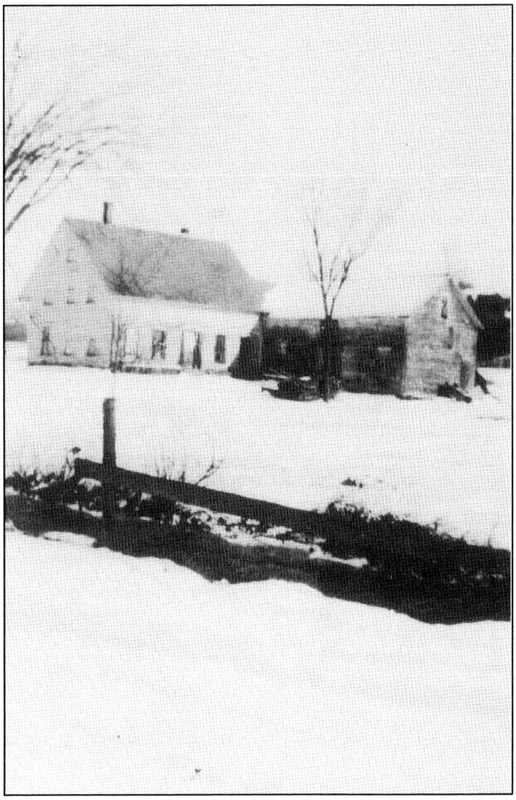

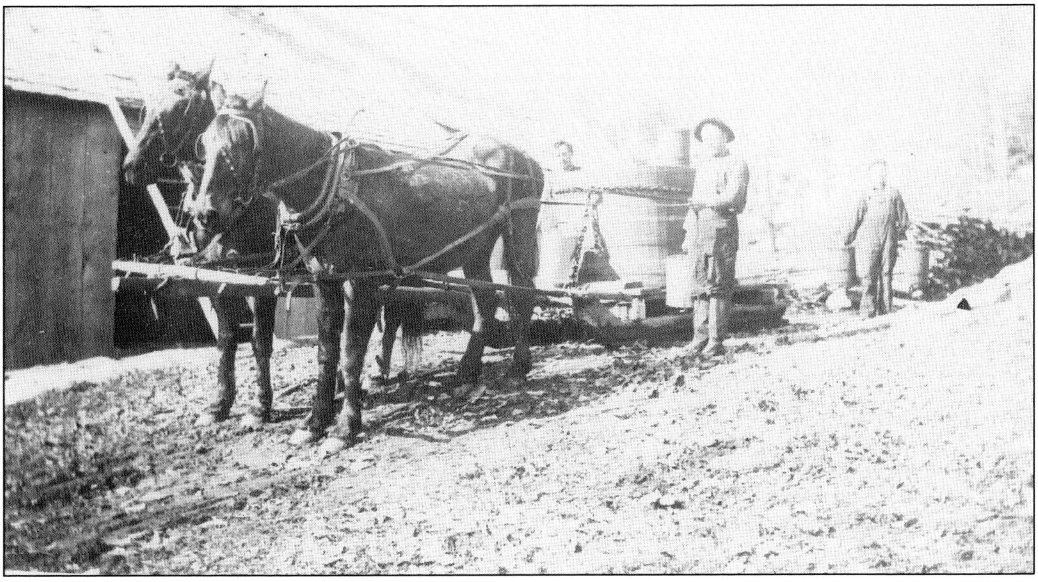

The Richardsons kept a maple sugar orchard up behind their village home, and like many rural families of the time, they added to their often small incomes by making maple syrup each spring. Here we see sap being collected into a wooden tub affixed to a horse-drawn sled.

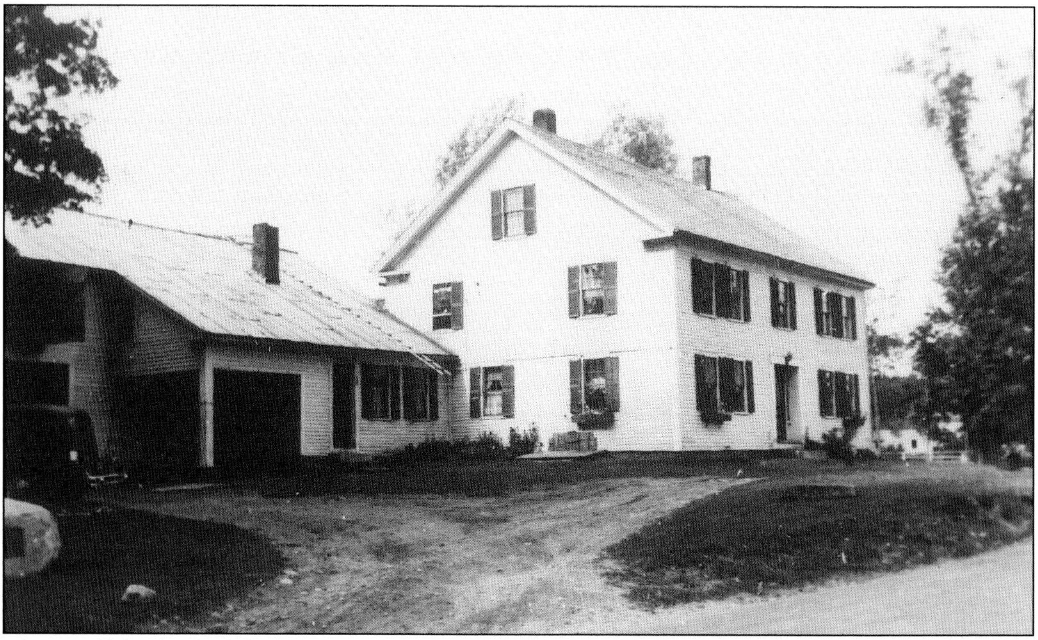

The small back el of this residence at 174 Etna Road is one of the earliest structures erected in Hanover, constructed by Moses Woolcott in 1767 and consisting of one principal room. Benjamin Fellows added the main house in 1820. For many years during the nineteenth century, the Bridgman family owned the property, and on brief occasions it was lived in by Laura Bridgman—the famous predecessor of Helen Keller. Since 1951, the family of Robert Storrs has been carefully maintaining and restoring the historic home.

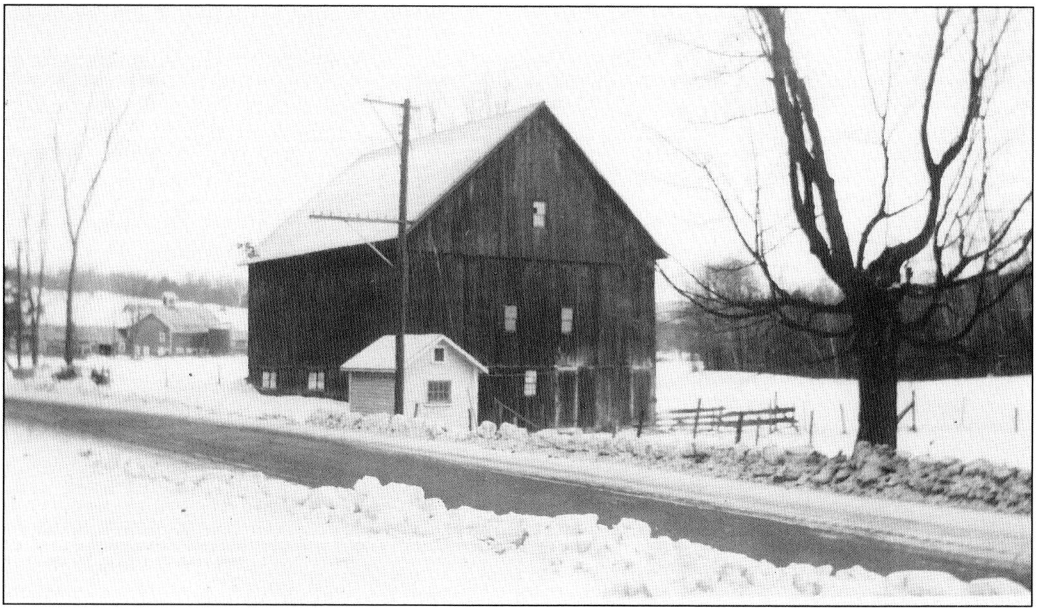

The barn on the east side of Etna Road, belonging to and across from the Bridgman/Storrs home, is believed to have been erected about 1911, replacing an earlier structure that had been hit by lightning and burned. Both this photograph and the view above were taken *c.* 1940, when the property was owned by Leon G. Hayes.

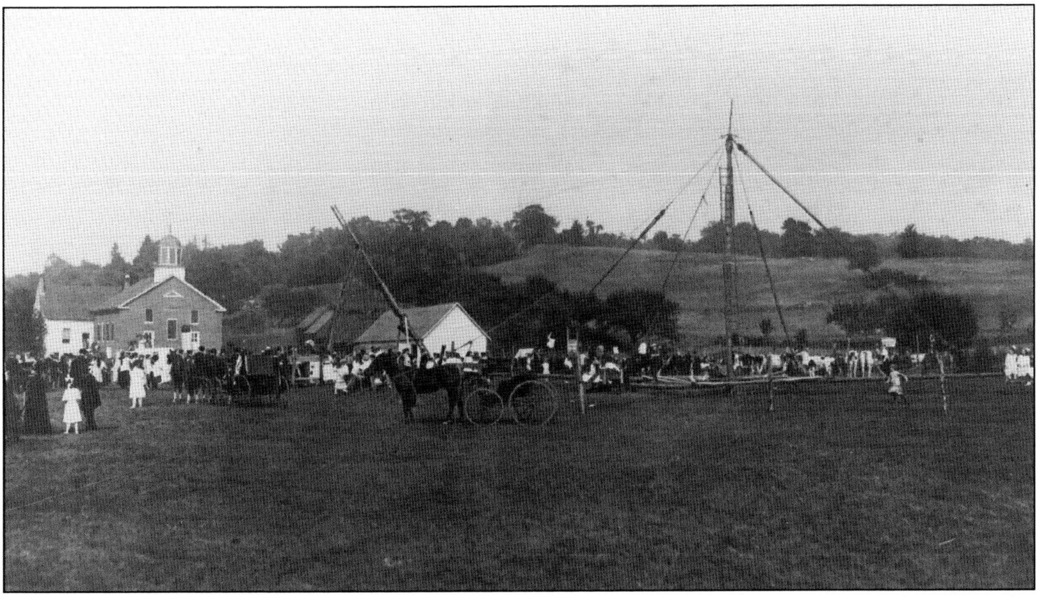

Starting in 1916, "Our Men's Club," an Etna civic organization, held an annual fair on the common, in front of the brick Baptist church. Proceeds from the event were used to fund local village improvements like streetlights and sidewalks, as an example. Here we see the first year of the fair in full operation.

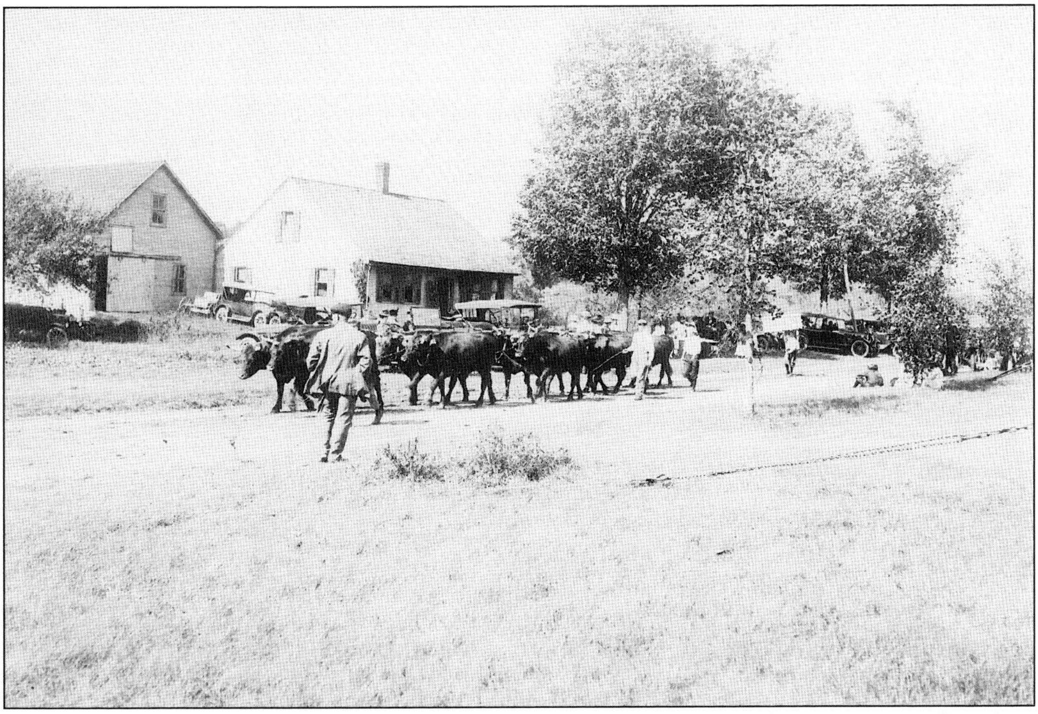

Because much of the focus of the annual fair was agriculture, it was only appropriate, therefore, to have a parade of livestock and their owners. In this view, steers from Arthur E. Fogg's farm on Dogford Road are part of the 1919 fair parade, passing by the church parsonage at 190 Etna Road.

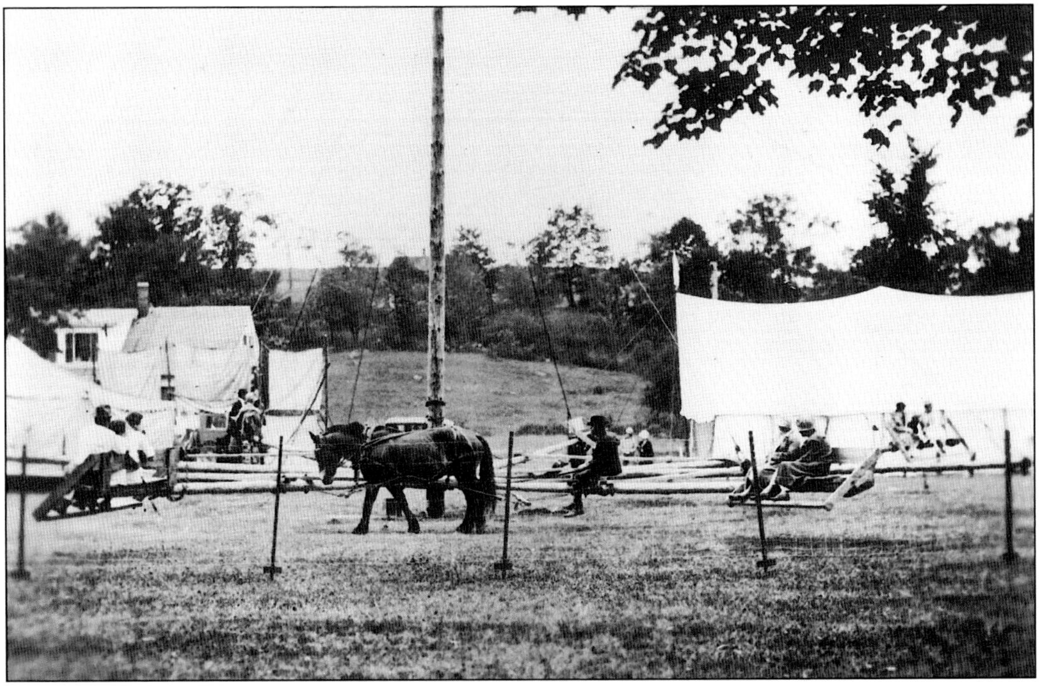

For many years, a popular attraction of the fair was this horse-powered merry-go-round, run by C.T. Camp, and set up on the common along with displays of agriculture, produce, culinary, and needlework. Band music was provided, as well as horse- and oxen-pulling contests and sporting events for the village youth.

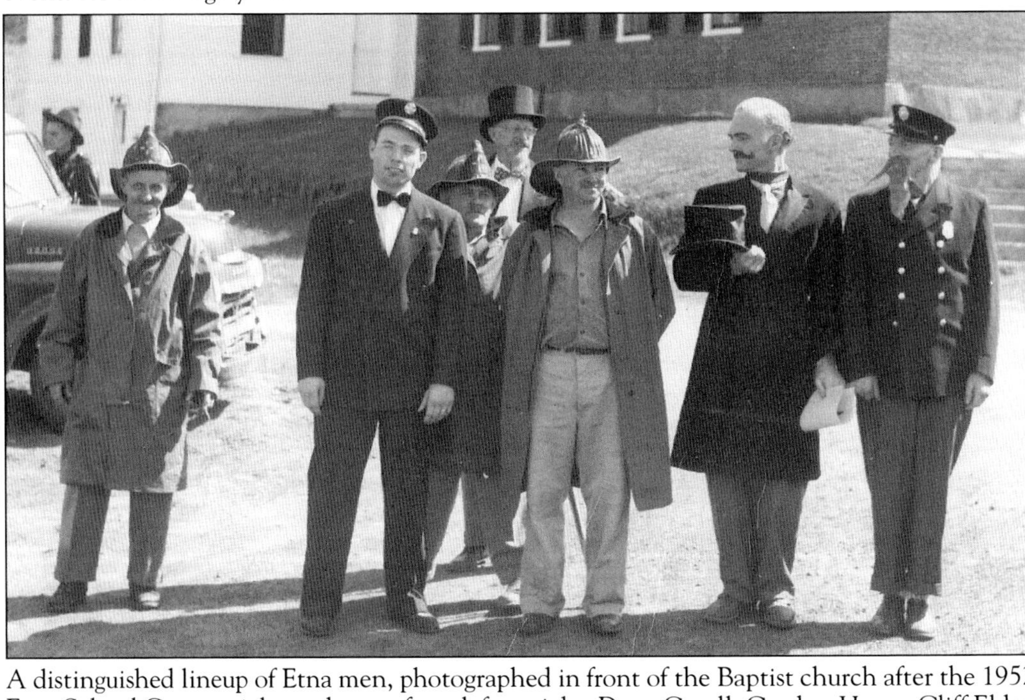

A distinguished lineup of Etna men, photographed in front of the Baptist church after the 1952 Etna School Centennial parade, are, from left to right, Dean Croall, Gordon Hayes, Cliff Elder, Harvey Camp, Morris Hayes, Bob Keene, and Leon Hayes.

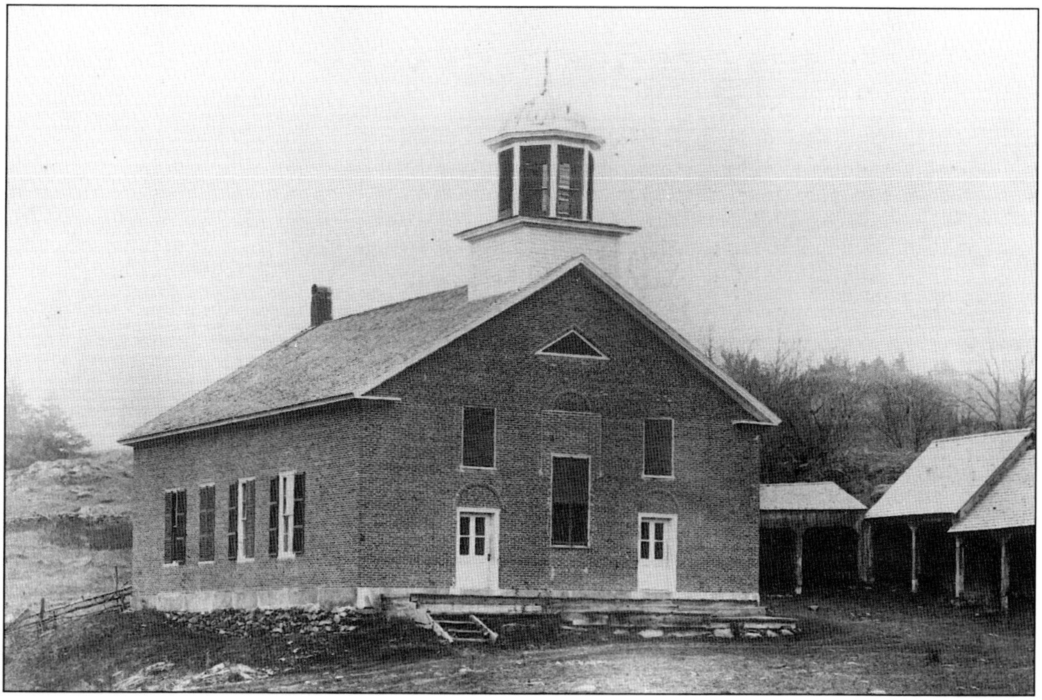

Church Elder Jesse Coburn was the designer of Etna's Baptist church, officially recognized as the First Baptist Church of Hanover. When the building was completed in 1827, after two years of construction, it ended up costing approximately $1,800. A vestry annex was constructed in 1898–99; and in 1954 a parish house was added—named Trumbull Hall after Etna resident Walter H. Trumbull.

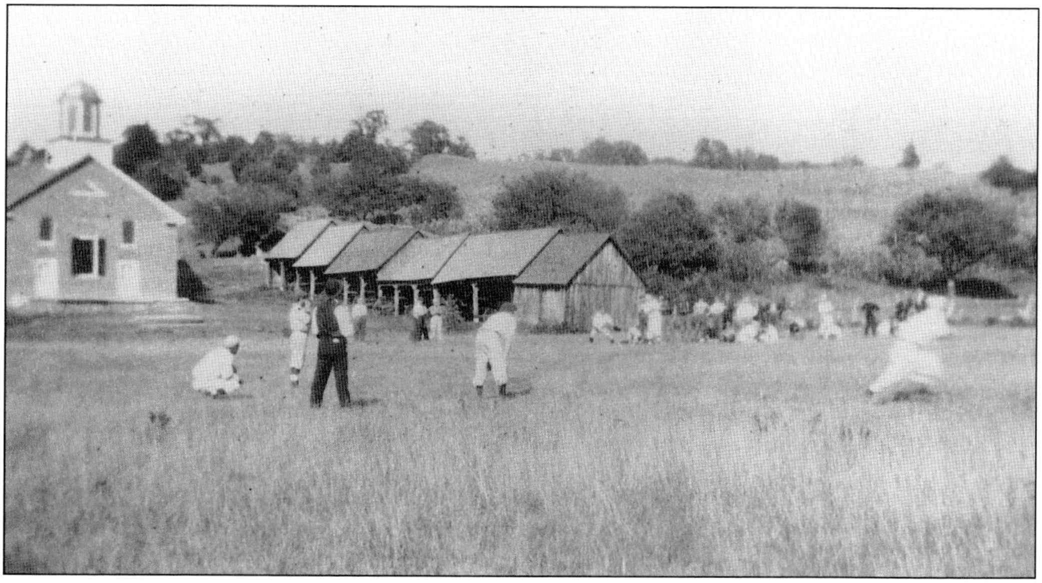

This is a turn-of-the-century view of Etna village boys playing baseball in front of the Baptist church. This common area was originally referred to as a "parade ground," meaning land for public exercises—military or likewise. It was established in 1829 with $120 of private subscription money; however, only since 1909 has it been owned by the Town of Hanover.

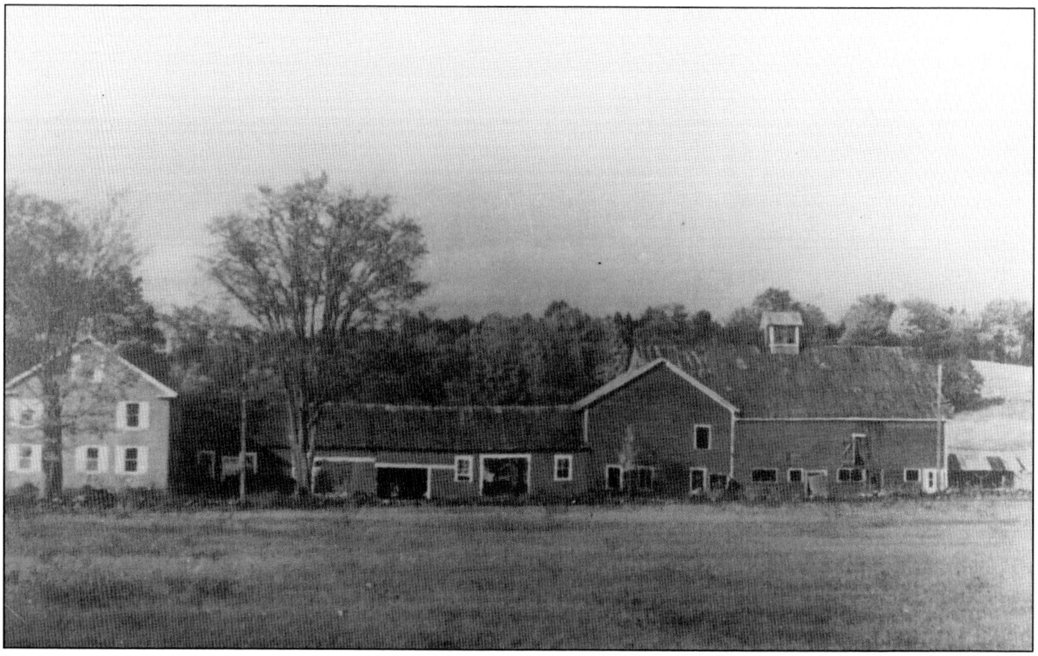

This beautiful Federal-period brick house at 2 Ruddsboro Road still keeps watch over the Etna common, as it has done since about 1820 when constructed by Ithamar Hall. Once part of a large dairy farm operation with sizable land holdings, owned by Harvey Camp, the extensive complex of barns was still attached to the house when owned by Jack and Phoebe Stebbins, seen here in this *c*. 1955 view.

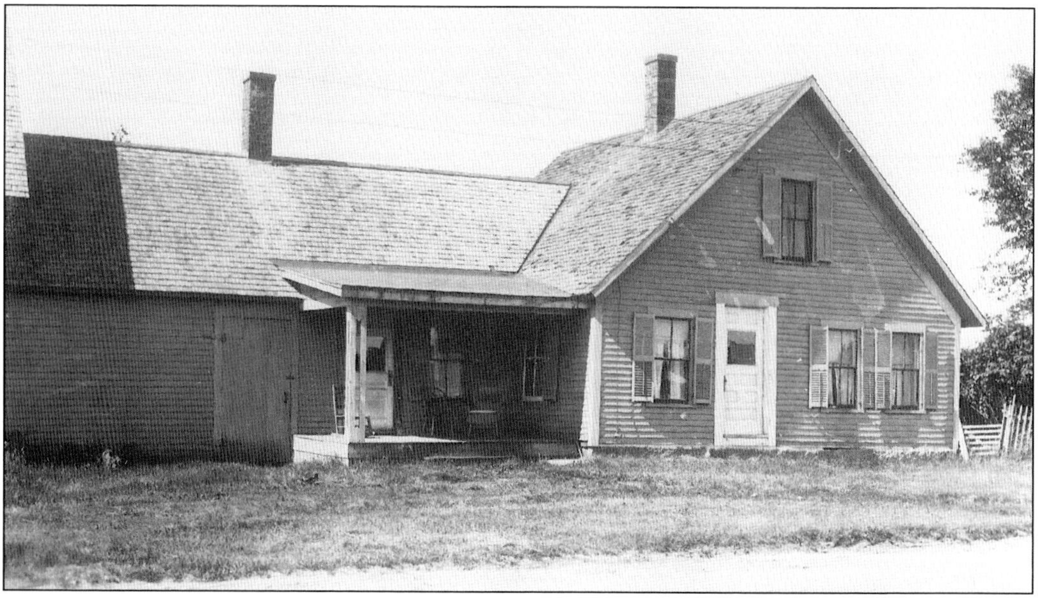

In 1889, Harrison Trumbull, a Civil War veteran formerly of Canaan, New Hampshire, purchased this early wood-framed dwelling located at 5 Ruddsboro Road. Like so many of the older residences in the rural areas of Hanover, little history is known of this building, including the date of its construction. When this photograph was taken, *c*. 1890, a large barn was attached to the easterly side of the house, and it remained there well into this century.

Three

A Rural People and Their Pastoral Land

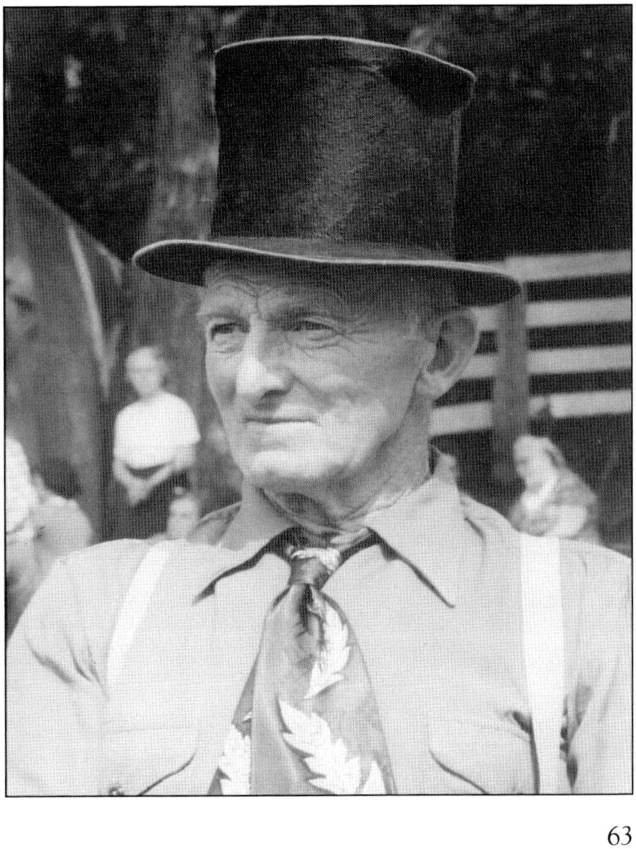

Lifelong Etna resident Leon G. Hayes keeps a watchful eye on things during the 1952 centennial celebration commemorating Etna's beloved village schoolhouse. Leon was descended from David Hayes, an early settler to Hanover who came by boat up the river from Connecticut and established for his family a farm on the high hill in Etna that still today bears his family's name.

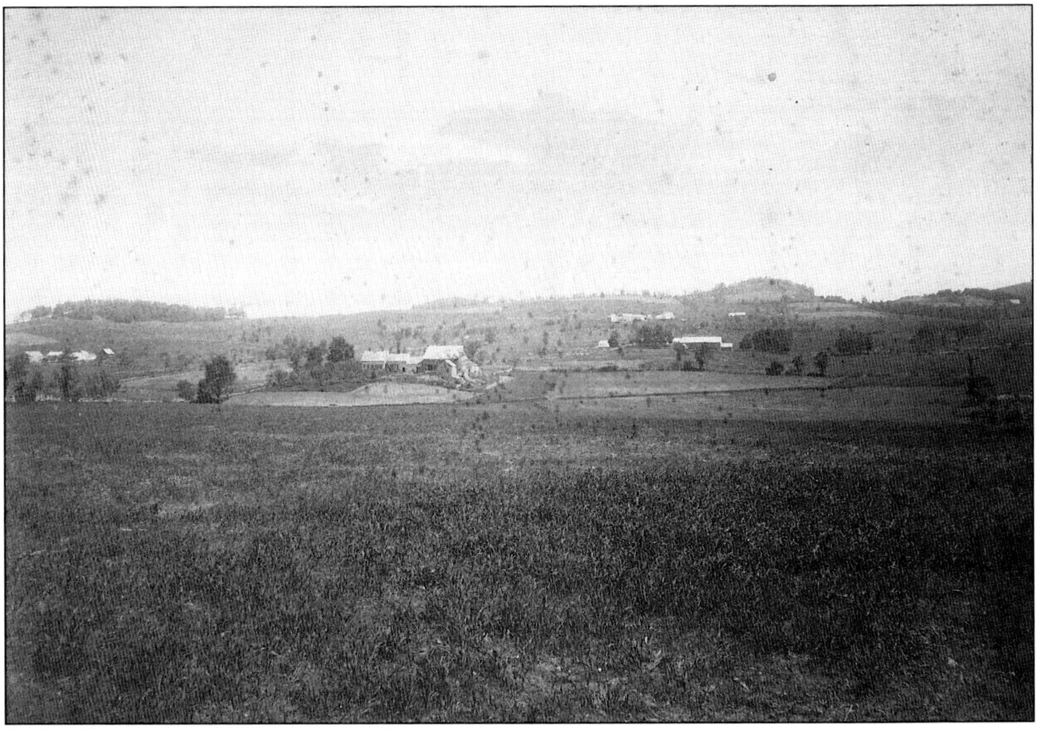

This *c*. 1890 view looks northerly from about the intersection of Trescott and Knapp Roads, into the small valley that is today part of the Hanover Waterworks protected watershed area. Four farms, totaling more than 600 acres, can be seen—those belonging to Charles W. Stone, William Hill, Charles J. Mason, and, in the distance, the town's poor farm.

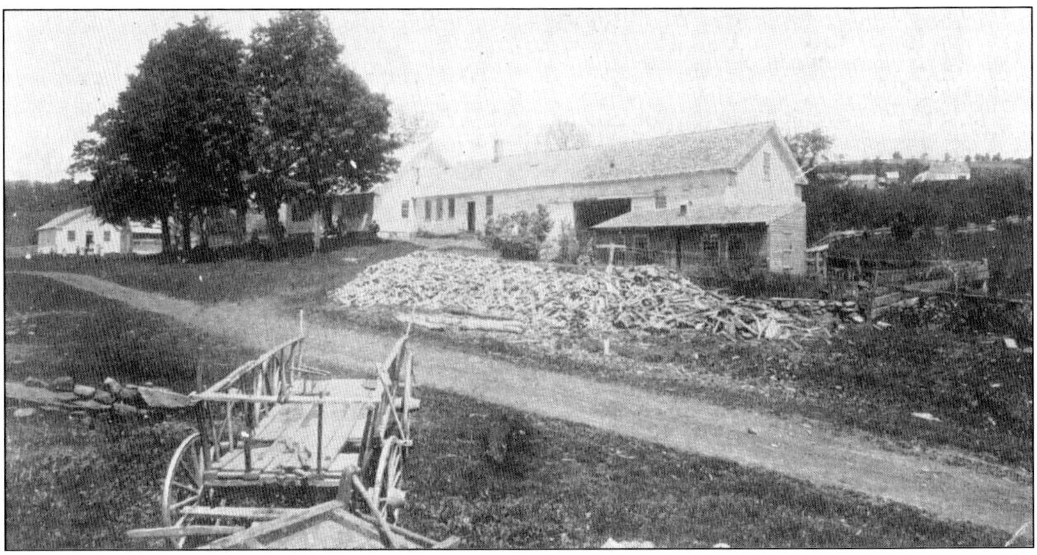

Charles J. Mason's 160-acre farm was located at the intersection of Wolfeboro and Knapp Roads, about 1890. The District No. 4 schoolhouse building can be seen to the far left; and the town's poor farm is up on the hill to the far right. In addition to orchards with 200 maple and 100 apple trees, Mason's farm had about 12 dairy cows and 70 Merino sheep for their fine wool. By 1903, the farm had been purchased by the Water Company for $4,000.

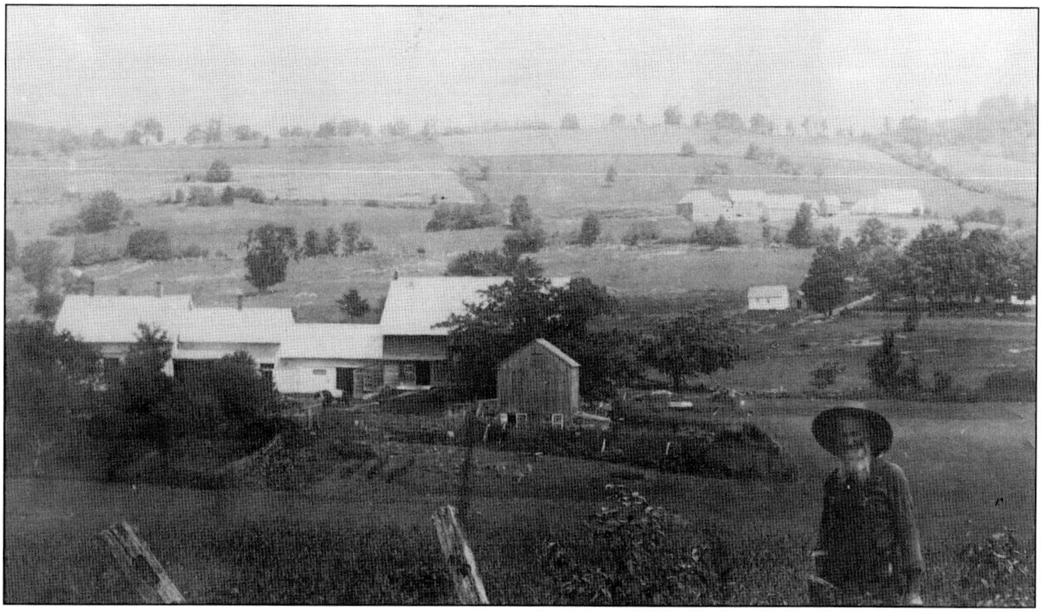

William Hall is in the foreground of this c. 1890 photograph looking down on his 105-acre farm, once situated where the dam is now located that impounds 150,000,000 gallons of water for the second reservoir, created in 1924. To the right is the District No. 4 schoolhouse; beyond that is the town poor farm. Hall, too, had a sugar orchard of approximately 500 trees, kept about 24 dairy cows, and raised Merino sheep.

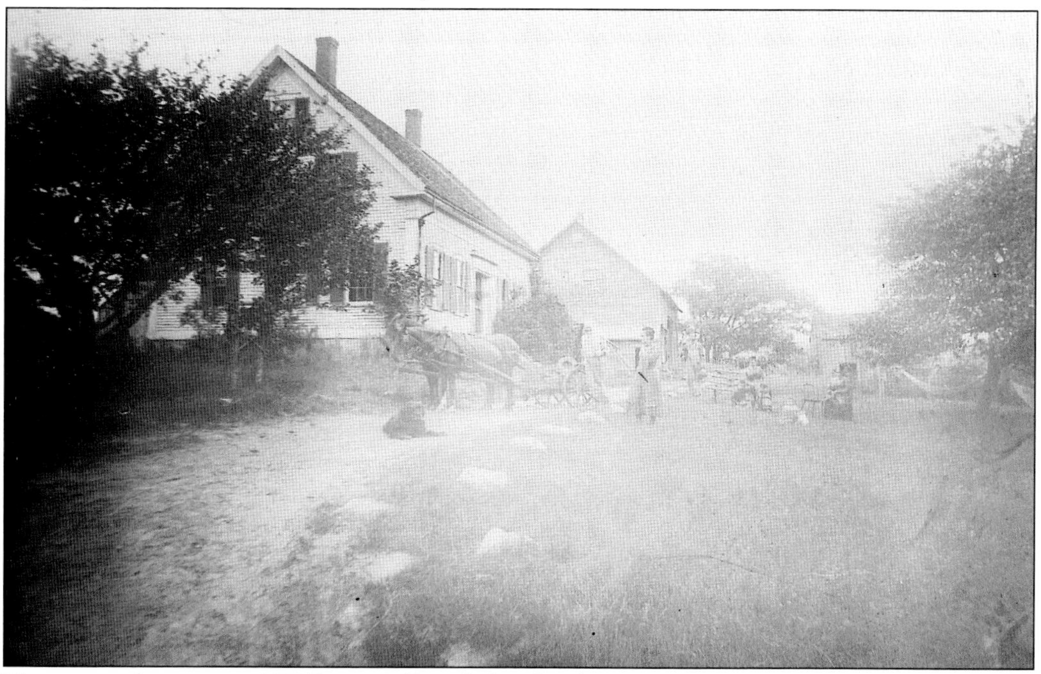

This is another view of William Hall with his family and farm, looking easterly from Knapp Road. This farm was not part of the initial 50 acres that created the first reservoir in 1893, but rather was purchased in 1903 for $4,750, in response to a water-borne typhoid fever scare and the resultant need to have more vacant land to protect the water supply.

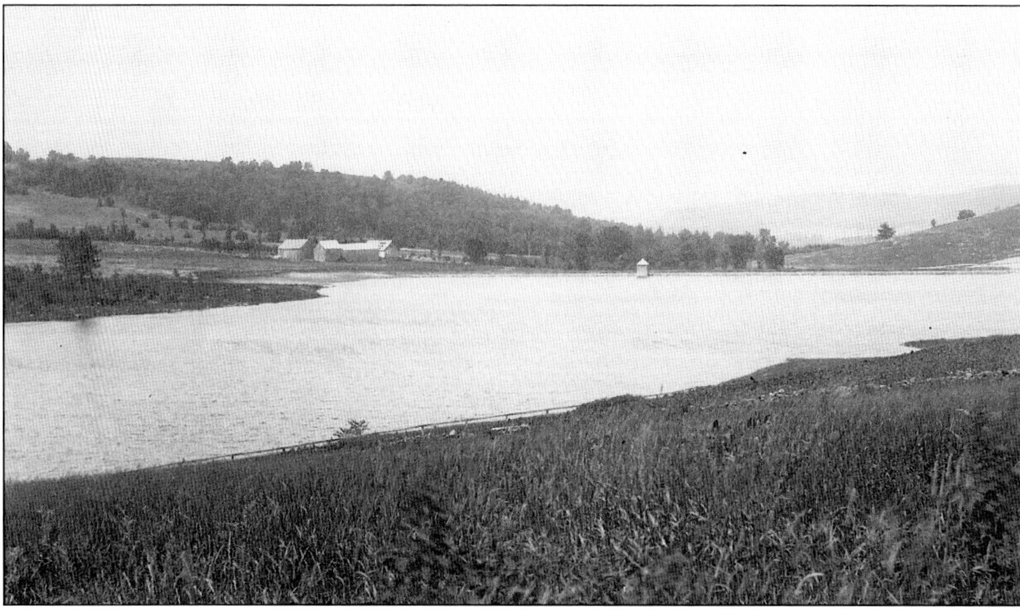

This view is of the first reservoir, constructed in 1893, and it looks southwesterly from Charles W. Stone's farm across to Henry H. Marshall's 200-acre farm. In the distance can be seen the newly constructed earthen dike and gatehouse creating the artificial pond. Today, the Marshall farmhouse still stands at 41 Grasse Road. Marshall, similar to many Hanover farmers, made maple sugar in the spring and kept sheep for their wool.

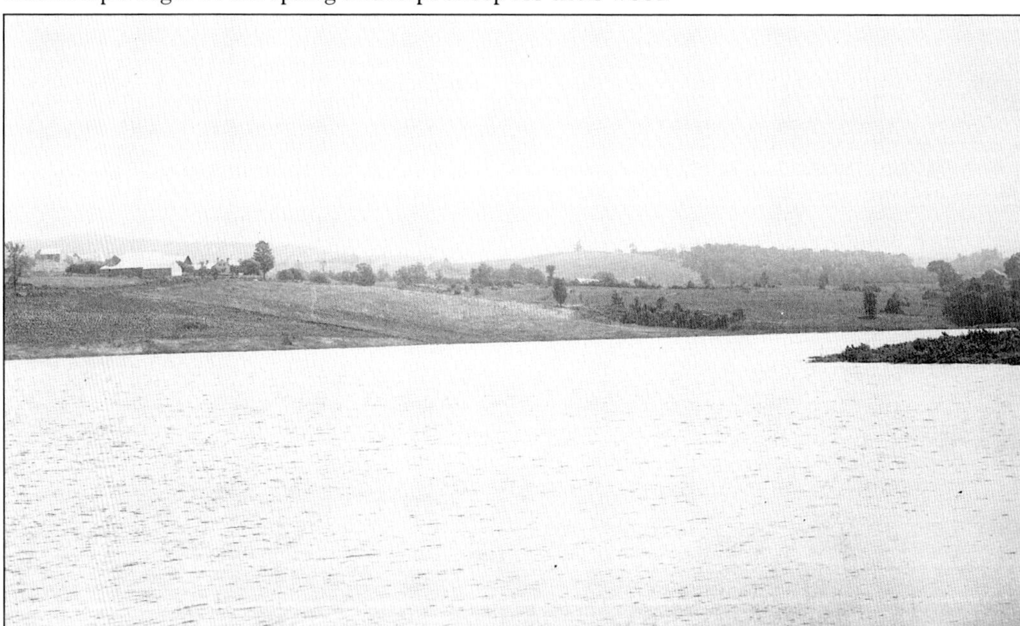

This view looks northeasterly across the same body of water at Charles W. Stone's 200-acre farm. In 1903, when the Water Company purchased this large parcel, the Stone family moved down to the newly acquired Benton farm, along Mink Brook and South Main Street, which they farmed until 1948. Stone's farm was primarily a dairy operation, as would most twentieth-century Hanover farms in time become.

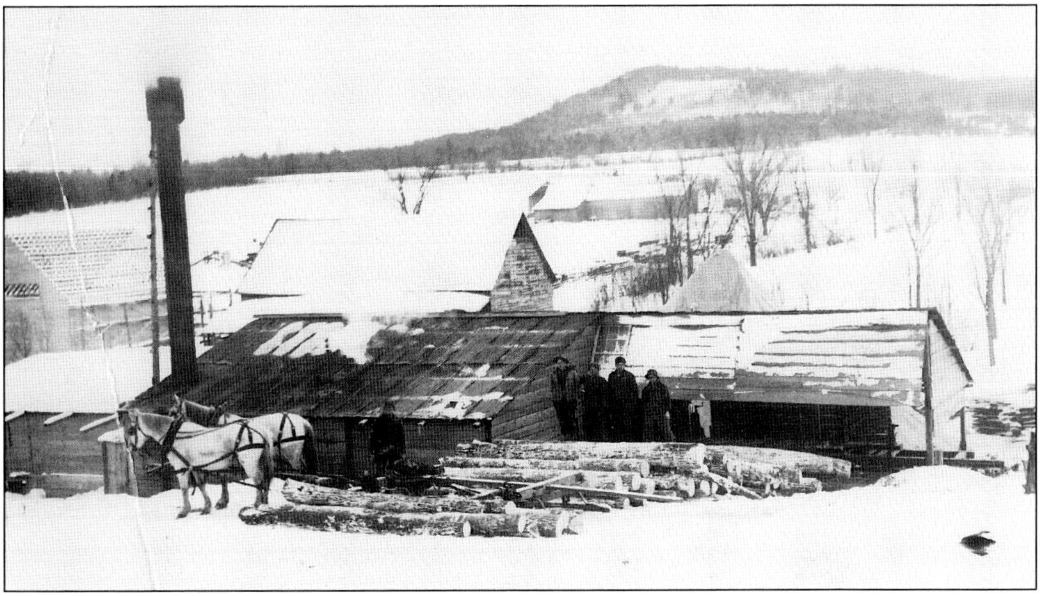

Apparently for a period of time, *c.* 1910, the town poor farm had a sawmill set up and in operation, as seen in this view. To the left can be seen a large icehouse under construction, and the buildings in the far center are part of the Mason farm. The hill in the background is the back side of the Velvet Rocks. Probably much of the timber for the sawmill came from maple sugar orchards that were once part of the farms acquired by the Water Company.

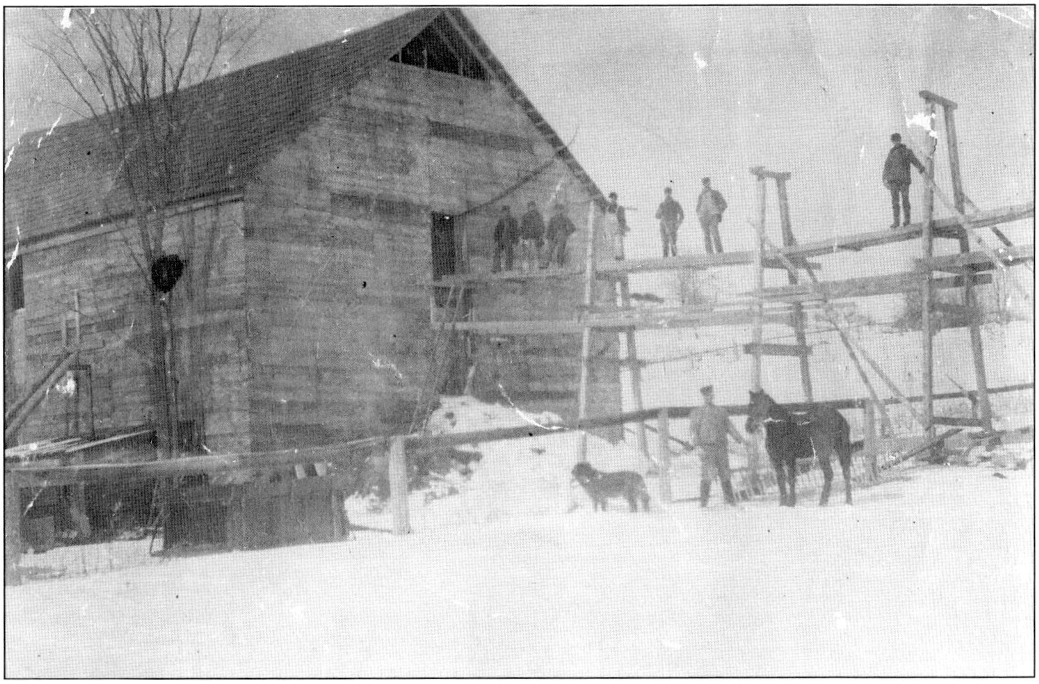

A rather tattered photograph shows men working at the town poor farm's icehouse. The newly created first reservoir, now known as the Fletcher Reservoir, furnished a ready and convenient supply of ice that during summer months was used by the college and the hospital. The adjacent sawmill supplied plenty of sawdust to pack around and preserve the ice.

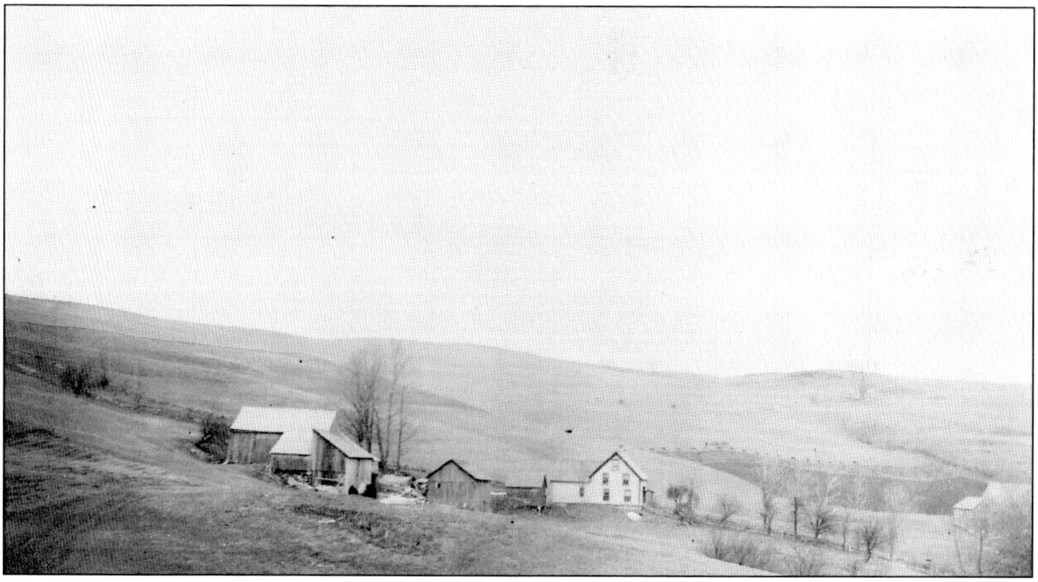

Through most of the last century, until the establishment of county poor farms by the State of New Hampshire, every town had their own—including Hanover. Always the subject of lively debate at the annual town meeting, Hanover's 202-acre poor farm was located on the south side of Pinneo Hill, adjacent to Pinneo Road. This view shows the farm perhaps 20 years before it was purchased by the Water Company in 1903 for $4,000.

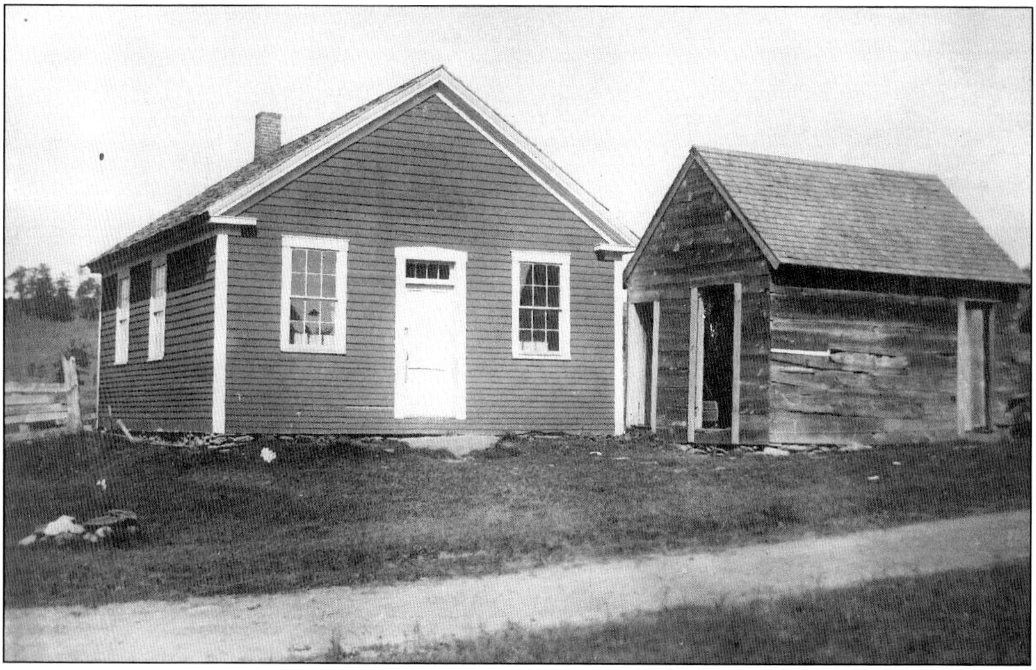

The District No. 4 schoolhouse was located at the northwest corner of Wolfeboro and Knapp Roads, shown *c*. 1890. No records appear to exist indicating when this little building was erected, although it might well have been shortly after 1807 when the Town completed a major school district redistricting. No. 4 was also known as the "Town Farm" district. Note the crude combination privy and woodshed beside the neatly clapboarded building.

Here are two generations of Hayes men, both farmers and descended from one of Hanover's earliest families to settle in the Etna area. Leon G. Hayes is standing beside his father, Roswell M. Hayes, in this *c.* 1940 view. In addition to farming, Childs' 1886 *Grafton County Gazetteer* listed the elder Mr. Hayes as a house and carriage painter.

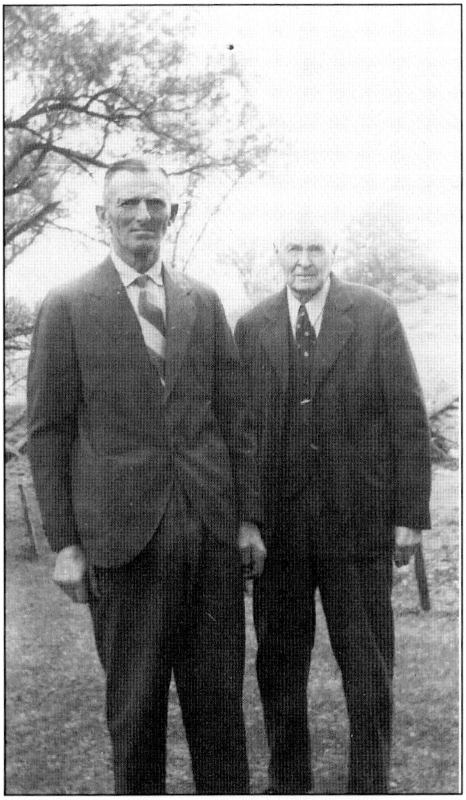

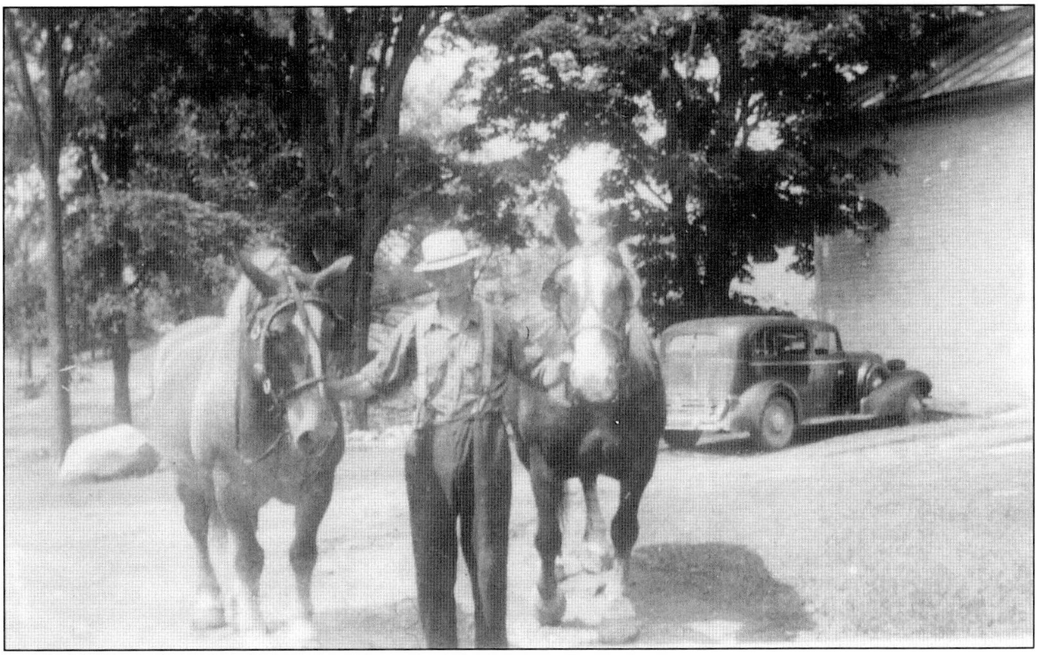

A 1940s view shows Leon G. Hayes with his two favorite workhorses, named Molly and Dolly. This photograph was taken in front of the so-called Laura Bridgman house, then owned by the Hayes family and today the residence of Jean Storrs at 174 Etna Road.

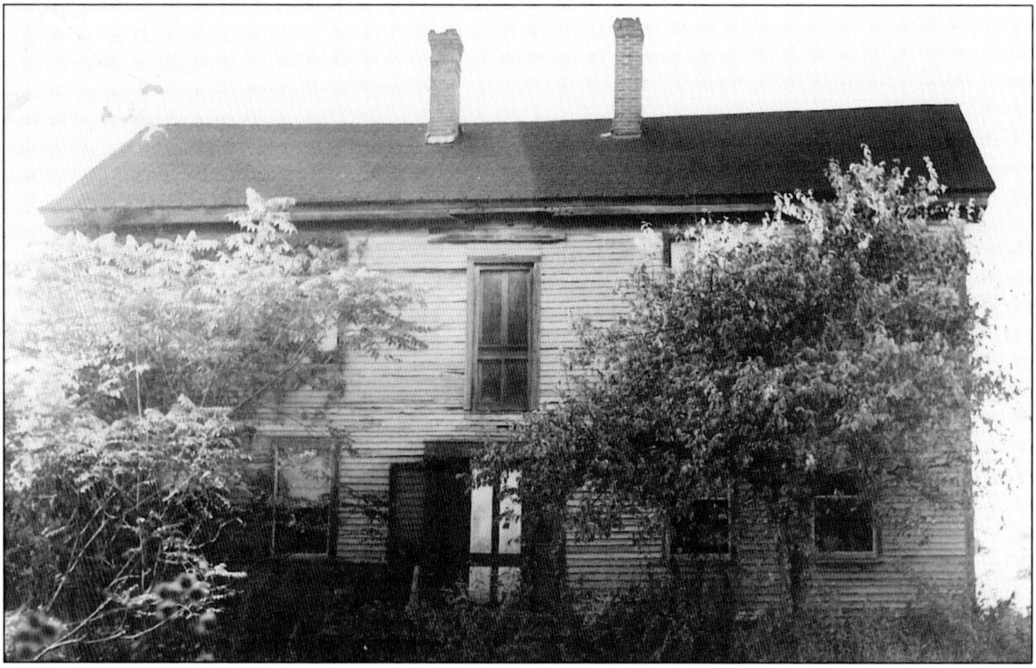

This 1960 photograph shows the remains of the George F. Adams house, situated on Jones Road overlooking Etna Road below. In the late 1960s, all of the land that went with this early farmhouse became the Trescott Ridge subdivision, and by then, the old, abandoned farmhouse had been torn down.

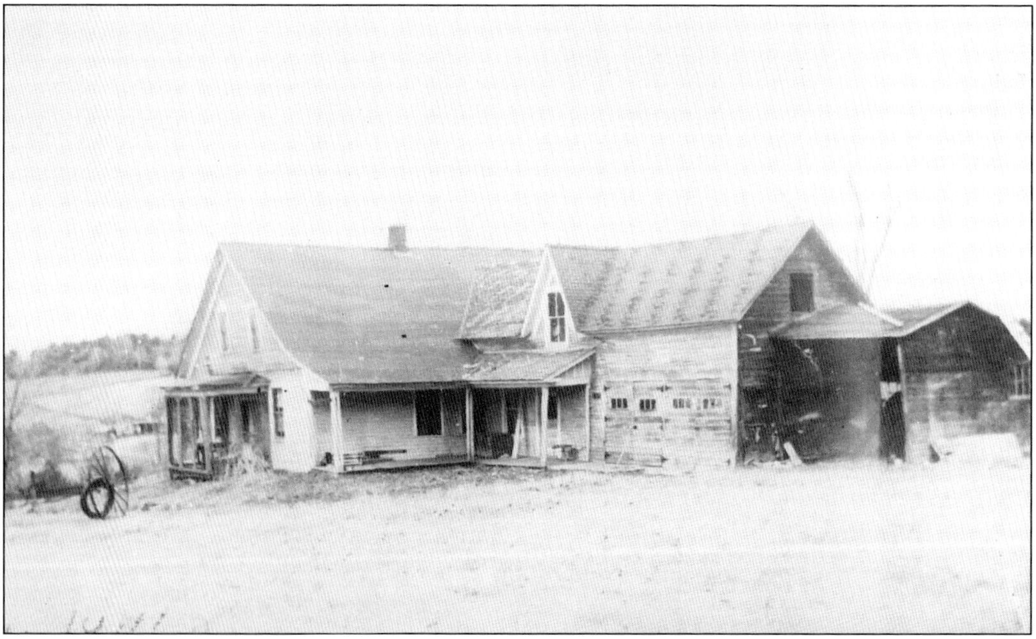

This early home, seen here in about 1946 and now the residence of Elaine Bent up on Bent Road, was erected by Webster Hall in 1781, and it is one of the older dwellings in the area. Much of the land that was part of this house and farm in earlier days has been kept undeveloped by the Bents.

David Croall bought the 120-acre Foss farm on Lower Dogford Road in 1927. Although the builder and date of construction of the one-and-a-half-story farmhouse is no longer known, it is thought to be of early-nineteenth-century origins. David Croall passed away in 1970, and his son Dean still resides on the farm.

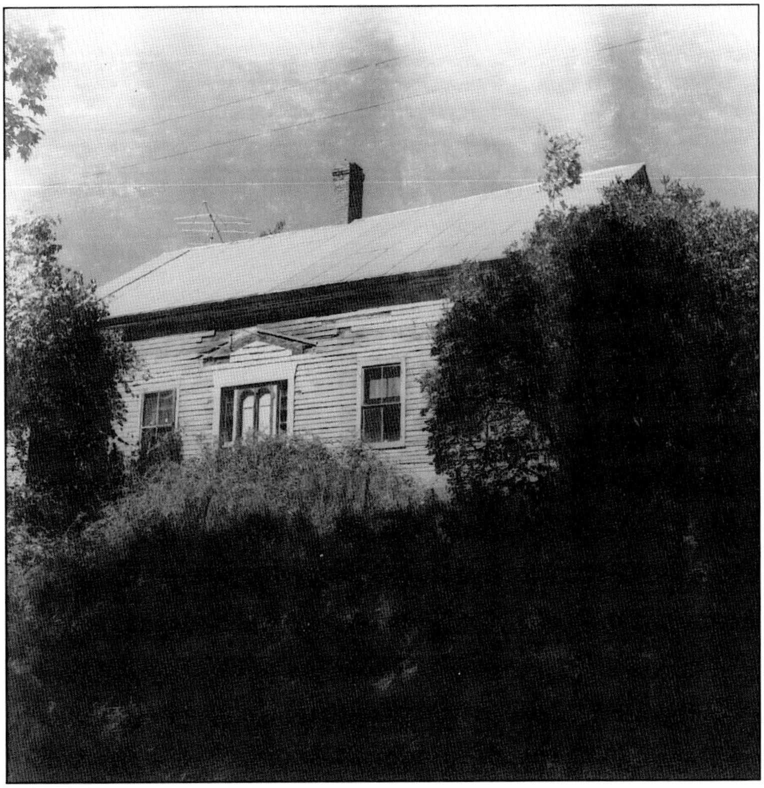

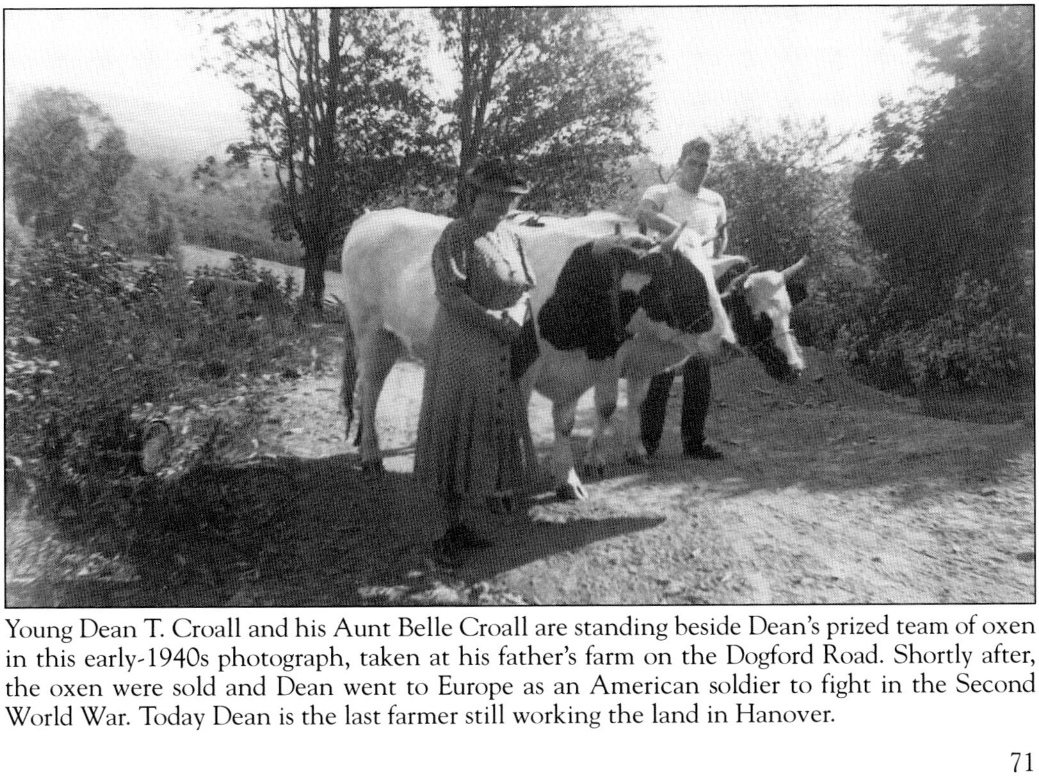

Young Dean T. Croall and his Aunt Belle Croall are standing beside Dean's prized team of oxen in this early-1940s photograph, taken at his father's farm on the Dogford Road. Shortly after, the oxen were sold and Dean went to Europe as an American soldier to fight in the Second World War. Today Dean is the last farmer still working the land in Hanover.

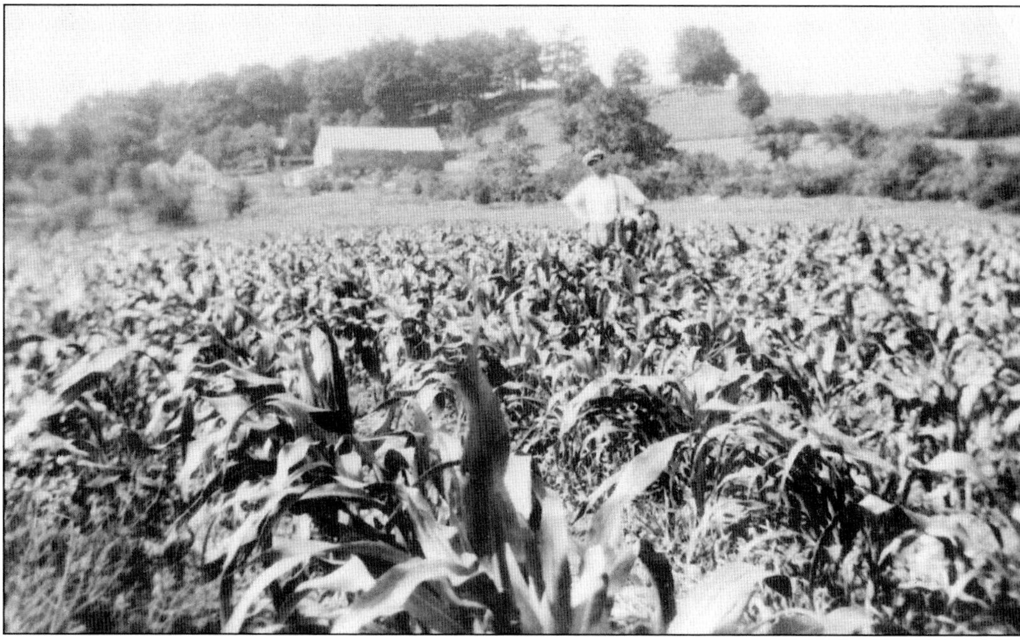

Arthur Elwin Fogg, seen in this *c.* 1920 view looking over his cornfield with his daughter Valma, owned a farm on the Dogford Road at its intersection with the Wolfeboro Road. In the distance are the farmhouse, barn, and Pinneo Hill. Today not a trace of this farm remains except for some scattered foundation stones.

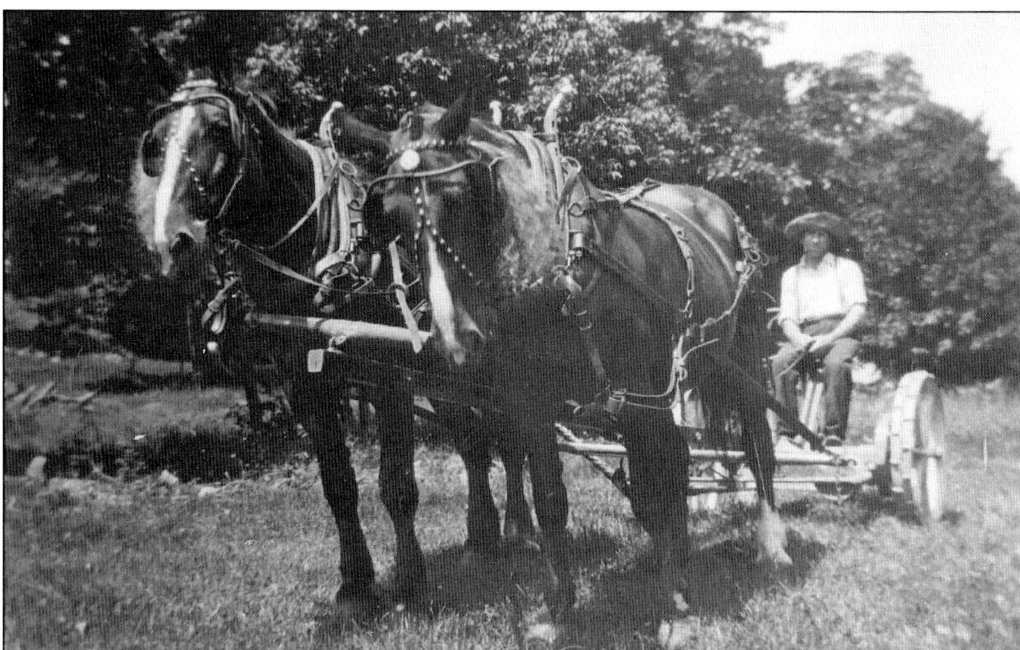

Another view of Arthur Elwin Fogg, *c.* 1920, shows him here sitting on his cast-iron mowing machine, being pulled by a team of workhorses. Arthur's daughter Valma later married Eugene LeBrun, and they too were farmers with a sizable spread of land that straddled the Hanover-Lebanon town line adjacent to the Lower Ruddsboro Road.

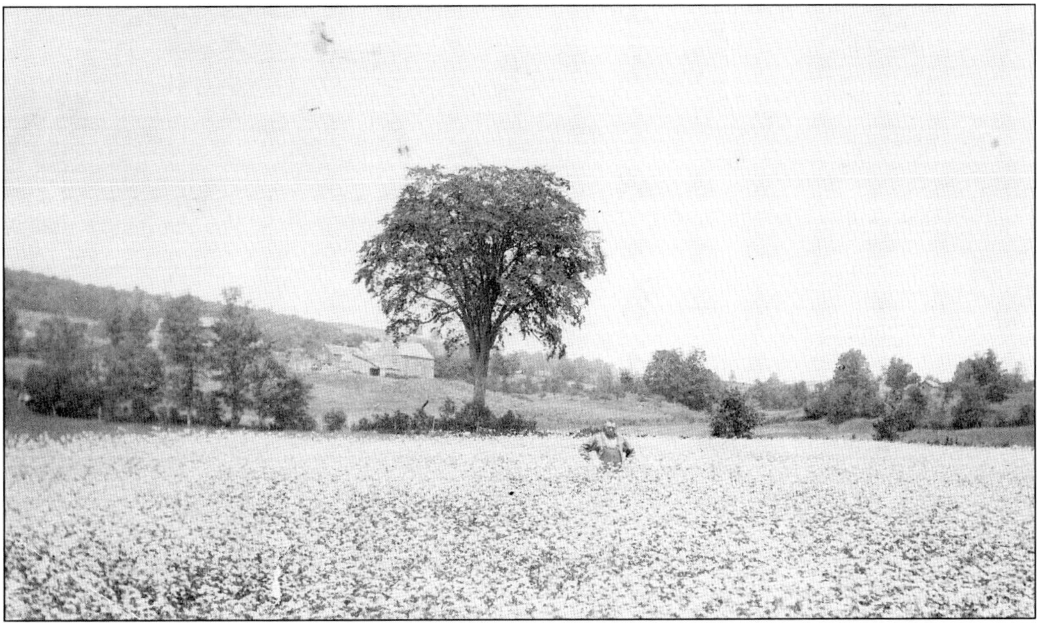

George Hill is standing in a field of buckwheat, *c.* 1910, where the present-day Hanover Center reservoir, constructed in 1962, is now located. In the background, above the Hanover Center Road, are his farm buildings—the farmhouse not quite visible to the left behind a clump of trees.

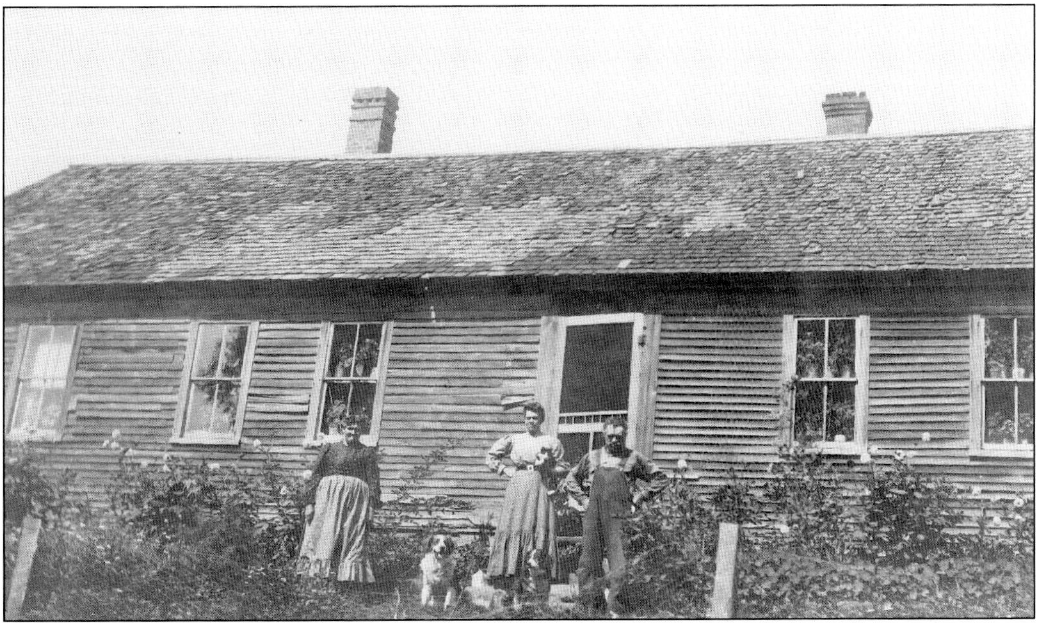

George Hill is posed with his wife, Susan (left), and daughter Nellie (center), in front of their farmhouse in this *c.* 1910 photograph view. Although the window sash have been changed, this building appears to have been a very early dwelling, by virtue of its low, simple lines. Today none of these farm buildings remain; and except for the reservoir, the land has grown back to forest.

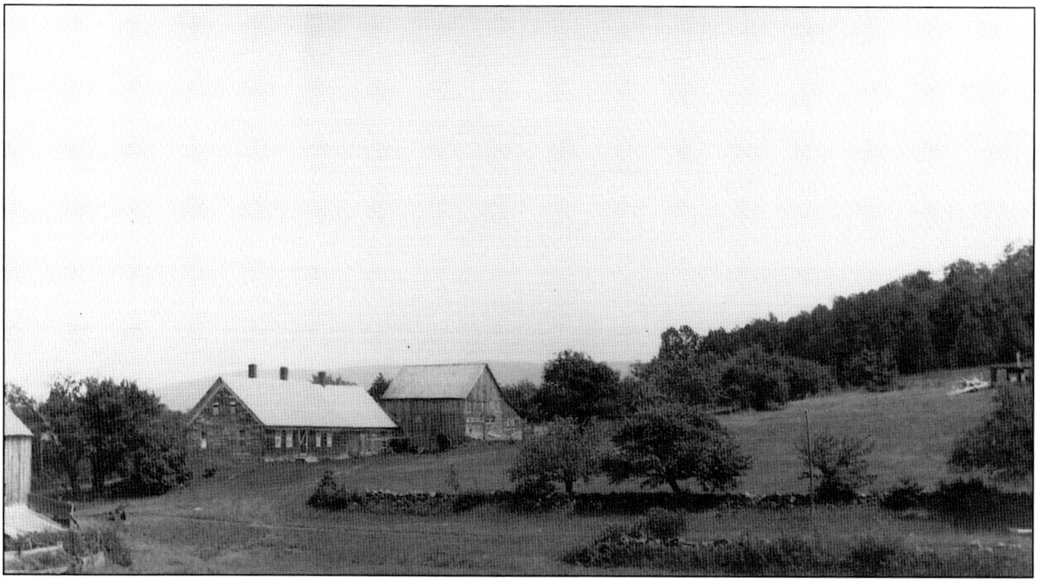

This view looks easterly from Spencer Hill across Dogford Road toward the Spencer farm, *c.* 1900. The 160-acre family farm, located around the intersection of Dogford and Spencer Roads, has been owned by the David Nutt family since 1946, and its land kept intact and mostly open.

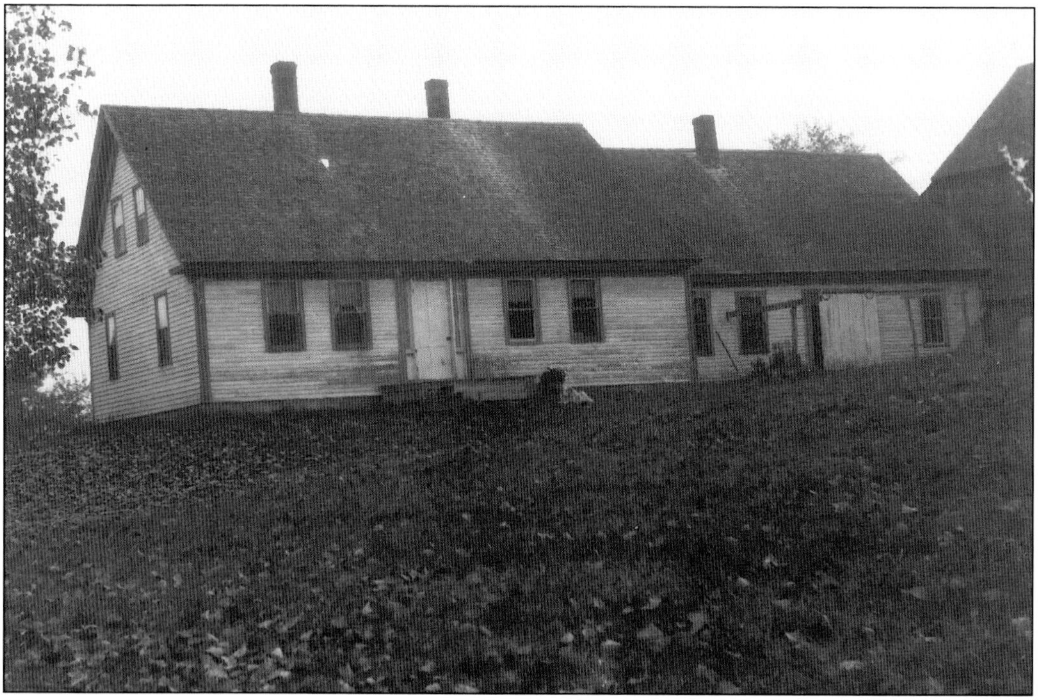

This is another turn-of-the-century view of the Spencer farmhouse, erected in 1848, and quite typical of that period. By this time, gone were the earlier central chimneys with their drafty, open fireplaces; instead, cast-iron wood stoves were hooked into individual small chimneys, seen here extending above the roof of the main house and its attached el that contained both summer kitchen and woodshed areas.

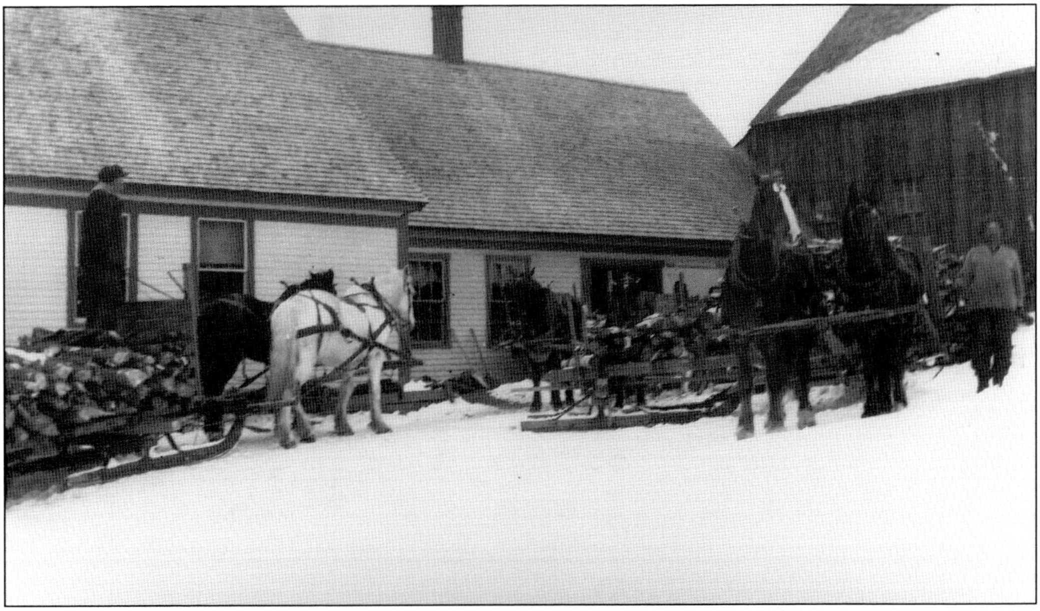

Annually, it took many cords of firewood, the only fuel readily available, to provide heat for both comfort and cooking on a typical rural New England hillside family farm. This early, turn-of-the-century view shows the Spencer family getting some firewood stored into the woodshed on an overcast winter's day—a job made easier with low sleds and snow on the ground.

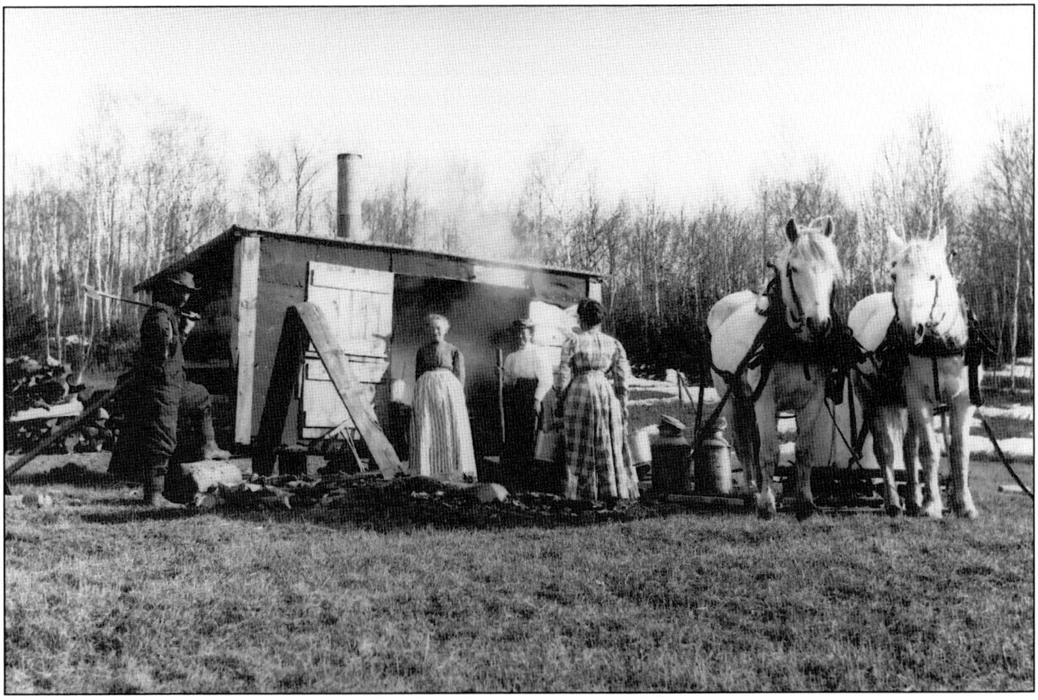

The making of maple sugar was a discovery of North America's Algonquin Indian tribes; however, it soon became an important cash commodity for the typical New England family farm and also an annual rite of spring. This *c.* 1910 view shows the Spencer family maple sugaring—boiling the sap tapped from the 150 trees in their well-developed maple orchard.

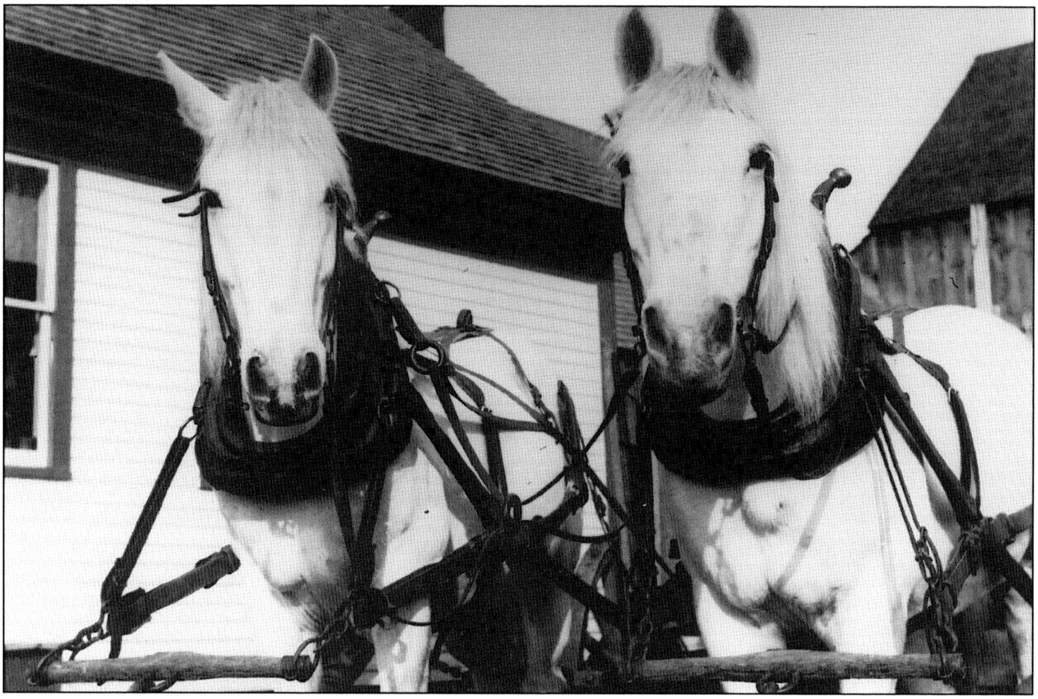

This portrait shows one of the teams of horses that helped the Spencers work their farm. Records indicate that in addition to making maple sugar, the family kept about 30 sheep for their wool, milked half a dozen dairy cows, and in the fall sold apples from the 75 trees in their fruit orchard. Together with at least one good team of horses, this was a common nineteenth-century way of life for many rural Hanover residents.

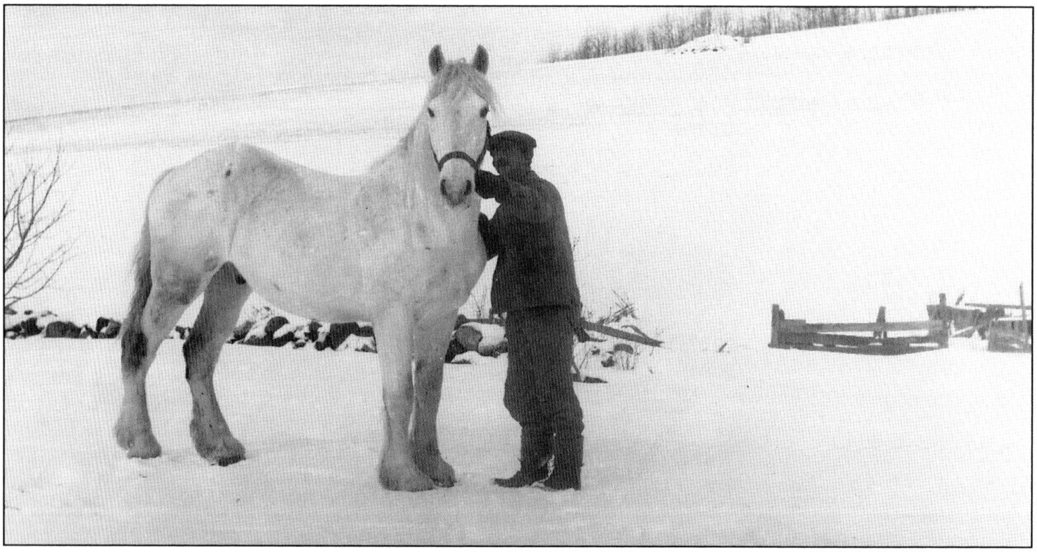

Son Jim Spencer is shown standing beside one of his workhorses in this c. 1910 view. Jim was considered a large man for his generation, and therefore the size of the horse can be judged to also be quite large! Records of the Town of Hanover from this period indicate that there were more then 500 horses in use within the community in these years—the dawn of the automobile age and about a decade away from the mass production of the farm tractor.

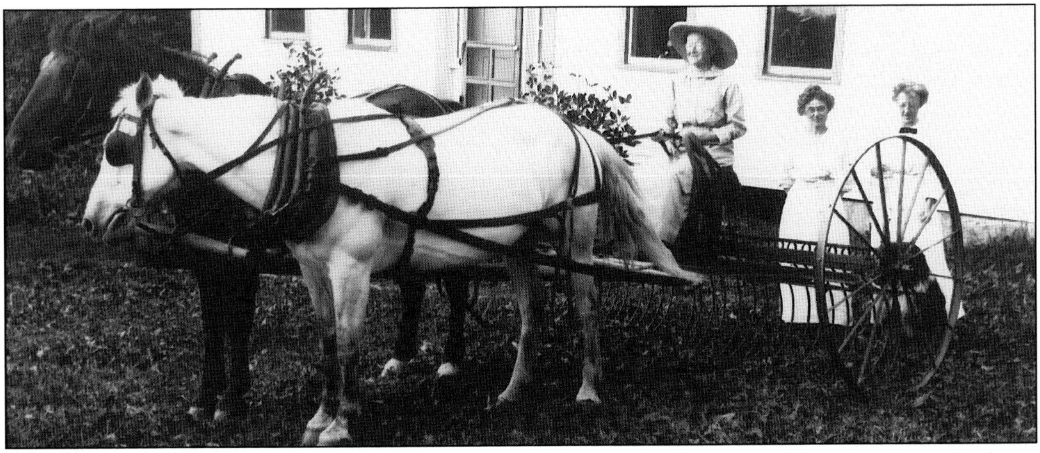

The elder Mrs. Spencer is seen seated on a steel "dump rake," as two of her daughters look on with amusement. Their farmhouse sparkles in the background of this *c.* 1910 photograph. In the years following the American Civil War, industrial mass production made a wide array of farm implements available to rural people at ever cheaper prices. The popular dump rake was used to make rows out of freshly cut hay, which would then be conveniently picked up and taken to the barn.

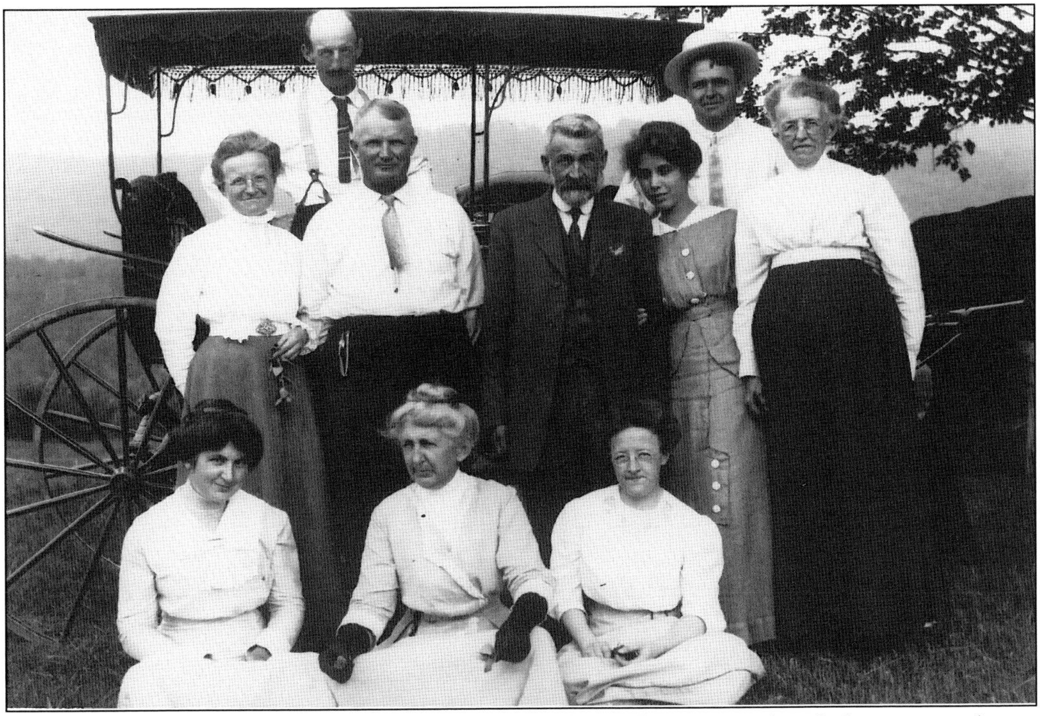

Family patriarch Uel Dea Spencer, the bearded gentleman in the dark suit, is shown surrounded by family in this formal photograph, taken *c.* 1910. As a young man, Uel was early to answer President Lincoln's call for troops to preserve the Union, and enlisted in the 7th New Hampshire Volunteers, Co. C, on October 14, 1861. During heavy fighting at Morris Island, South Carolina, on September 7, 1863, he was severely wounded, causing his honorable discharge the following February 1864. Thereafter he returned home to raise a family and work his 160-acre hillside farm.

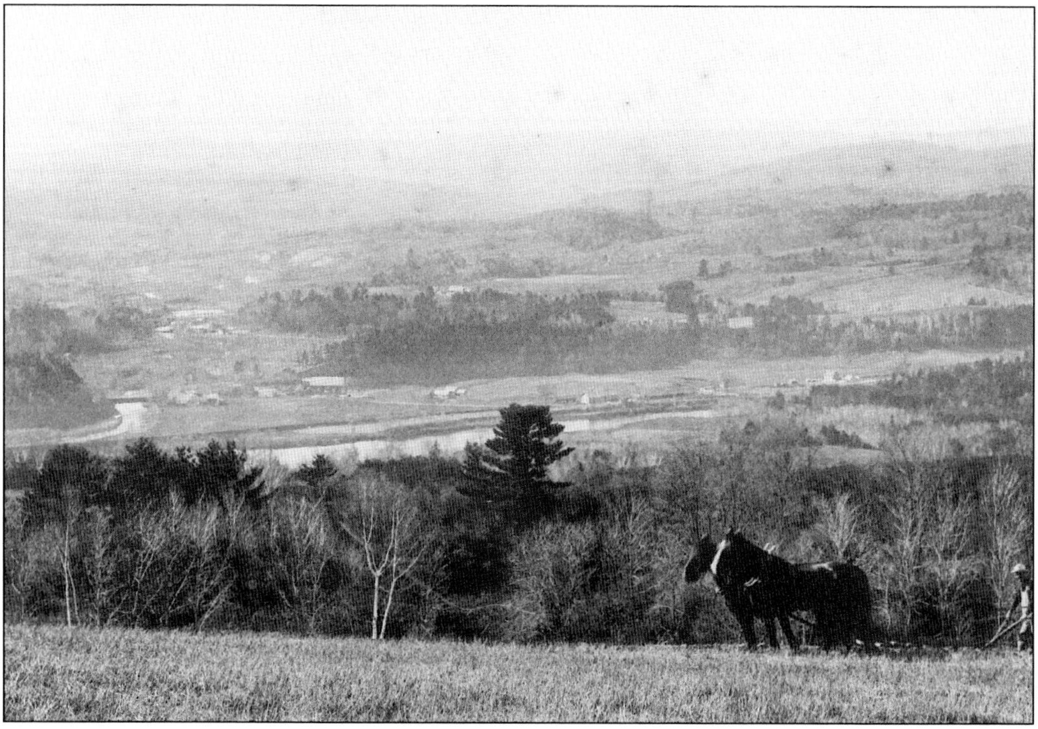

It is early spring in this *c.* 1910 view, and Jim Spencer is seen plowing a hillside field on the northeast slope of Spencer Hill. In the far left distance is the village of Pompanoosuc, Vermont, situated at the confluence of the Connecticut and Ompompanoosuc Rivers.

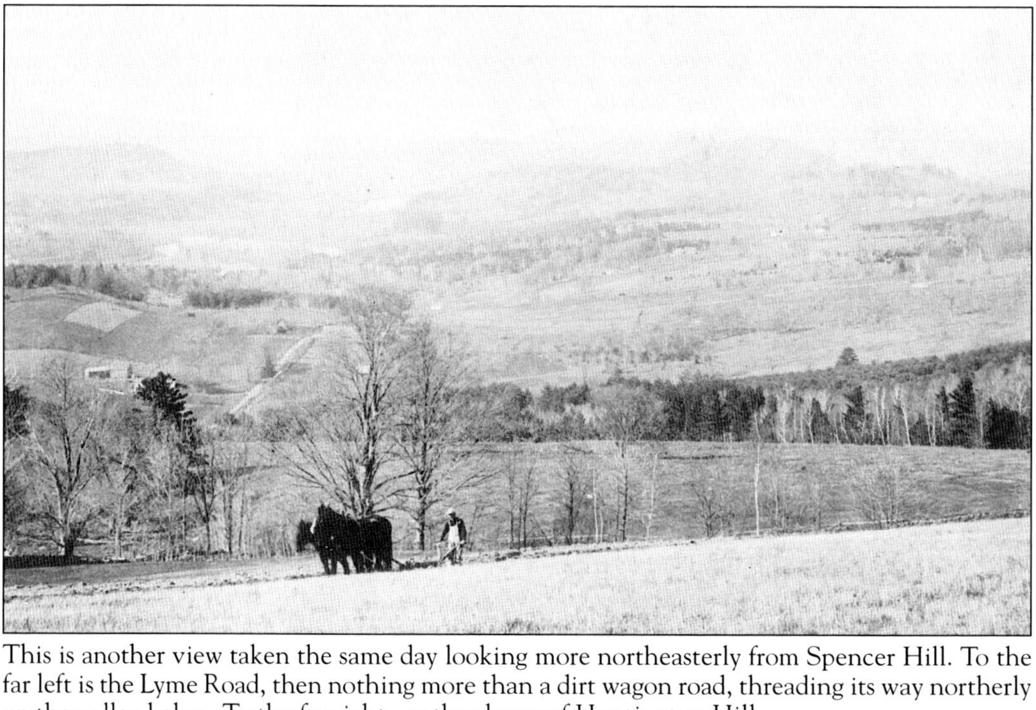

This is another view taken the same day looking more northeasterly from Spencer Hill. To the far left is the Lyme Road, then nothing more than a dirt wagon road, threading its way northerly up the valley below. To the far right are the slopes of Huntington Hill.

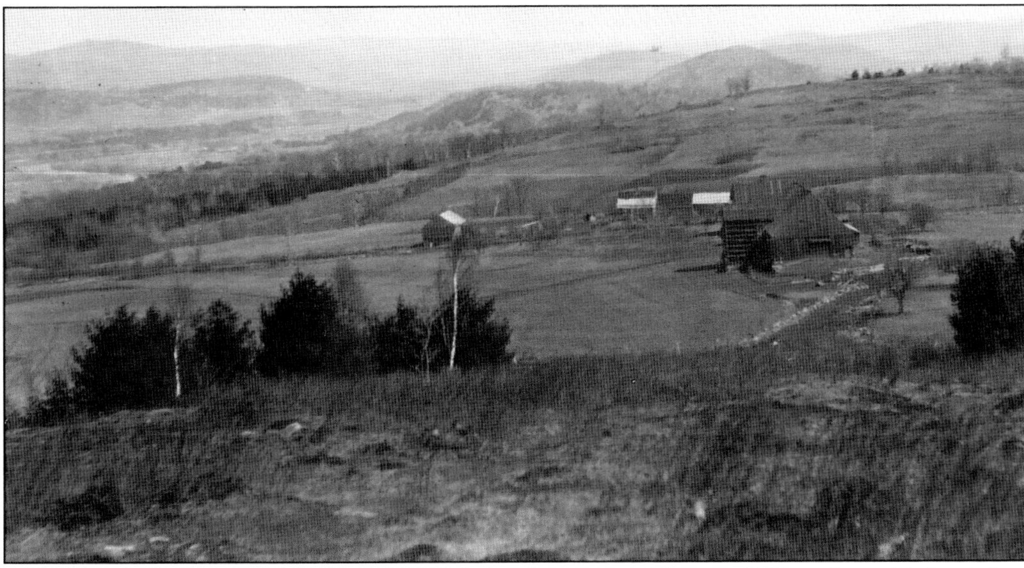

Andrew and Hezekiah Huntington settled in Hanover about 1787 and established their homestead upon the hill now bearing their family name. By the later nineteenth century, when this view was taken looking north at their 250-acre farm from Huntington Hill, the property was owned by Asa H. and Charles O. Ingalls, who kept more than 130 sheep, as well as maintaining orchards of 100 apple and 200 sugar maple trees.

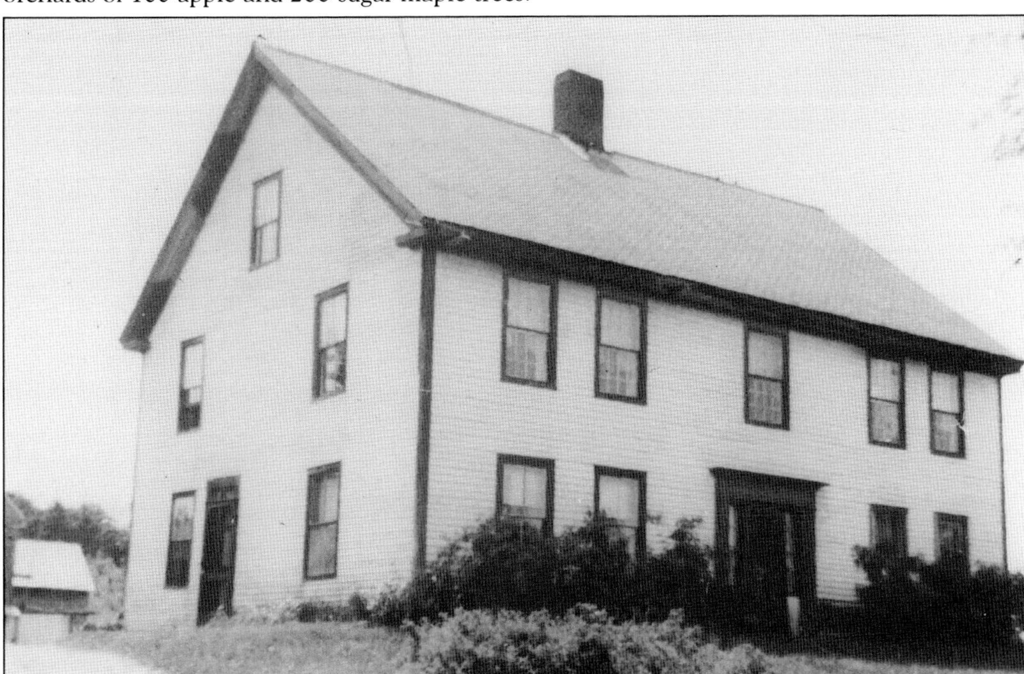

A 1948 view shows the large central chimney farmhouse erected just before 1800 by Hezekiah Huntington, on the hill that bears his family's name. Through much of the twentieth century, the land and buildings of the original Huntington, and later Ingalls farm, was owned by the Goodfellow family, for whom the present road over the hill is named. Since 1962, the property has belonged to Sam and Joanna Doyle.

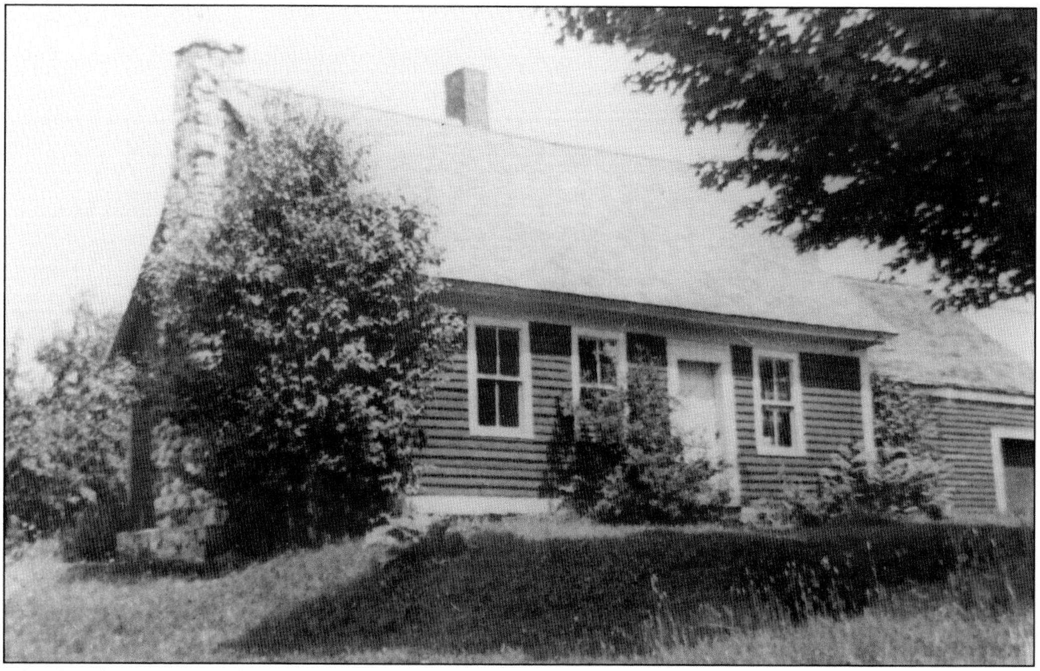

The first house erected up on the brow of Huntington Hill was this simple cape, built by Hezekiah Hungtinton perhaps several years before constructing his two-story home directly across the road. Tom and Etta Goodfellow lived in the house from 1905 until its tragic destruction by fire in March 1985. This photograph was taken in 1948.

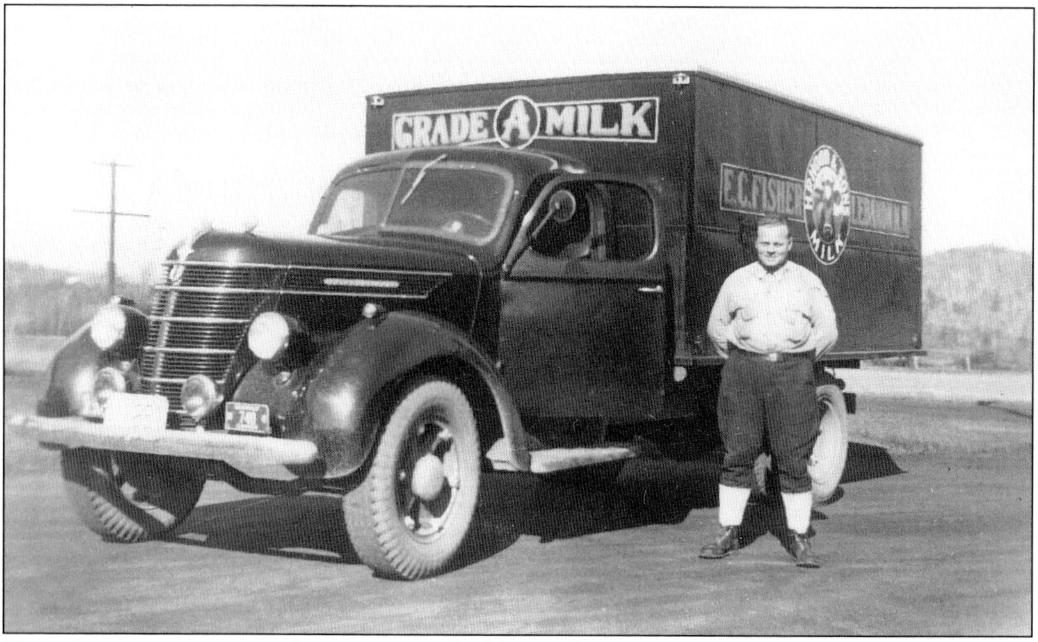

Elton Laraway appears to be quite proud of himself, standing beside Gabriel "Gabe" Elder's late-1930s sleek International milk truck. For many years Gabe's milk truck was a familiar sight around the rural parts of Hanover, picking up milk from the small family farms that there were at one time many of.

Four

Moose Mountain, Hanover Center, and the North Neighborhood

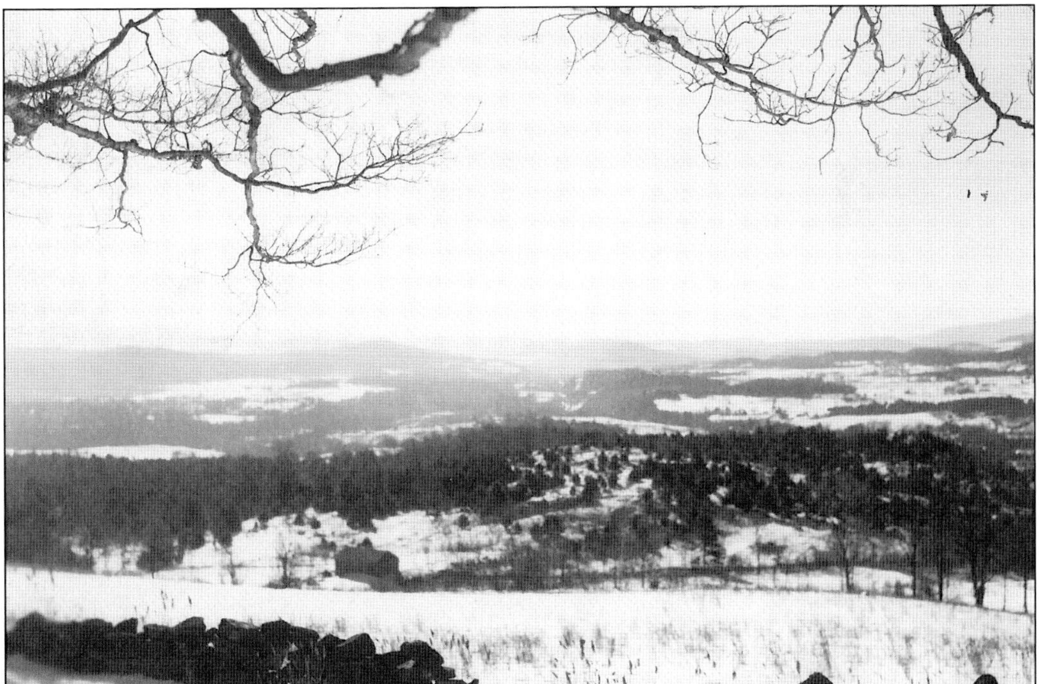

This wintry 1930s view looks westerly from up on Moose Mountain.

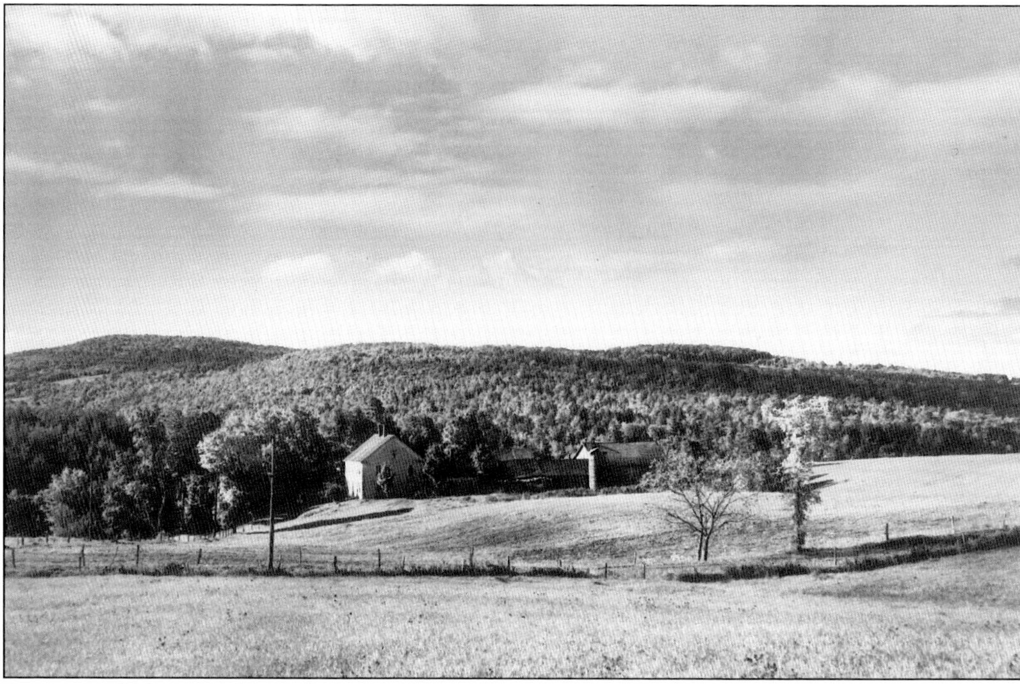

Dennis and Florence (Camp) LaCoss in 1912 purchased the 196-acre John R. Runnals farm. In addition to milking about 15 cows and shipping the milk to Boston, they also raised potatoes as a supplementary cash crop. In later years their youngest son, Niles, and his wife, Helen, maintained the farm until selling the cattle in 1962. This photograph was taken *c.* 1950.

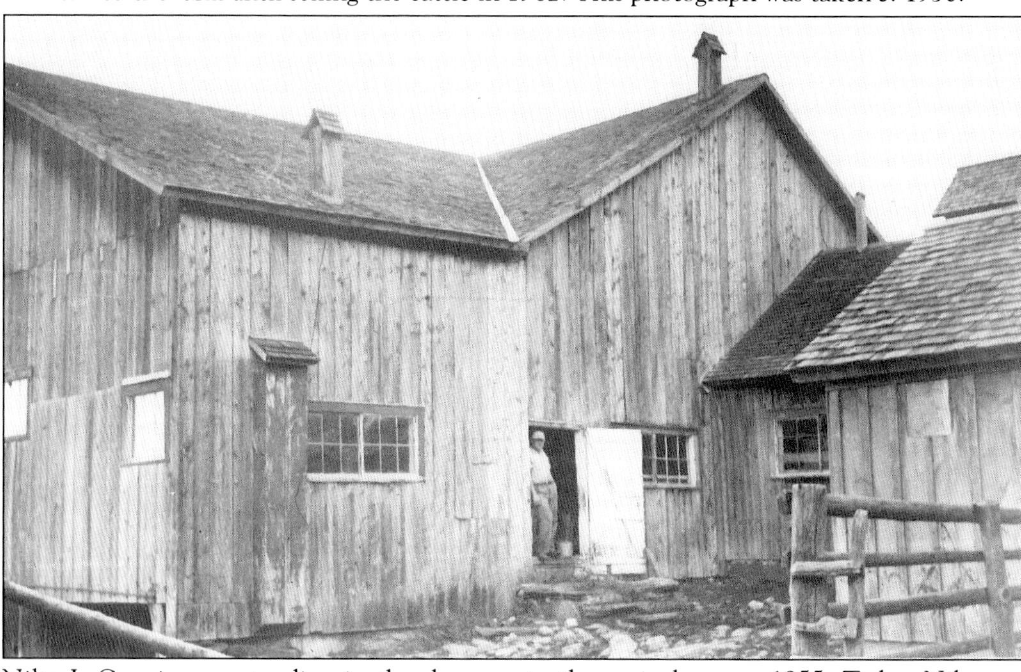

Niles LaCoss is seen standing in the doorway to the main barn, *c.* 1955. Today, Niles and Helen's daughter Nancy and her husband, David Cole, continue careful stewardship of the land and farm buildings—maintaining the beautiful openness of the landscape.

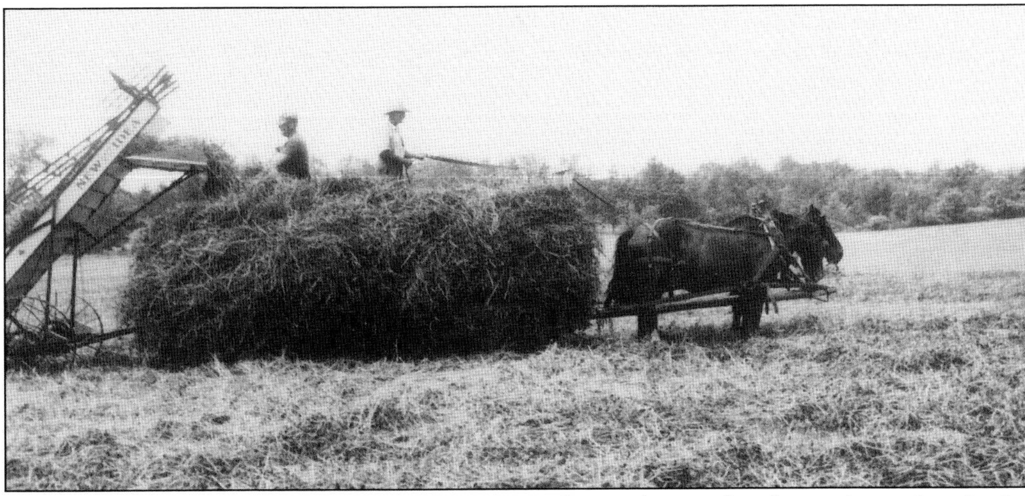

Niles and his father, Dennis LaCoss, are seen gathering hay with a horse-drawn hay loader, about 1948. The farm bought its first tractor in 1956, and a more modern hay bailer soon replaced the old hay loader.

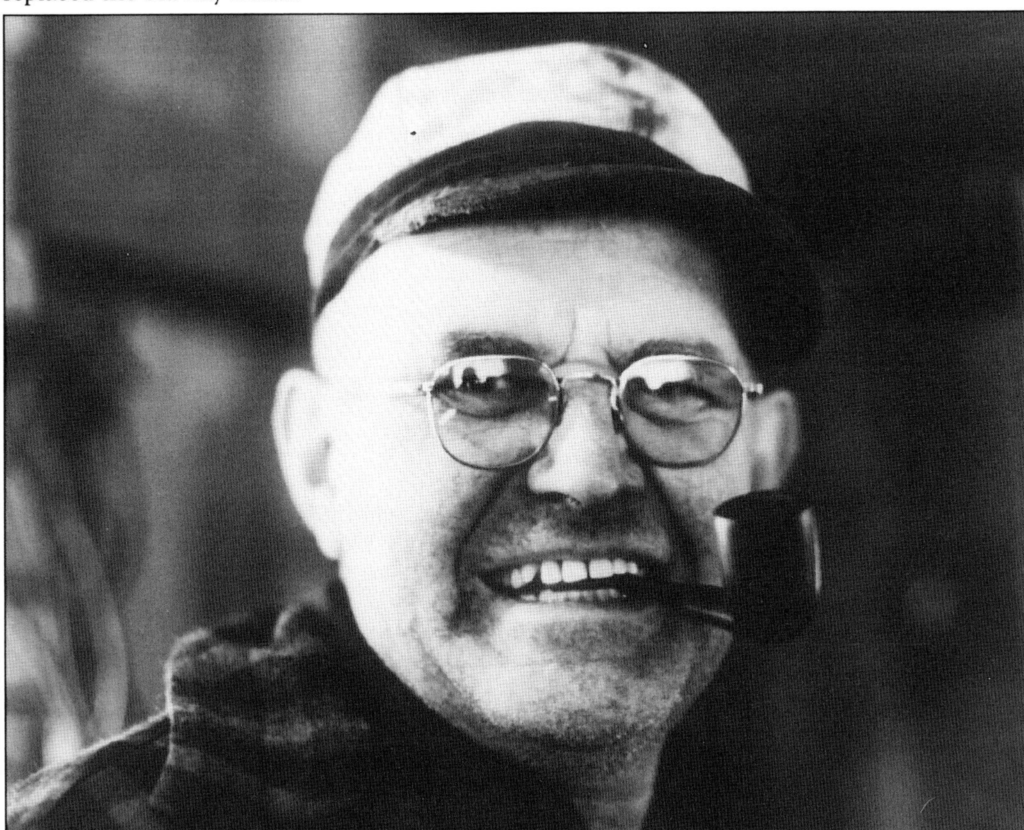

After retiring from farming in 1962, Niles LaCoss devoted more time to both his sawmill and blacksmith shop. In addition to his many mechanical talents, Niles also served the Town of Hanover for 22 years as selectman, in office from 1941 to 1963. This photograph was taken about 1965 in his blacksmith shop.

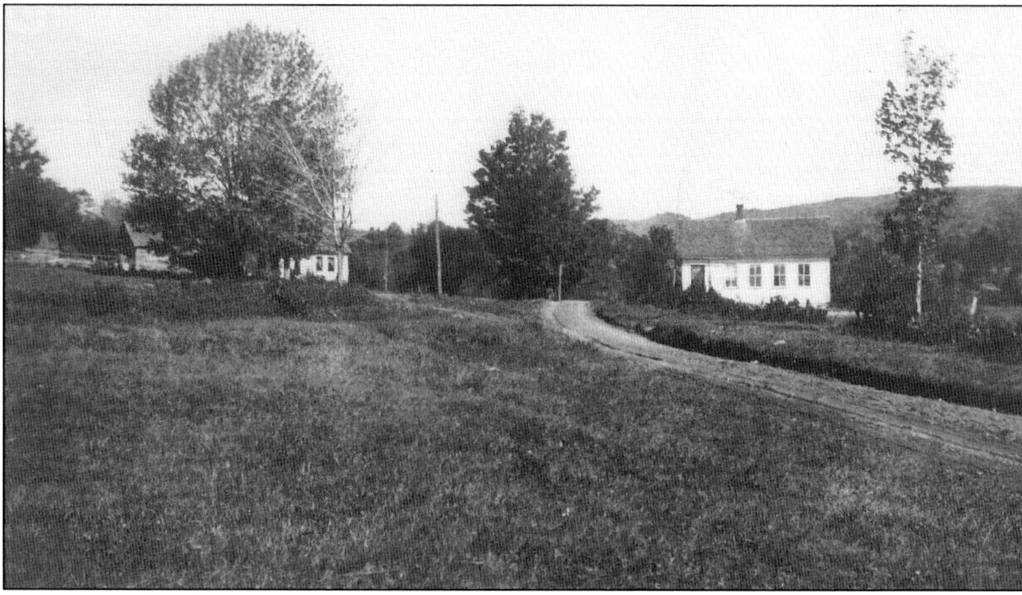

This quiet summer view c. 1920 looks northerly from the LaCoss farm up Three Mile Road toward the Dana farm on the left and the Arvin District schoolhouse on the right.

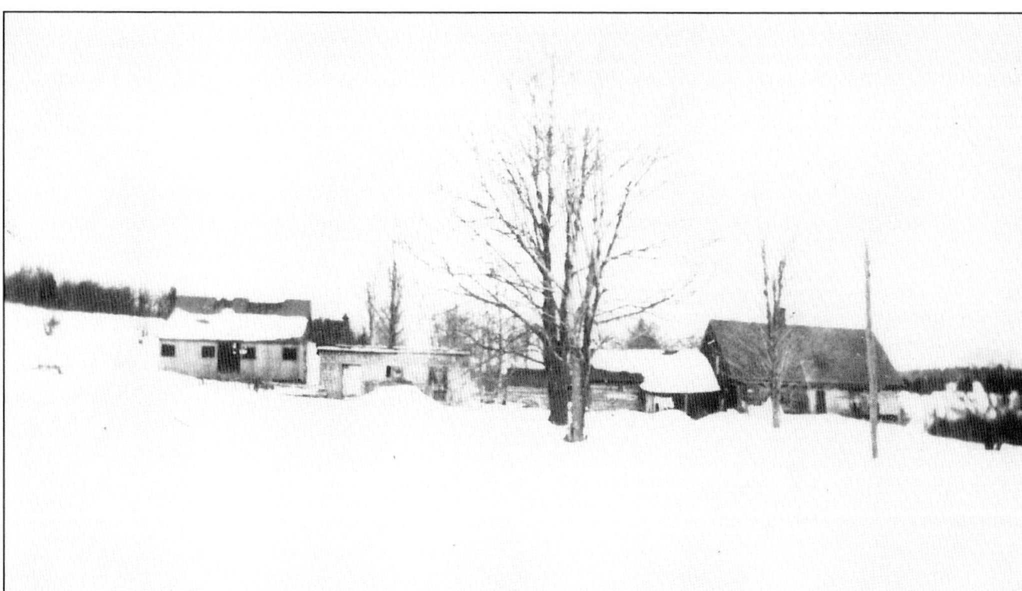

The Dana farm, c. 1920, appears here in a view looking from Chandler Road. John "Burt" Burton Dana and his wife, Anna (Camp) Dana, purchased this small farm in 1917. Today the farmhouse is home to Walker Weed at 30 Three Mile Road.

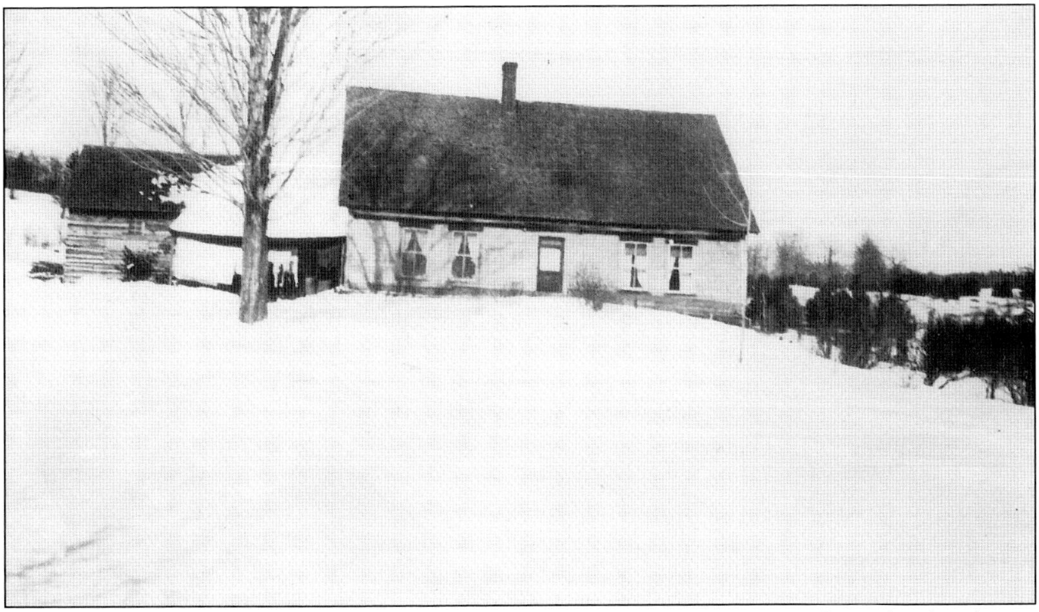

This is another view of the Dana farmhouse taken perhaps the same day. The farmhouse is believed to be a very early dwelling, built by Deacon Stephen Benton just before the American Revolution.

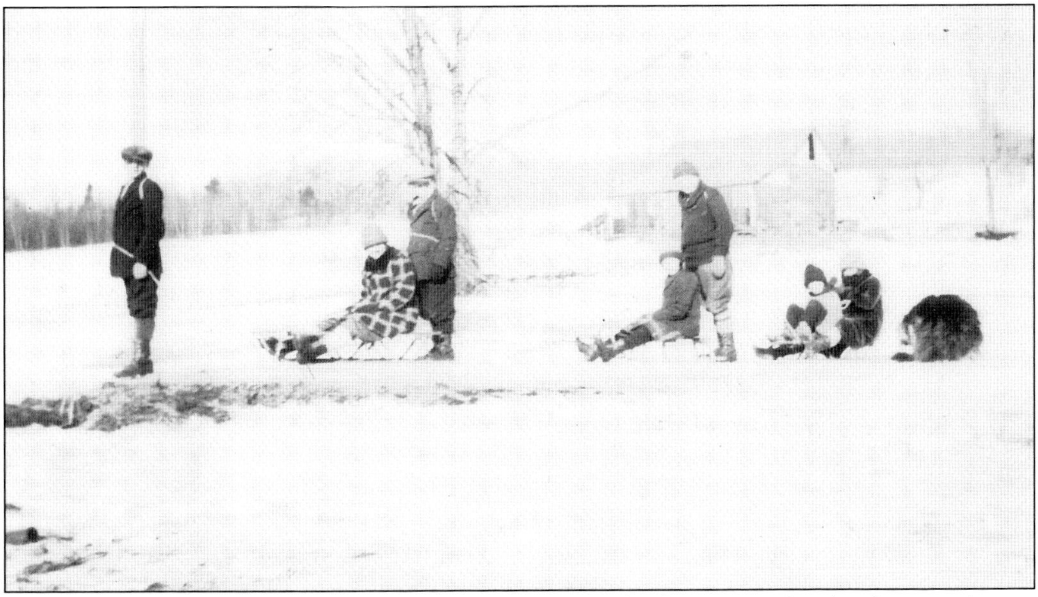

LaCoss and Dana children are shown sledding with the Dana family dog in this c. 1925 view. Florence (Camp) LaCoss and Anna (Camp) Dana were sisters whose farms bordered each other.

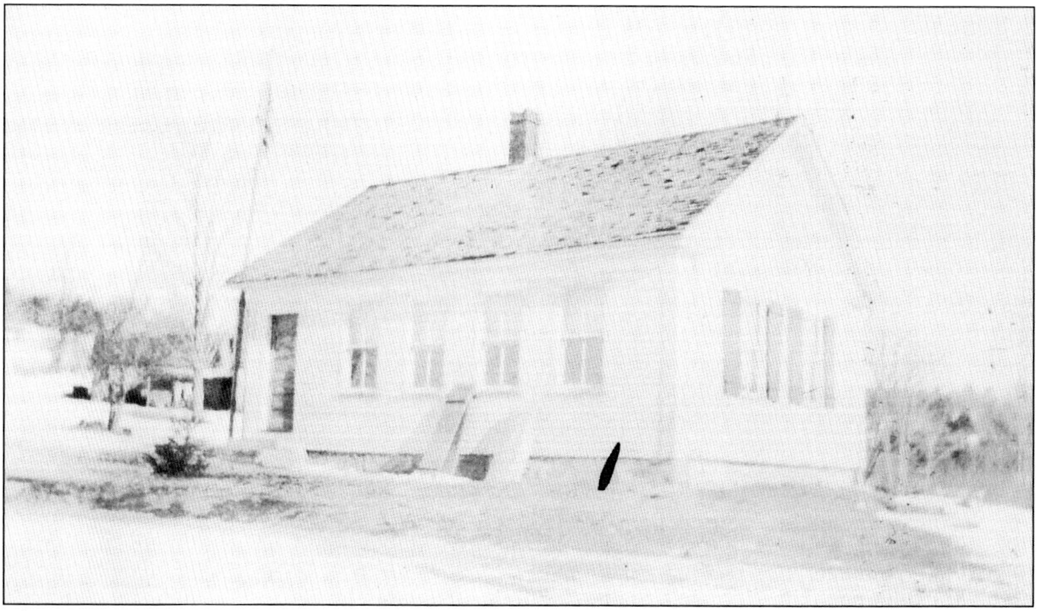

This 1920s view shows the Arvin District school, one of eighteen district schoolhouses to exist in Hanover at one time. This schoolhouse closed in 1925, and today not a trace of the building remains.

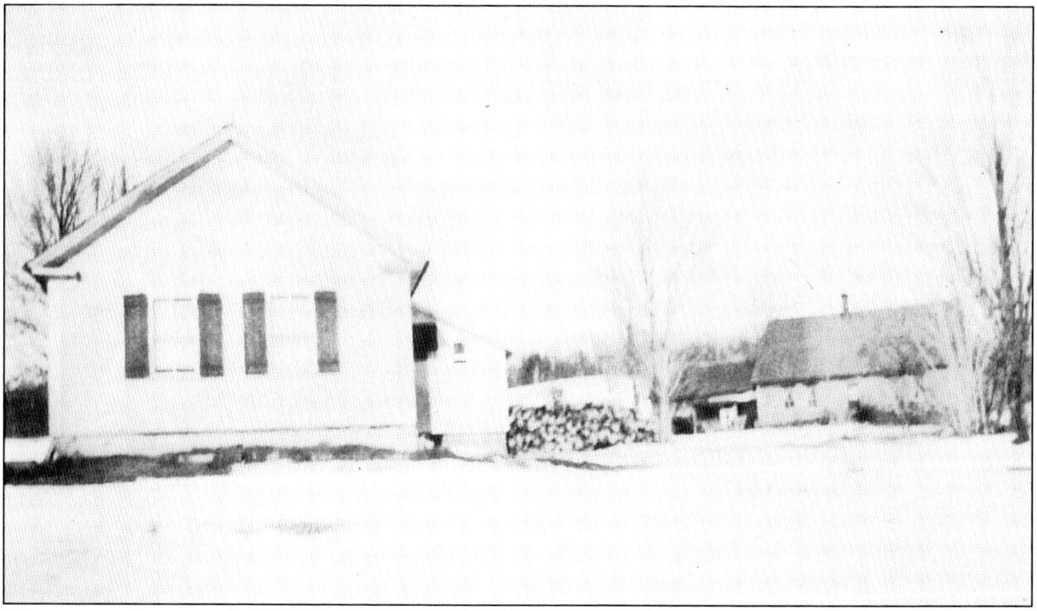

This is another view of the Arvin District schoolhouse, looking westerly. In the background is the Dana farmhouse at 30 Three Mile Road.

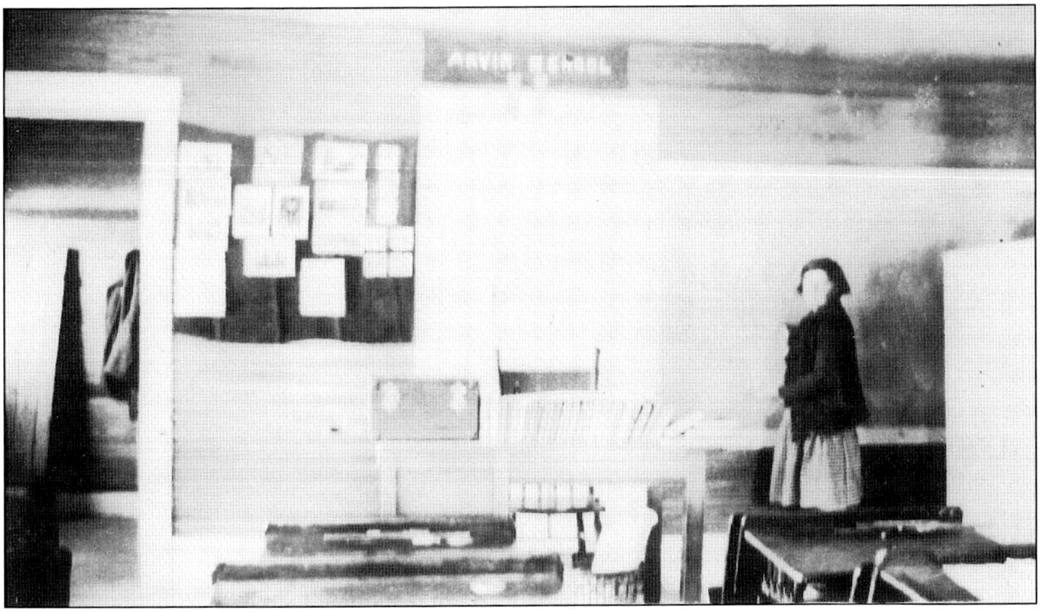

A long-serving teacher at the one-room Arvin schoolhouse was Muriel Armstrong Ferson, seen here *c.* 1925 at the front of her classroom.

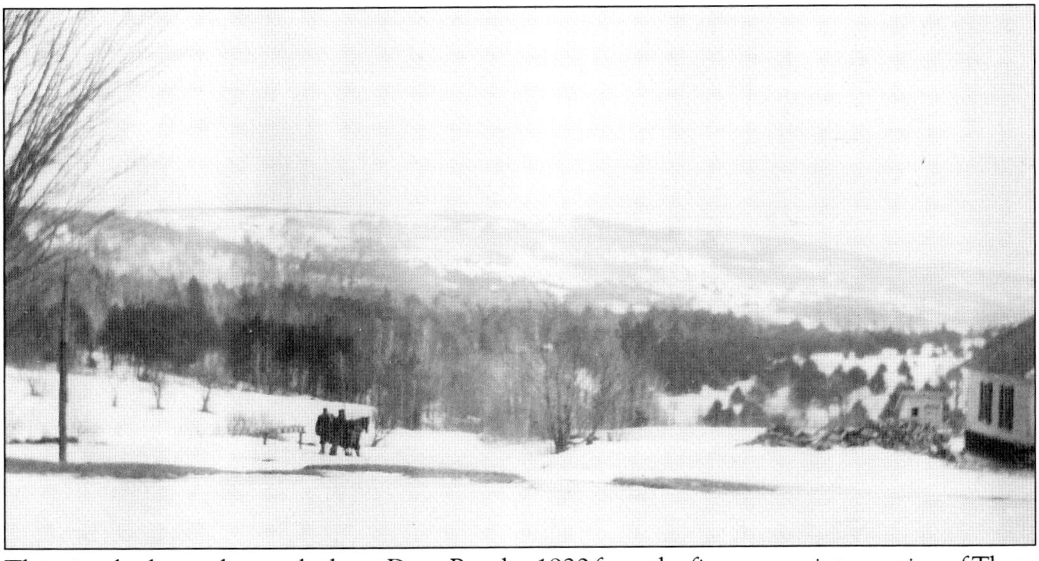
This view looks southeasterly down Dana Road *c.* 1920 from the five-corner intersection of Three Mile, Cory, Chandler, and Dana Roads. To the right is the back of the Arvin schoolhouse.

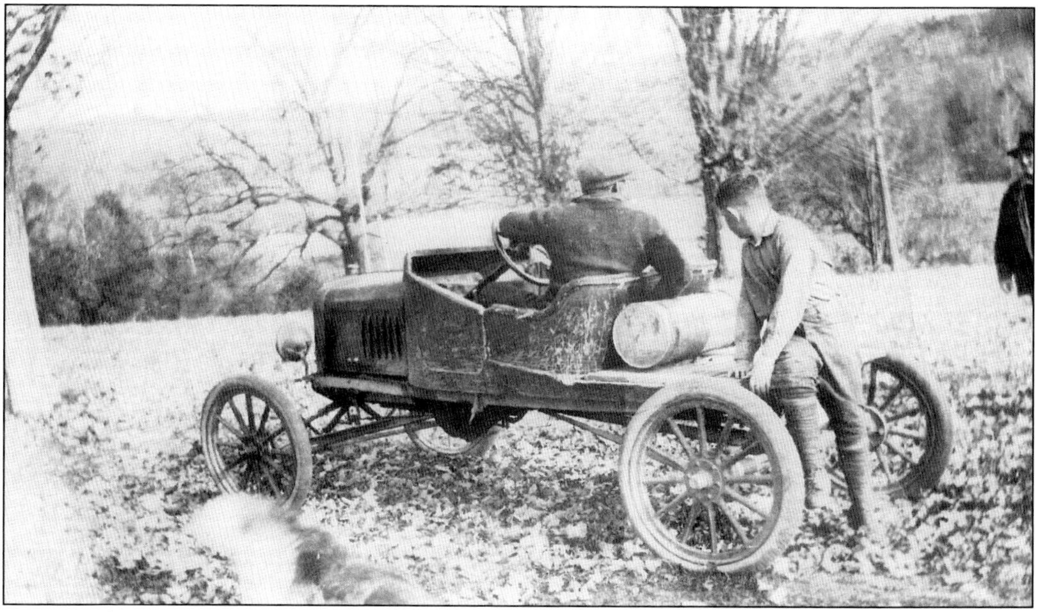

Young Niles LaCoss built himself a "doodlebug" out of a stripped-down, used Model T Ford, and he is seen here with one of the Dana boys on the back in this *c.* 1925 photograph.

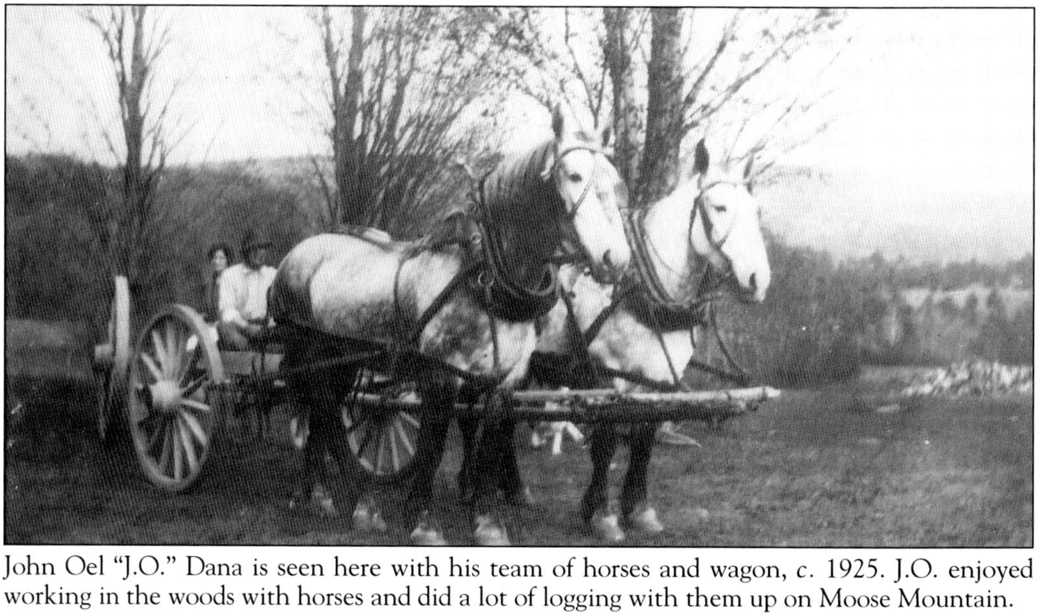

John Oel "J.O." Dana is seen here with his team of horses and wagon, *c.* 1925. J.O. enjoyed working in the woods with horses and did a lot of logging with them up on Moose Mountain.

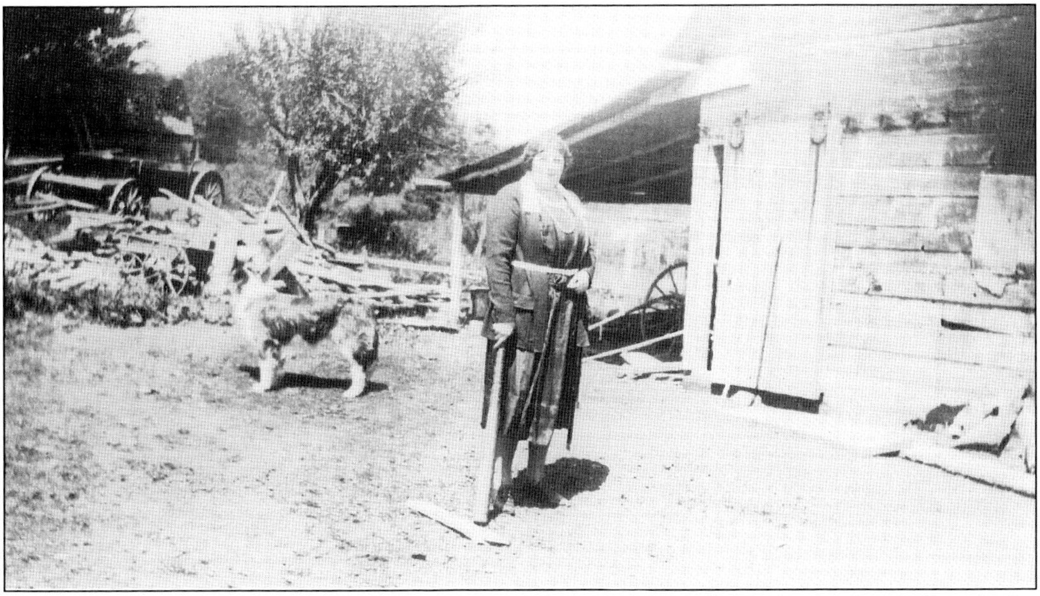

Arvin School District teacher Muriel Armstrong Ferson is seen here playing baseball with the LaCoss and Dana boys in the Dana farm dooryard, *c.* 1925.

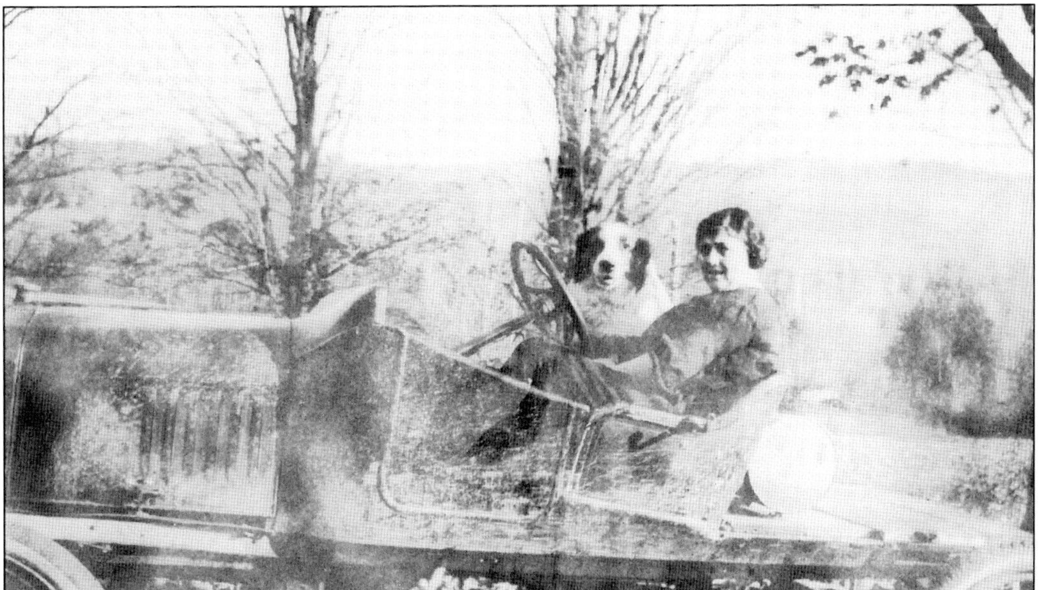

In this view, teacher Muriel Armstrong Ferson is ready to take a fast trip up Three Mile Road in Niles LaCoss's "doodlebug," with one of the Danas' dogs riding shotgun!

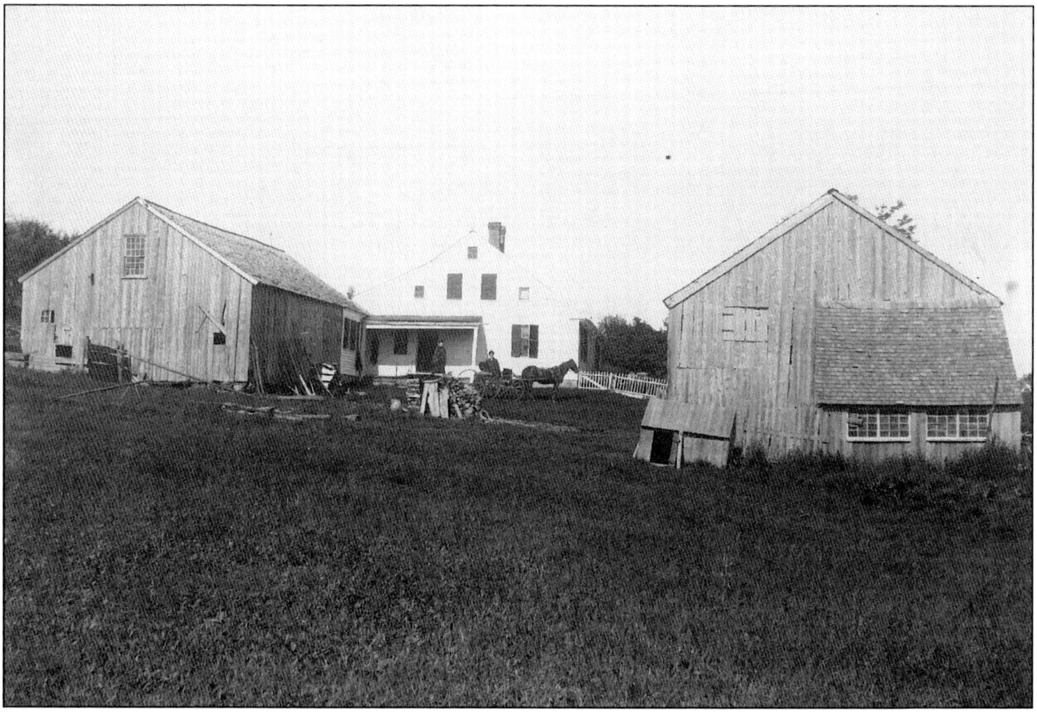

By the time this photograph was taken in 1890, the farmstead of Daniel Bridgman and his wife, Harmony, had long ago been sold to Asa and Mary Camp in 1860. However, it was here where on December 21, 1829, Laura Dewey Bridgman was born, who would become well known in Victorian-American history as the predecessor of the more famous Helen Keller.

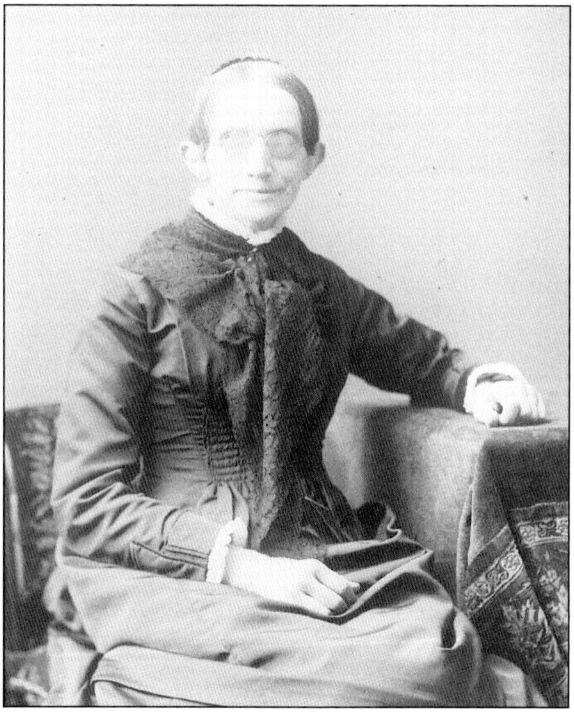

Although Laura Bridgman was not born blind nor deaf, she was none-the-less a sickly child who at age two was savagely stricken with scarlet fever and hence became bereft of all abilities and senses. At age eight, she became a student of Dr. Samuel Gridley Howes and his new school in Boston, Massachusetts—the Perkins Institute. By the time she died, on May 24, 1889, she had become world famous—permanently pushing back barriers for the blind and deaf.

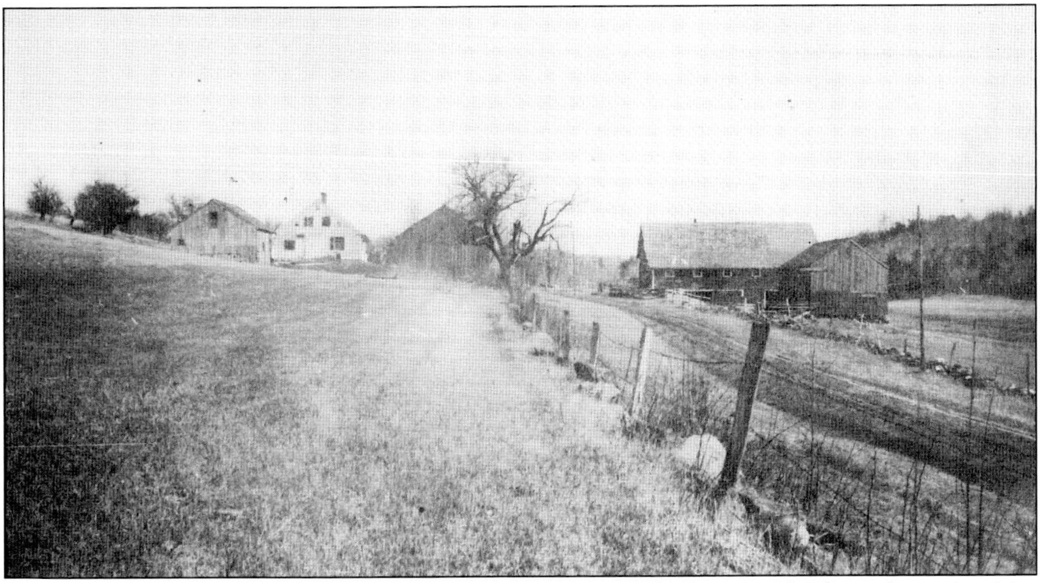

This is a view of Dana Road and the old Bridgman farmstead, about 1925. Through much of the twentieth century, this 275-acre farm has been owned by the Dana family, and Divina (Croall) Dana still resides in the *c.* 1812 farmhouse at 10 Dana Road.

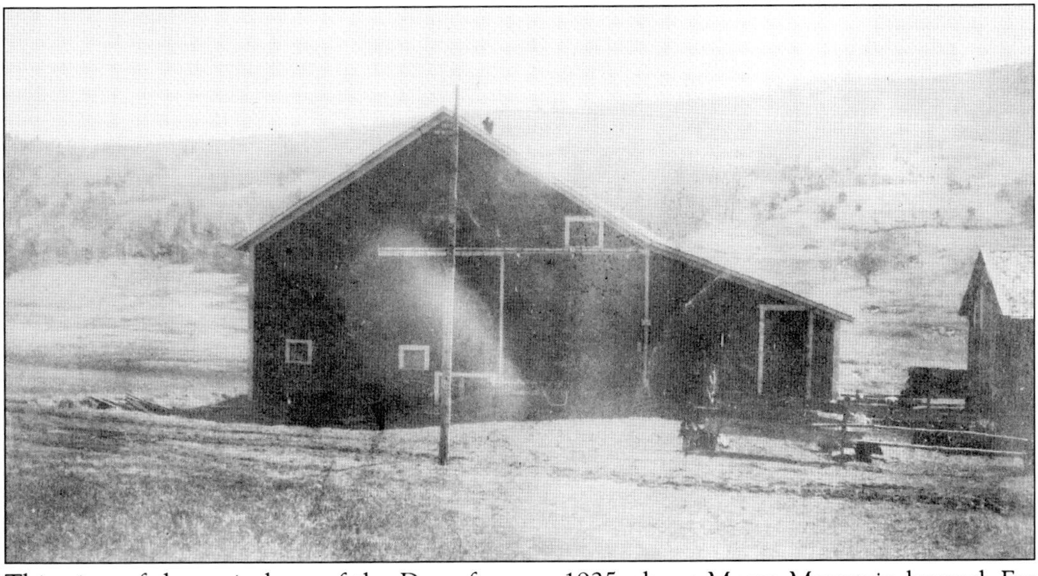

This view of the main barn of the Dana farm, *c.* 1925, shows Moose Mountain beyond. For many years Elmer and Divina Dana raised Ayrshire cattle and kept several teams of horses to help work this upland mountain side farm.

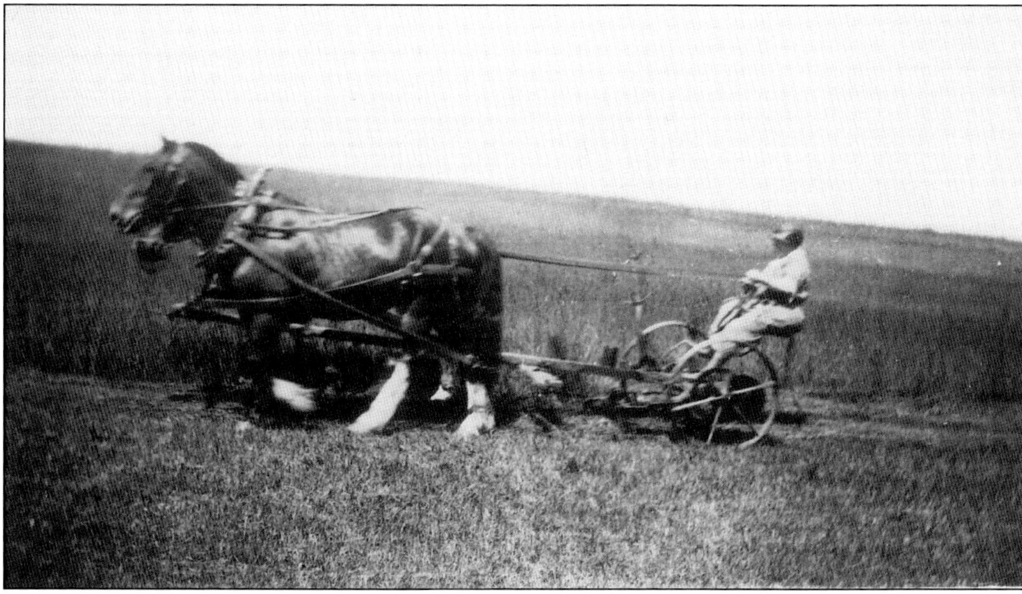

Elmer Dana's mother, Anna (Camp) Dana, is seen taking a turn or two around the hay field in this c. 1940 view. Pulling the mowing machine are Colonel and Socks. The field is on the west side of Dana Road.

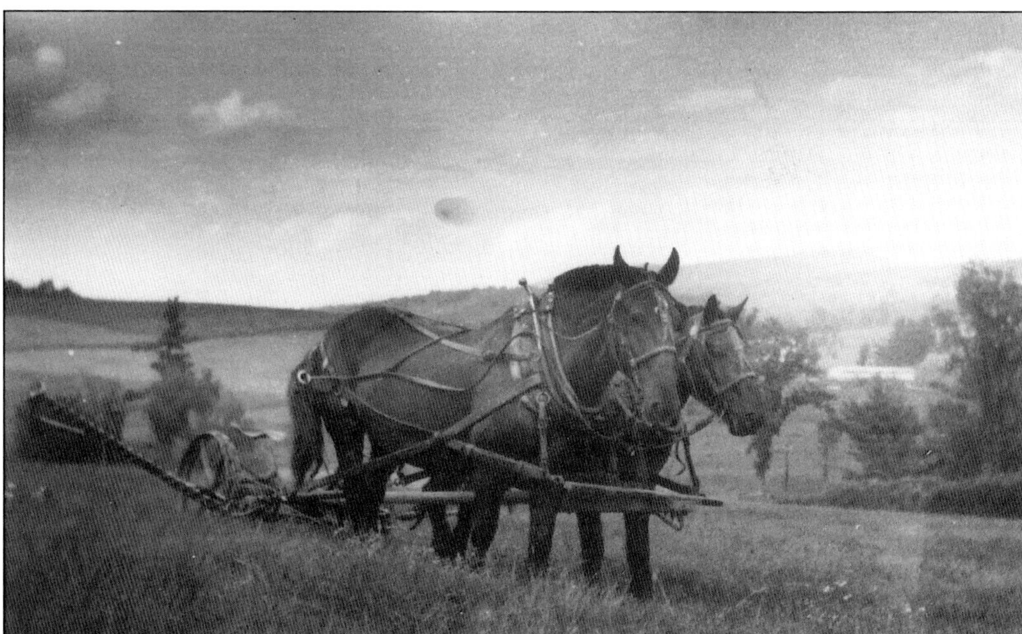

High up along the western side of Moose Mountain, another team of Elmer Dana's horses are cutting hay—probably just below the present-day Moose Mountain Lodge area.

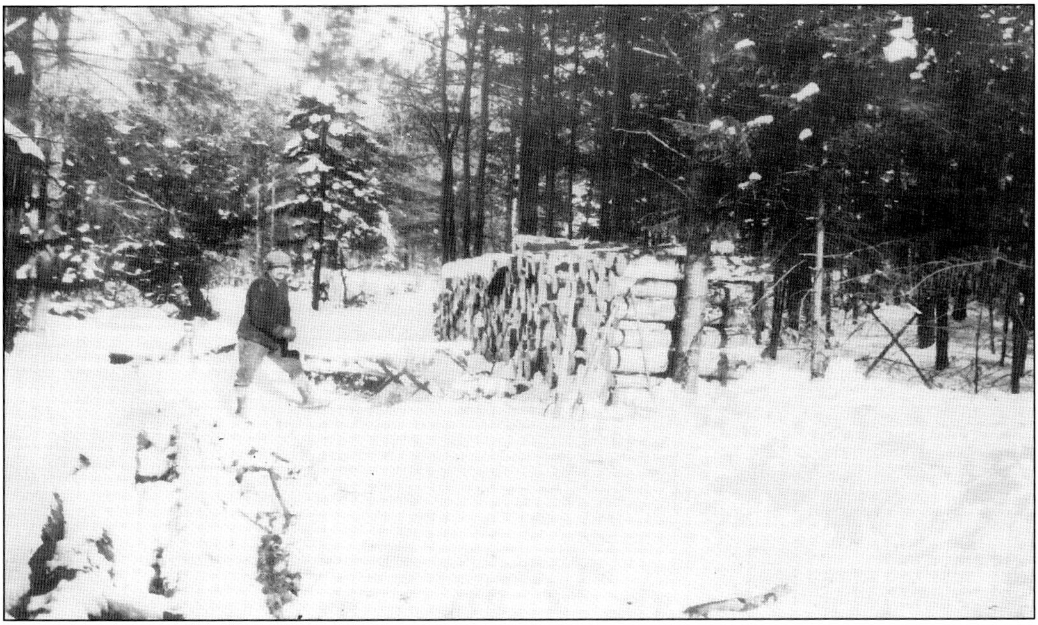

This picture shows the labor of cutting either pulp or firewood up on Moose Mountain, *c.* 1925. Many families who lived down in the Etna/Mink Brook valley kept wood lots up on the mountain for both fuel and cash crop purposes.

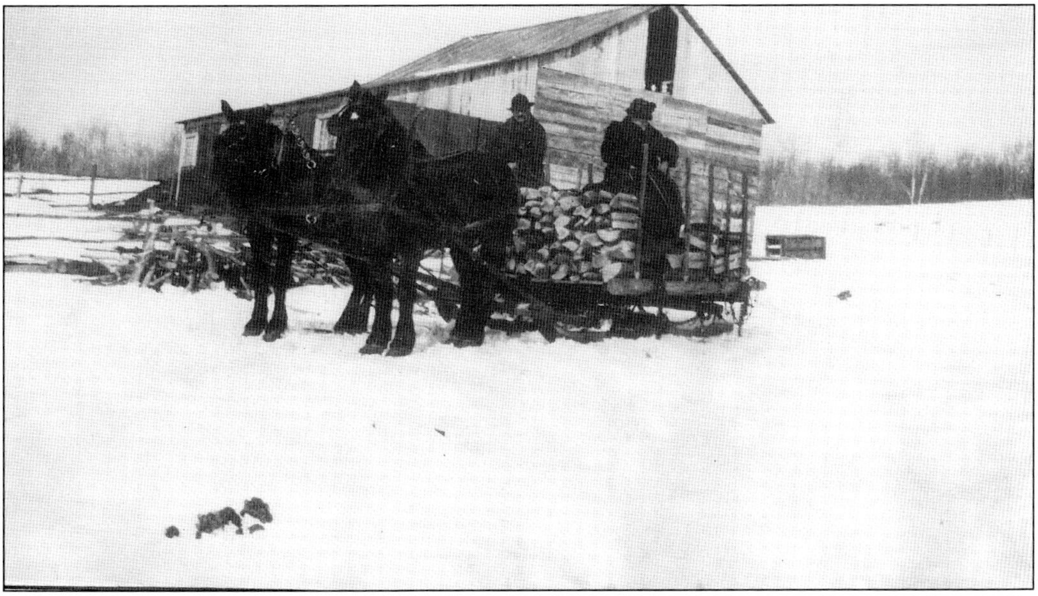

A load of firewood brought down off the mountain is drawn up to the Dana farm on Three Mile Road, *c.* 1920. Like most rural homes not too many generations ago, burning firewood was the only source of heat.

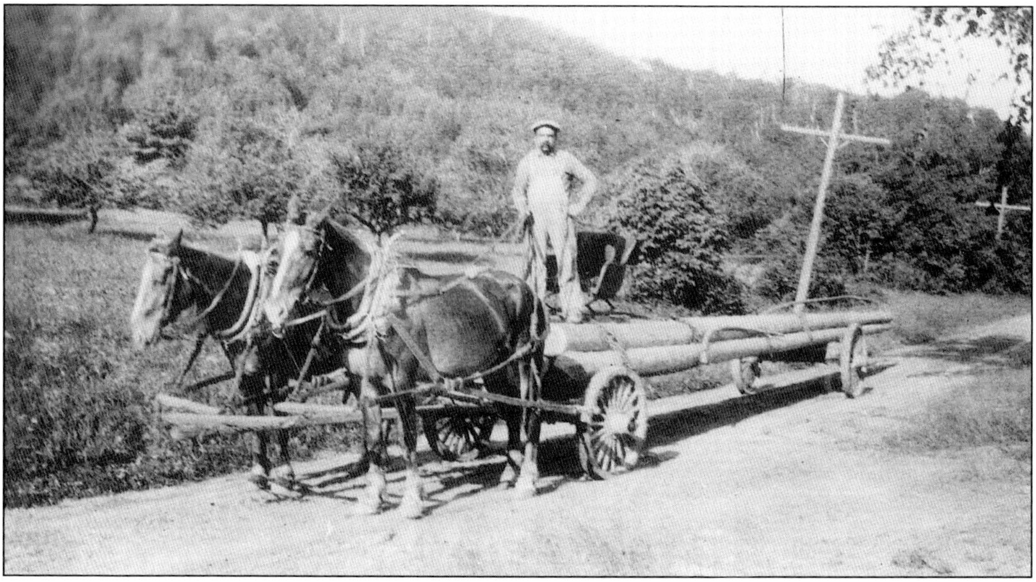

It would appear that the driver of this team of horses has a load of telephone poles in tow. The picture, *c.* 1920, is believed to have been taken at the intersection of King and Ruddsboro Roads looking southerly.

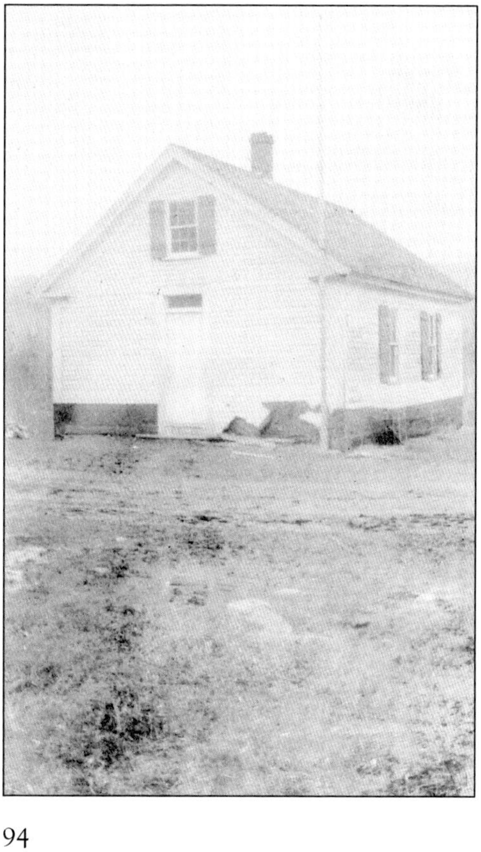

A *c.* 1910 photograph shows the so-called Ruddsboro District Schoolhouse, once located on the east side of Ruddsboro Road, about halfway between King and Dana Roads. It closed about 1920, and what few schoolchildren went there were sent to the Arvin District School. The building is no longer standing.

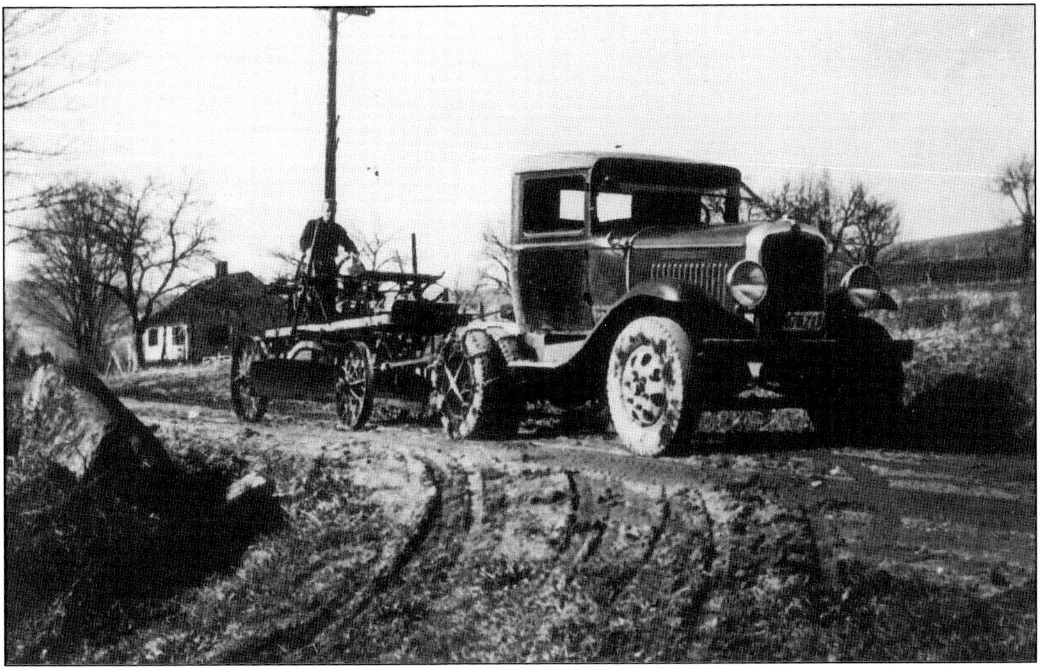

An early-1930s vintage truck is pulling an older hand-operated road grader along Dana Road, at about the intersection of Moose Mountain Road in 1938. In the distance is the Dana residence at 10 Dana Road.

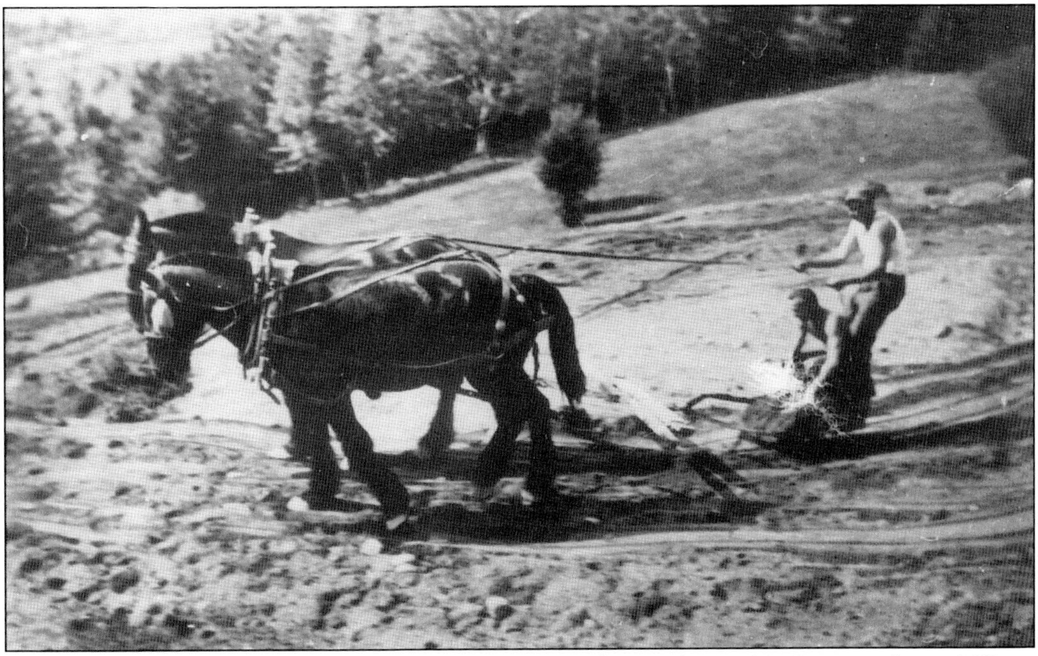

Construction has begun on the Moose Mountain Lodge in this 1938 photograph, and Elmer Dana is shown with a team of his horses excavating ground for the new building.

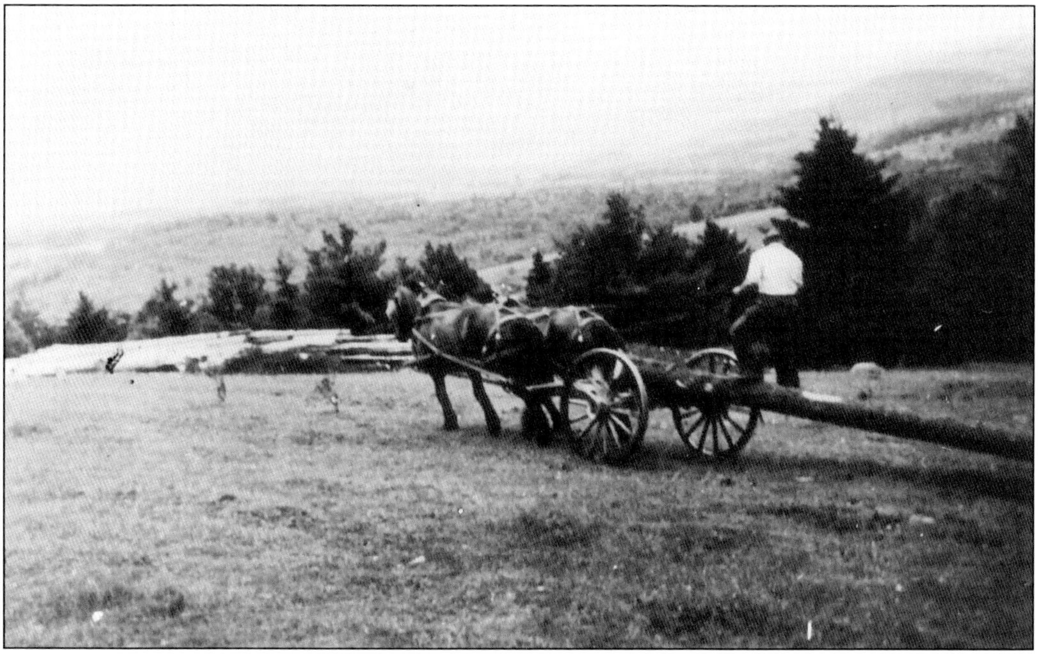

Much of the material used to construct the lodge came right from the top of the mountain. In this view, Elmer Dana and his team of horses are bringing logs out of the woods to the building site.

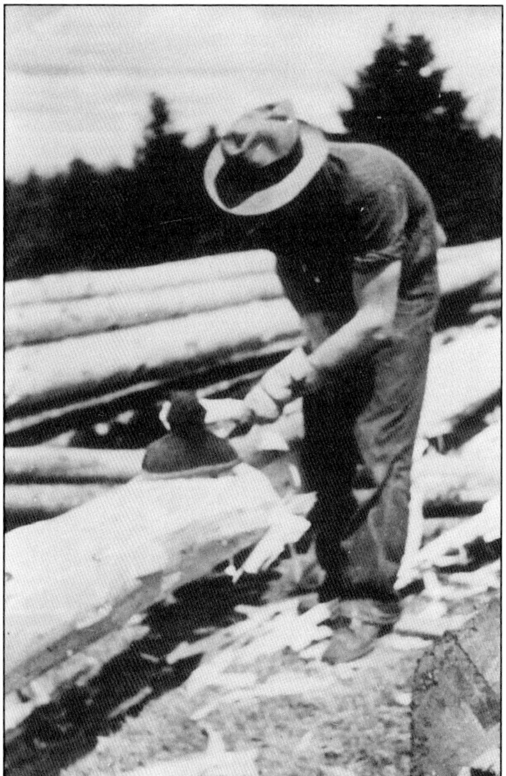

Most of the construction of the new Moose Mountain Lodge was with hand methods unchanged from pre-industrial times. Here, a worker fashions logs into beams for the floor assembly.

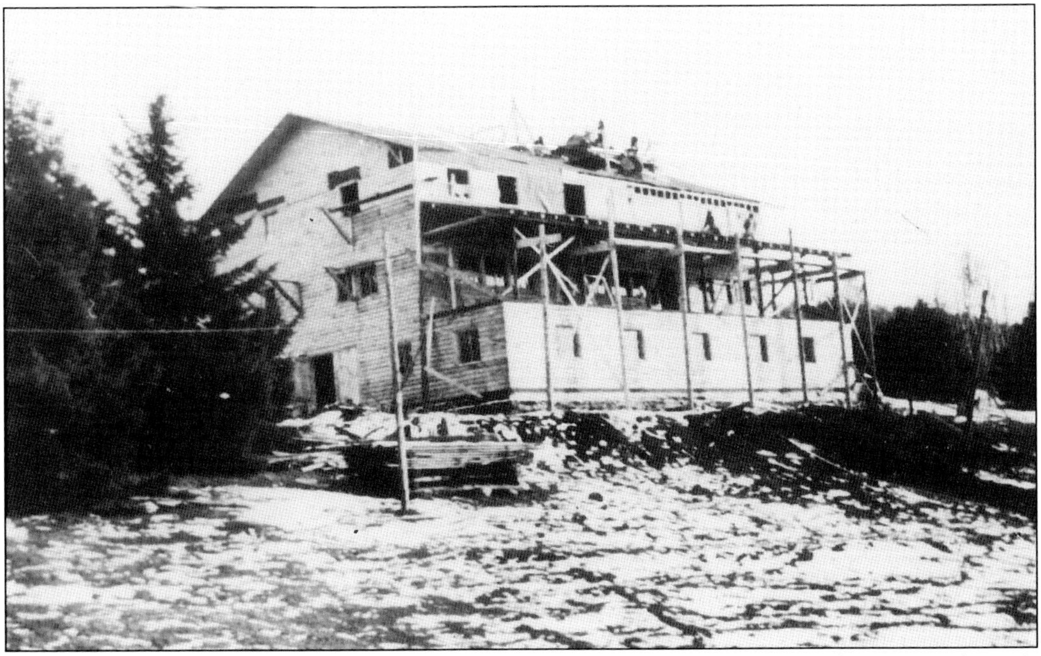

The new lodge building is taking shape in this 1938 view. The hurricane that swept through parts of northern New England in September of that year temporarily damaged the building by moving it from its foundations.

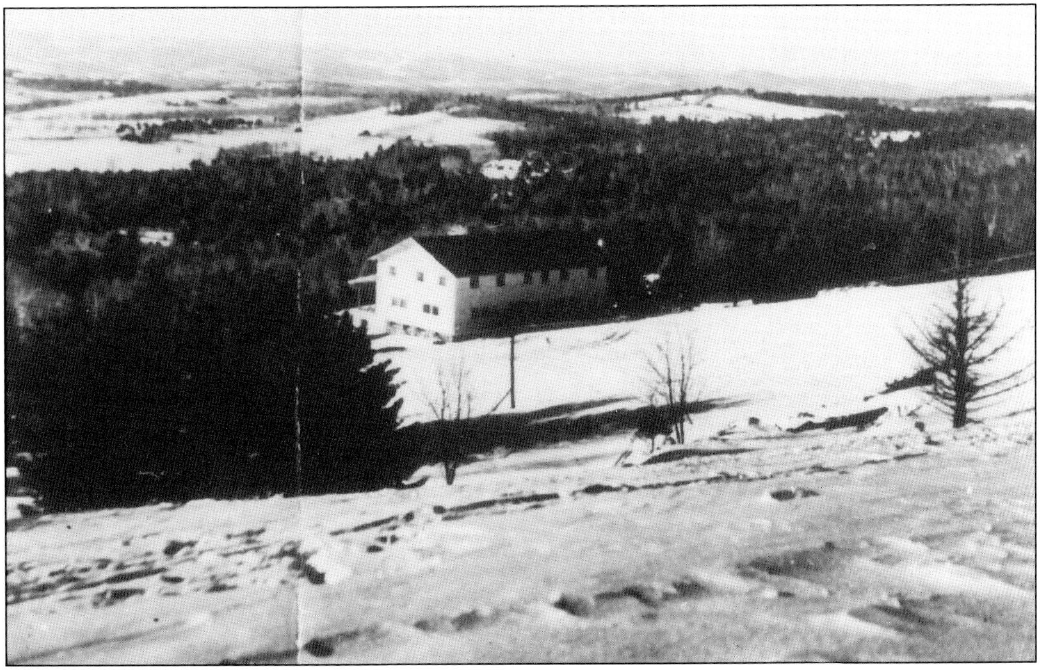

This view looks down on the newly finished lodge in late 1938. The facility was built by three brothers from eastern Massachusetts: Jack, Bill, and Julian Leslie. However, the outbreak of World War II temporarily halted their plans. Since 1975, the lodge has been owned and operated by Peter and Kay Shumway.

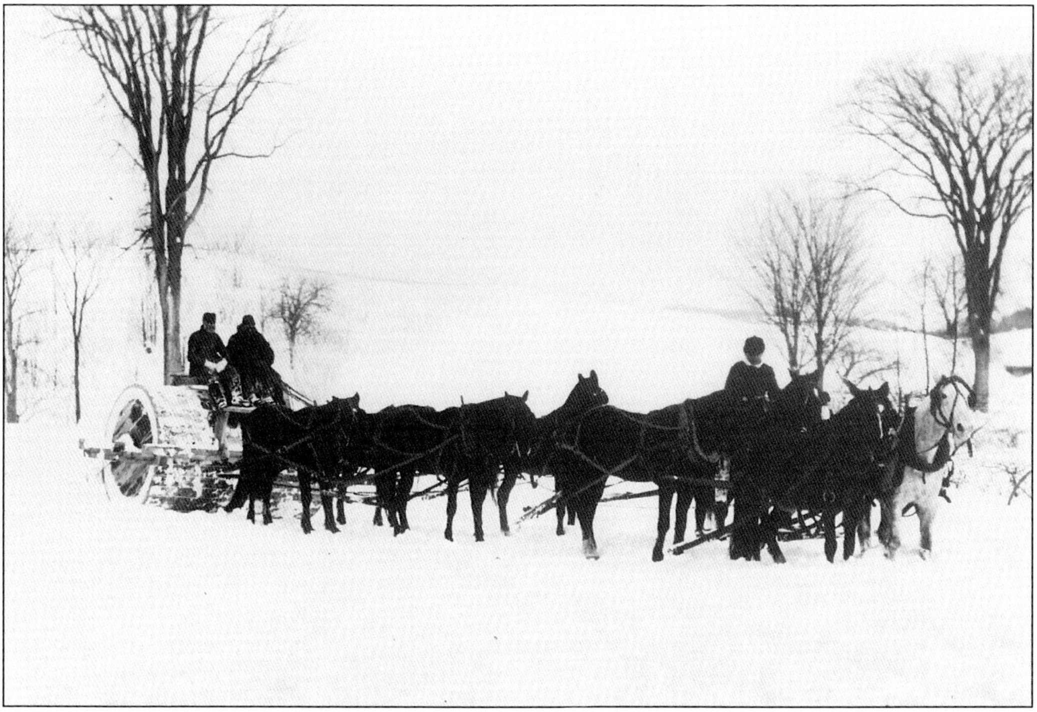

Prior to the popularity of automobiles and the need to plow snow from the roads to allow their passage, the snow was rolled, making a hard surface over which horse-drawn sleighs could glide. Here we see Ruddsboro Road between Two Mile and Dana Roads being prepared by a heavy wooden roller drawn by four teams of horses.

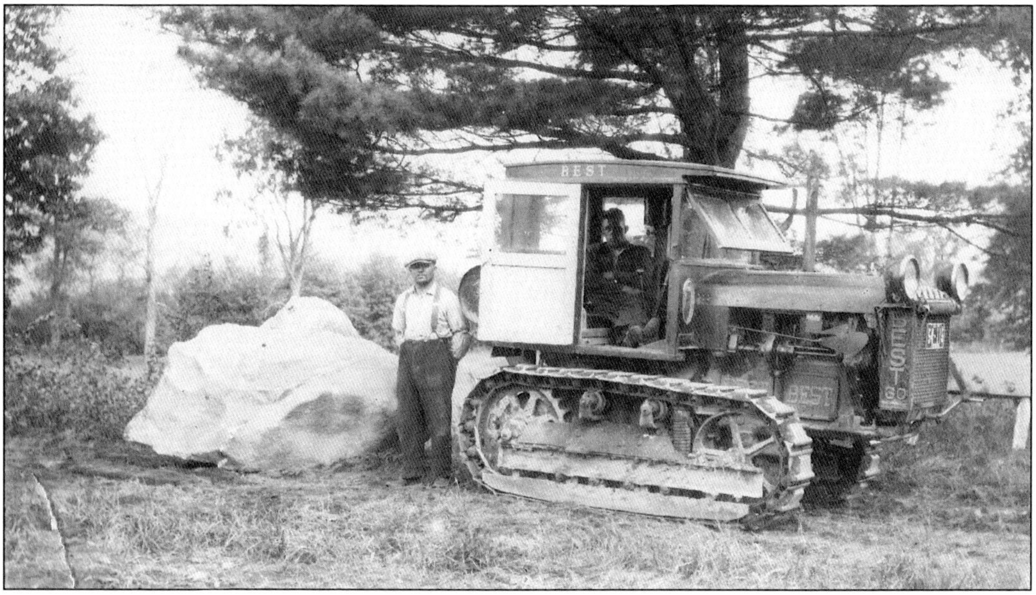

John Oel "J.O." Dana (standing) and Cliff Elder (in tractor) seem pleased with their efforts, moving a large rock from a Hanover road. Both men for many years worked on the town's highways, and the late-1920s vintage Best tractor was one of Hanover's first pieces of motorized equipment. This photograph was taken *c.* 1935.

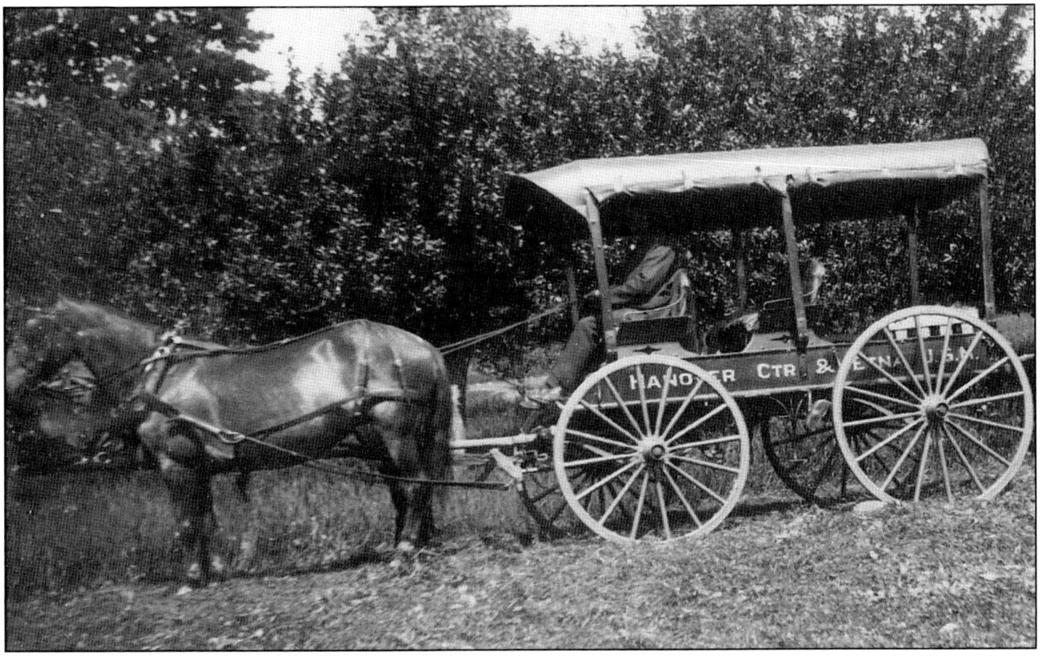

During the latter years of the nineteenth century, this horse-drawn stage was a common sight in the rural areas of Etna and Hanover Center. Its official purpose was to deliver mail, but it also provided transport to residents as well, especially schoolchildren.

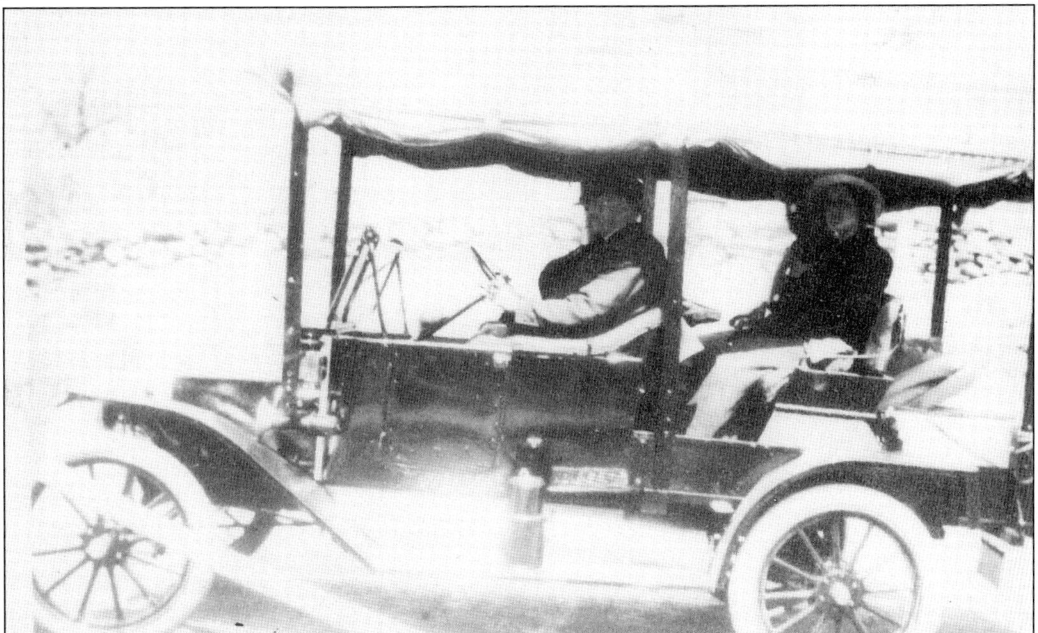

Alvin Fitts converted his 1914 Model T Ford touring car into a mail and passenger carrying stage, and for many years traveled the roads between Lebanon and Hanover Center. The gasoline-powered internal combustion engine was liberating rural America!

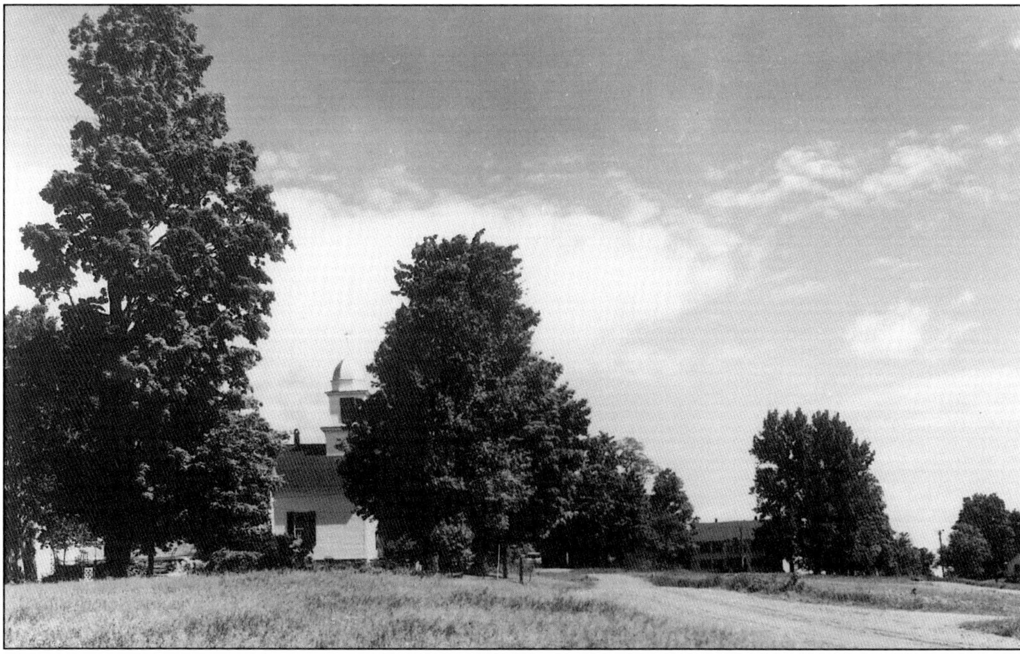

This view looks north across the Hanover Center "Parade Ground" toward the Jonathan Freeman house in 1960. The village common–like area, comprised of slightly more then 5 acres, was conveyed to the Town of Hanover in 1795 by Solomon Jacobs for a "Military Parade" ground, in exchange for certain assignments of road allowances.

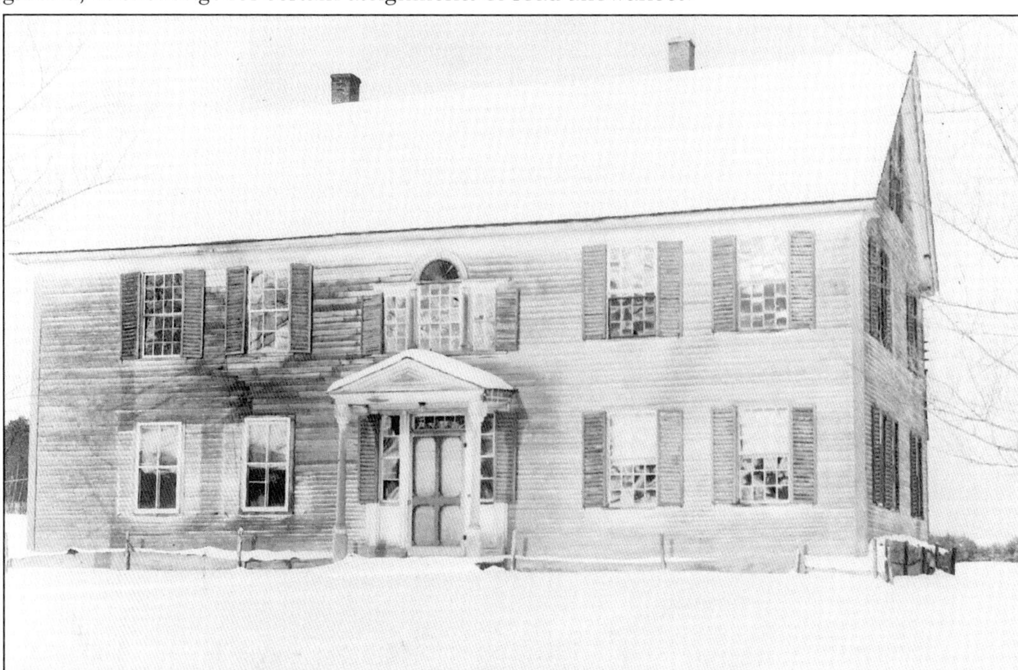

The front of the Jonathan Freeman house appears here in 1936. The Freemans were the first family to spend a winter in Hanover, migrating from lower Connecticut, and Jonathan, of that family, built this fine two-story home about 1798.

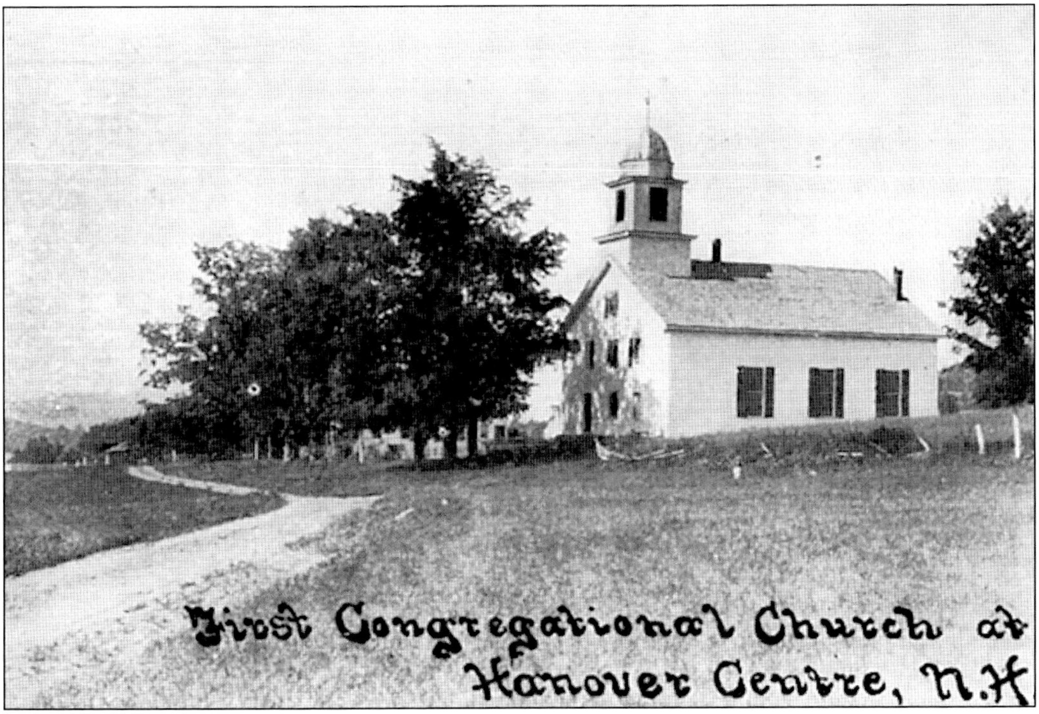

A postcard view taken about 1905 shows the present Hanover Center Church, erected in 1840 at a cost of about $2,100. It was the fourth meetinghouse to have stood at a location in the village facing the Parade Ground.

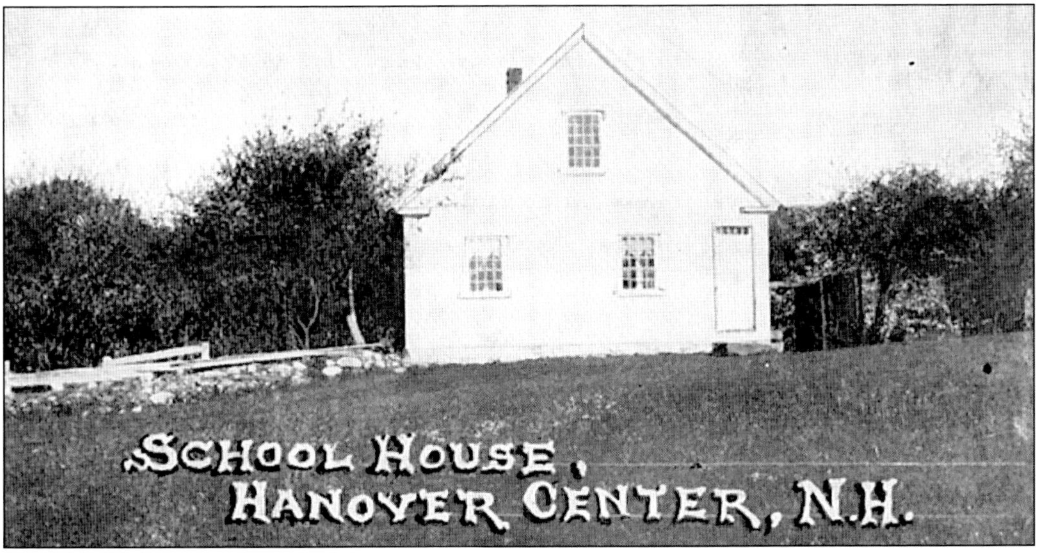

A companion postcard to the view shown above is of the Hanover Center District Schoolhouse, officially known as District No. 13 after the town was further redivided into increasingly smaller school districts in 1826. This building, constructed in 1826, still stands in the village facing the Parade Ground.

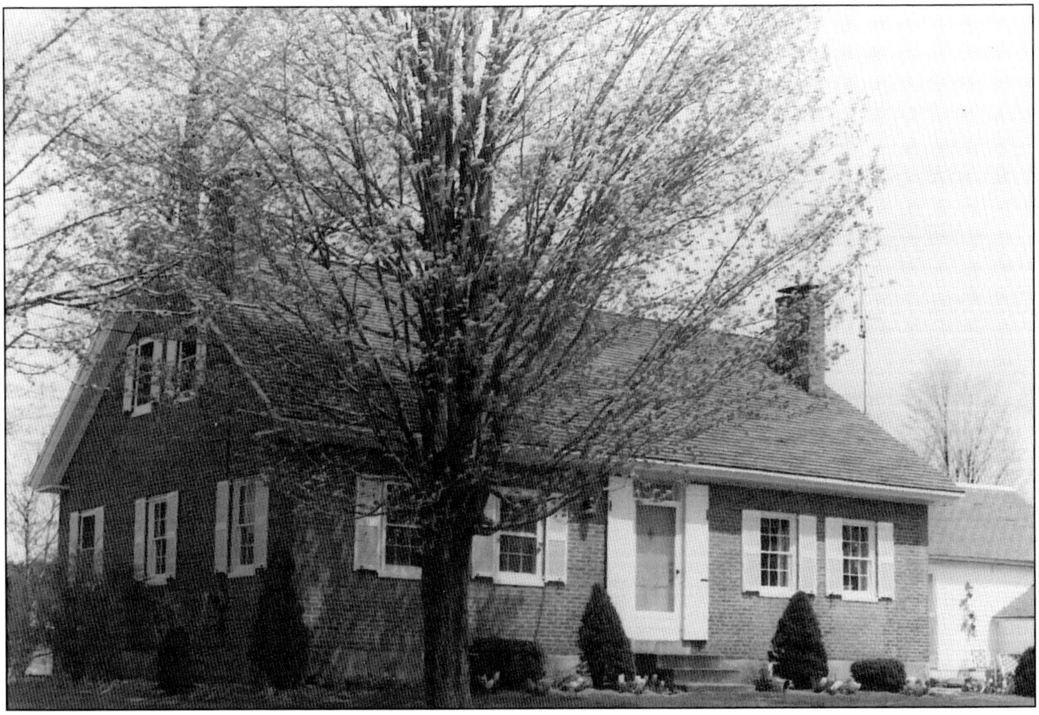

This handsome brick "cape"-style home at 385 Hanover Center Road was constructed in 1835 as a parsonage for the First Congregational Society. During the 1940s, the residence was restored by Dartmouth Engineering Professor John H. Minnich and his wife, Charlotte (LaBombard). This photograph shows the house in 1960.

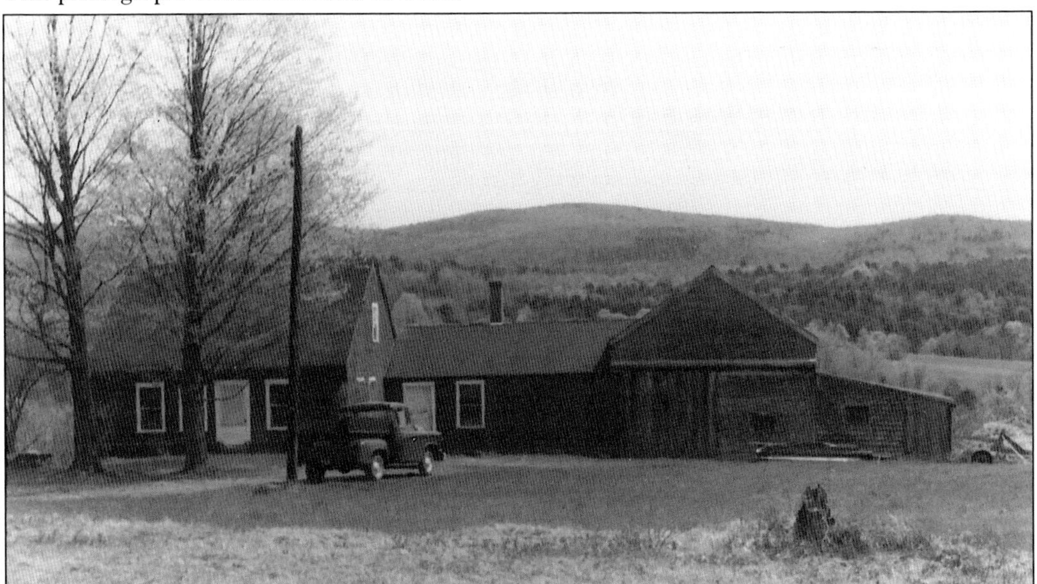

It has long been thought that this delightfully simple early home is the oldest structure still standing in Hanover Center, although the builder and date of construction are not definitively known. In fact, this might be the first permanent home to have been erected in the village. This photograph shows the house at 393 Hanover Center Road in 1960.

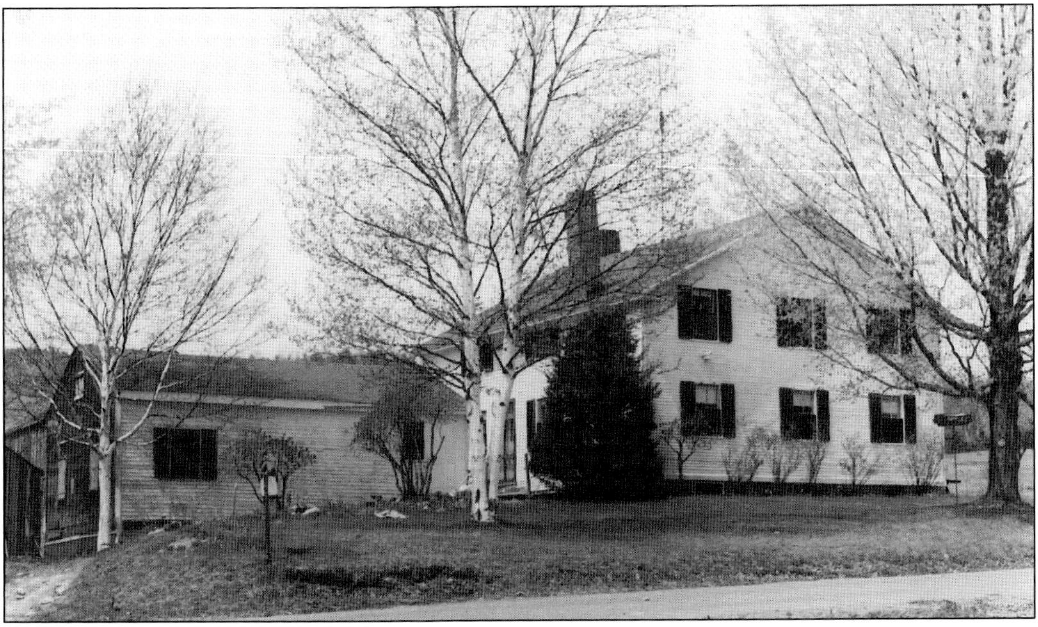

This architecturally interesting house at 4 Parade Ground Road was reportedly built by John Smith, probably very late in the eighteenth century. Mr. Smith kept a store just south of his home, which also is rumored to have had the character of a public house. Today this residence, shown here in 1960, is the home of John Storrs Stebbins, a direct descendant of one of Hanover's very first families.

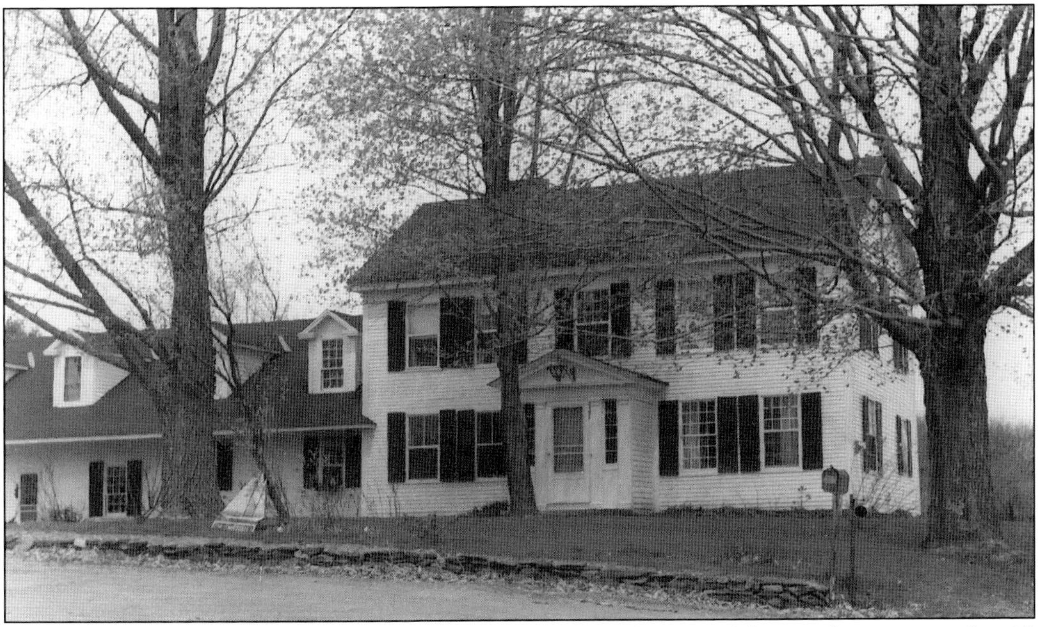

Like other older houses in the village, very little history is known of this residence situated at 10 Parade Ground Road. The building is thought to have been constructed in the early nineteenth century as a store, located just south of the present schoolhouse. In the 1830s, the building was purchased by a Dr. Edward Smith, who then moved the structure to its present location and converted it into a residence.

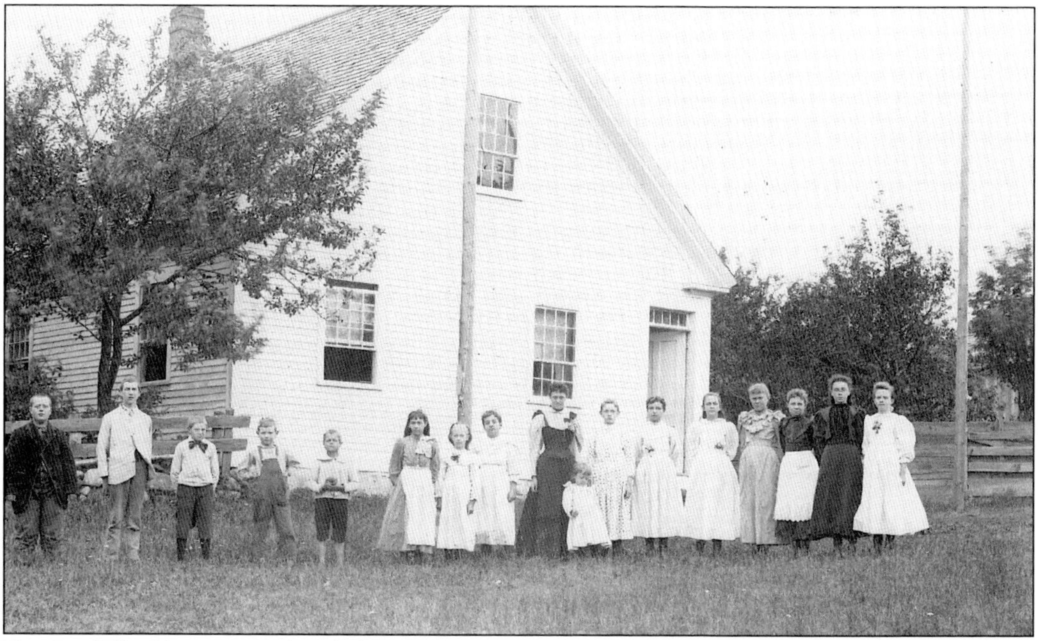

Teacher Effie Fitts is posed with her students in front of Hanover Center's schoolhouse in this formal turn-of-the-century photograph. Note that everyone appears to be wearing their best clothes for the occasion. The "centre" school permanently closed in 1945.

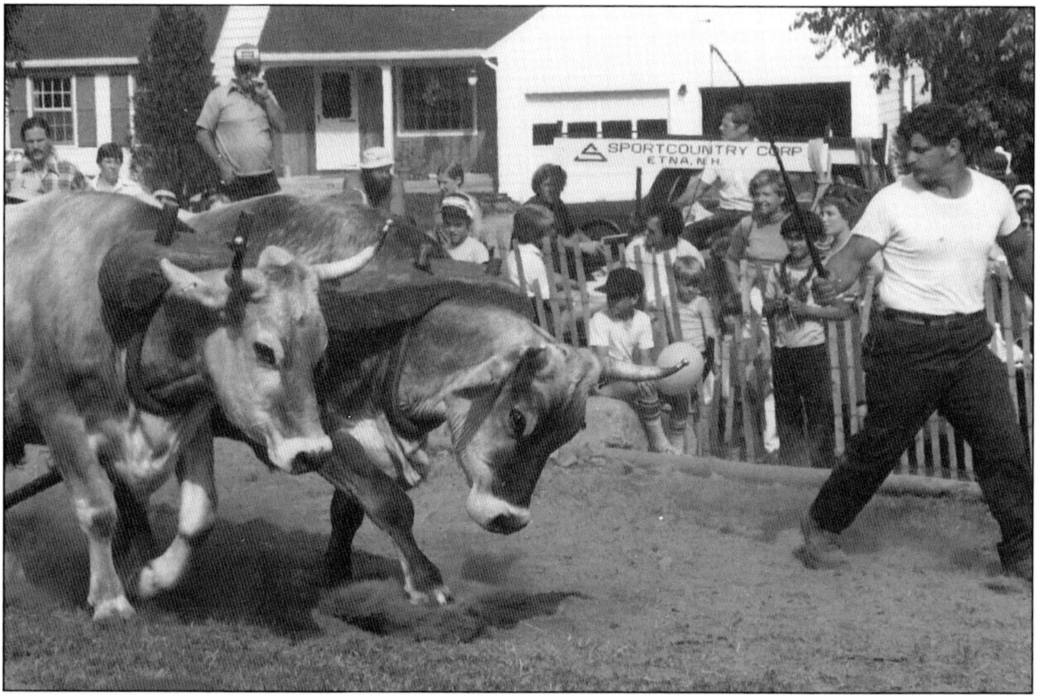

The Hanover Center Old Timers Fair has been for years an annual Hanover tradition, and of all the fair's events, the Saturday afternoon ox pull is the highlight. John LaHaye Jr. is coaxing his team forward. Although a photograph only perhaps 15 years old, the scene and its subject are in fact timeless.

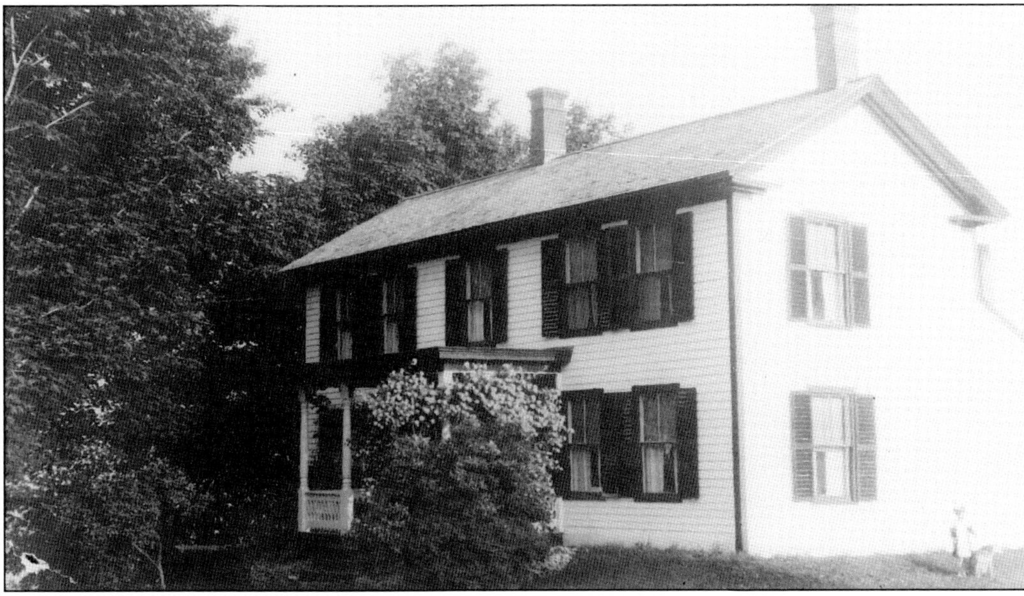

This two-story dwelling at 19 Wolfeboro Road was built about 1790 by Isaac Bridgman Jr., son of Isaac Bridgman, who was one of the first settlers in lower Etna Village. George LaBombard purchased this home in April 1913 after his farmhouse, north of Hanover Center, burned—it is at that time that this photograph was taken.

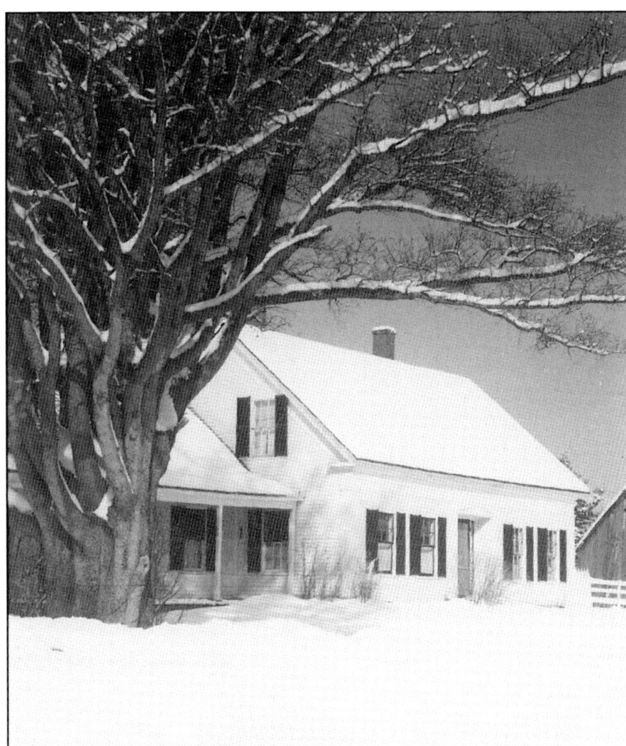

During the first half of the nineteenth century, the so-called Greek Revival style of architecture was a popular way to dress up an otherwise typical and straight-forward farmhouse. This dwelling, still standing at 494 Hanover Center Road, is a nice example of that period, as seen in this c. 1930 photograph.

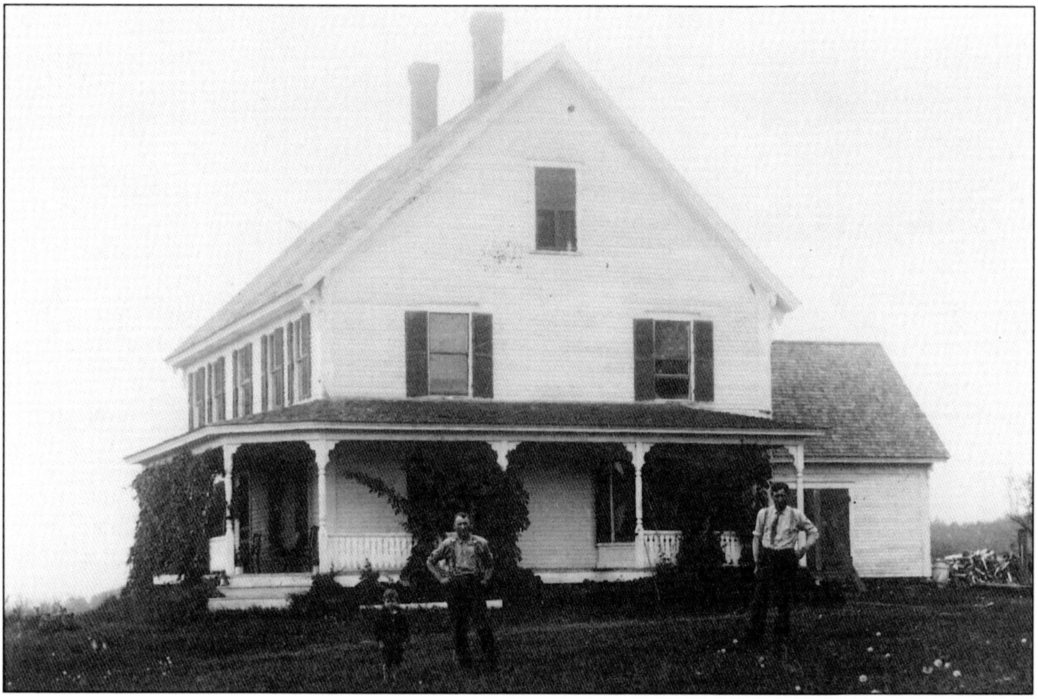

Late one night in April 1913, George LaBombard's farmhouse was completely destroyed in a fire caused by paint-soaked rags stored in the back el—the house's exterior had just been repainted. About 30 years later, George's son Lester built a new house on the same site at 441 Hanover Center Road.

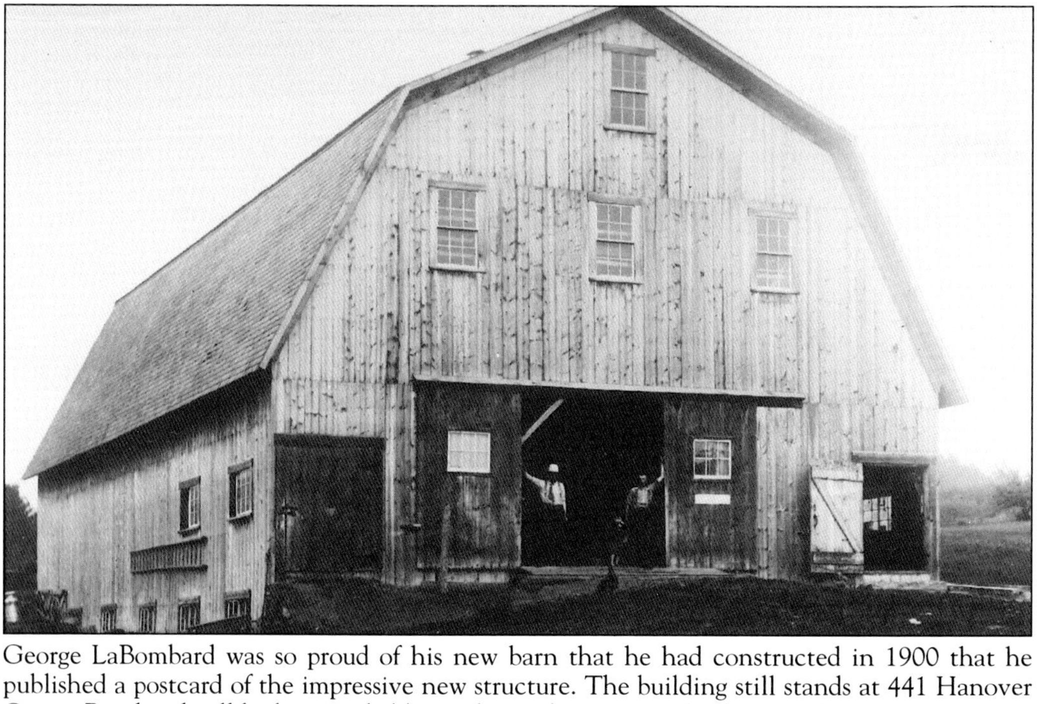

George LaBombard was so proud of his new barn that he had constructed in 1900 that he published a postcard of the impressive new structure. The building still stands at 441 Hanover Center Road and still looks remarkably similar to this view made almost 100 years ago.

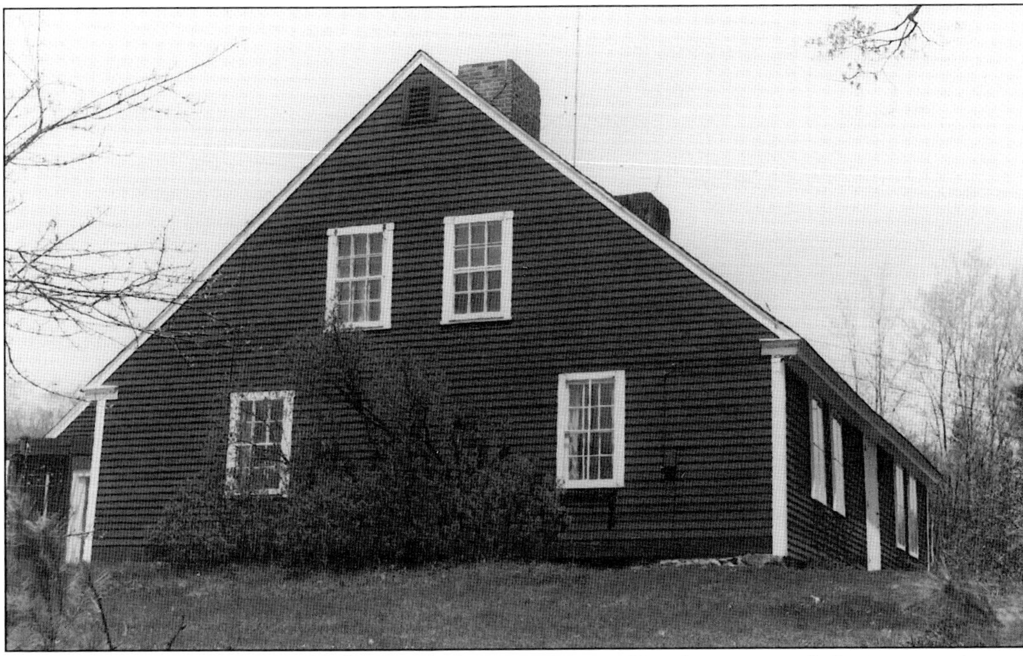

At the intersection of Goodfellow and Hanover Center Roads is situated this very early cape style dwelling, erected in the mid-1780s by Salmon Dow and shown here as it looked in 1960.

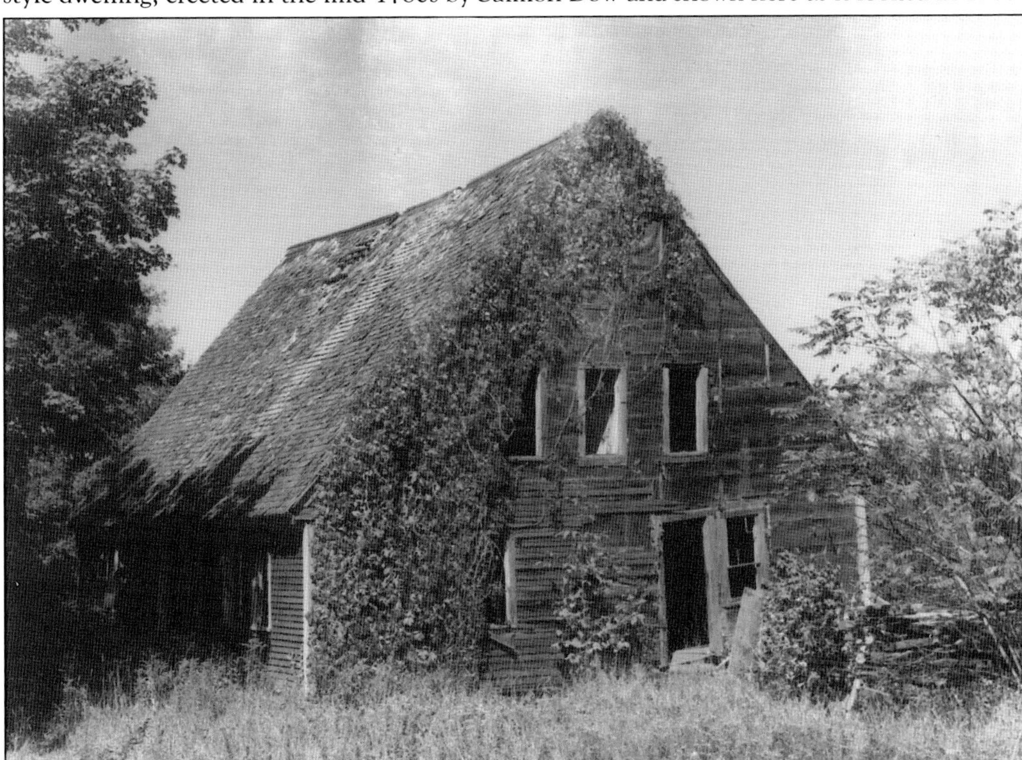

On the Wardrobe Road there existed until quite recently the remains of this also very early mid-1780s dwelling, built by Nathaniel Hurlbutt and shown here in decrepit condition in 1960.

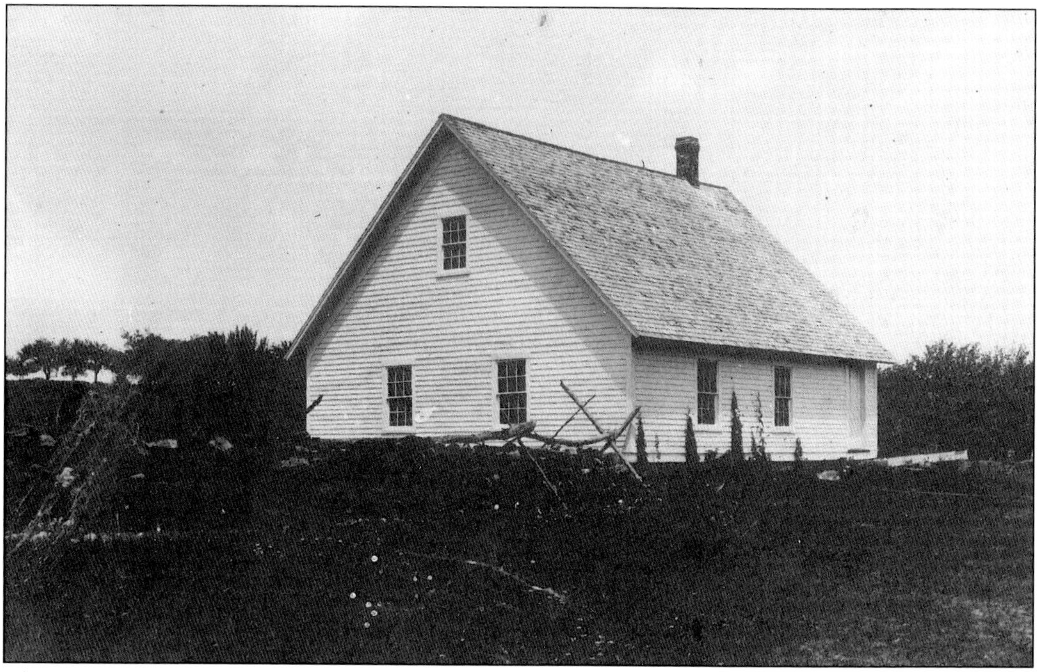

The area around the intersection of Hanover Center and Ferson Roads has long been known as the North Neighborhood, and for years even had its own school, seen here perhaps *c.* 1880. Nineteen twenty-nine was the last year that the school was open. Today the building still remains at 566 Hanover Center Road, the home of George and Dorothea Stibitz.

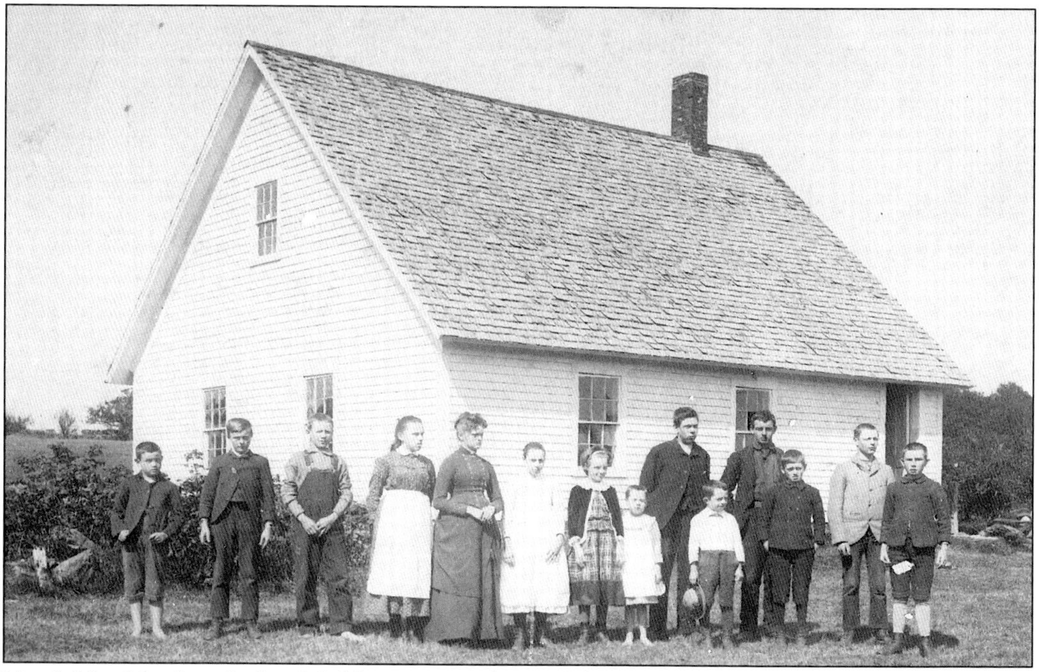

North Neighborhood schoolchildren pose in front of their schoolhouse, perhaps *c.* 1890. Often, depending upon the population of school-age children in the area, small schools such as this might be closed for years at a time, and then reopen again when need so required.

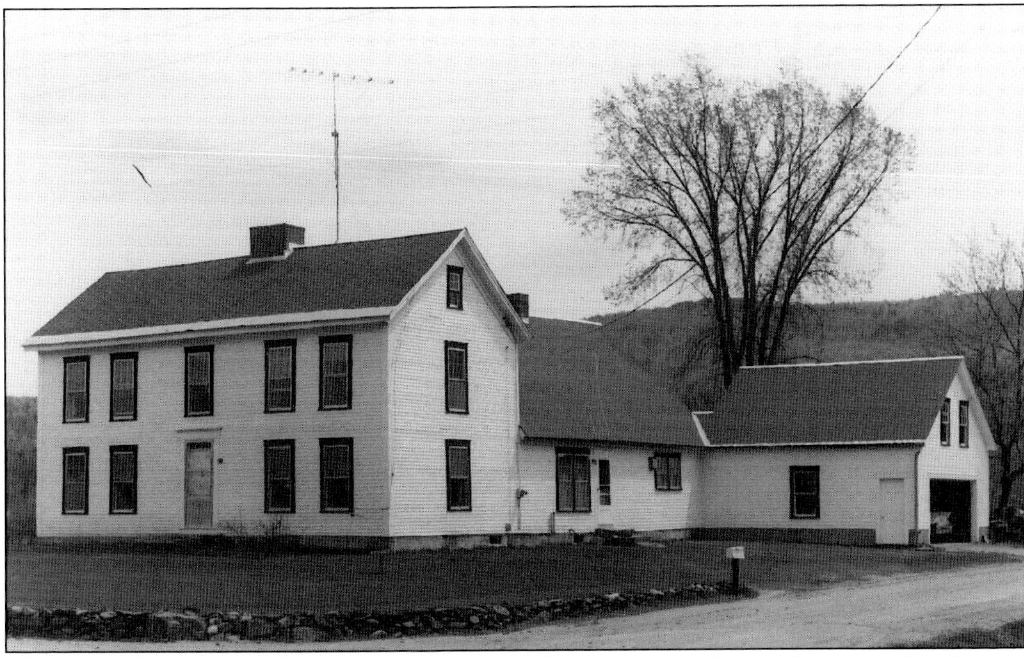

Samuel Slade, an early settler to Hanover, erected this home for himself before 1791, although exactly when is not definitively known. The house still stands at 2 Ferson Road and is presently the residence of Harthon and Barbara Munson.

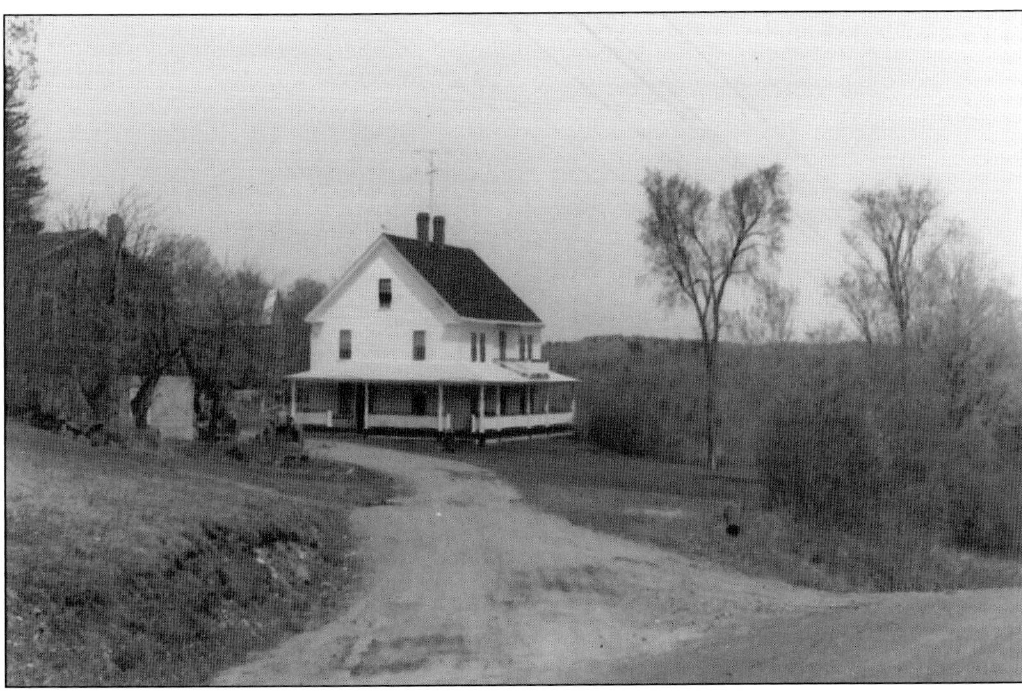

Elijah Miller constructed this North Neighborhood home at 572 Hanover Center Road sometime soon after 1800. In more recent years, the farm, totaling as much as 300 acres, was owned by Edward Rennie, who later sold it to Dartmouth College—the property's present owner.

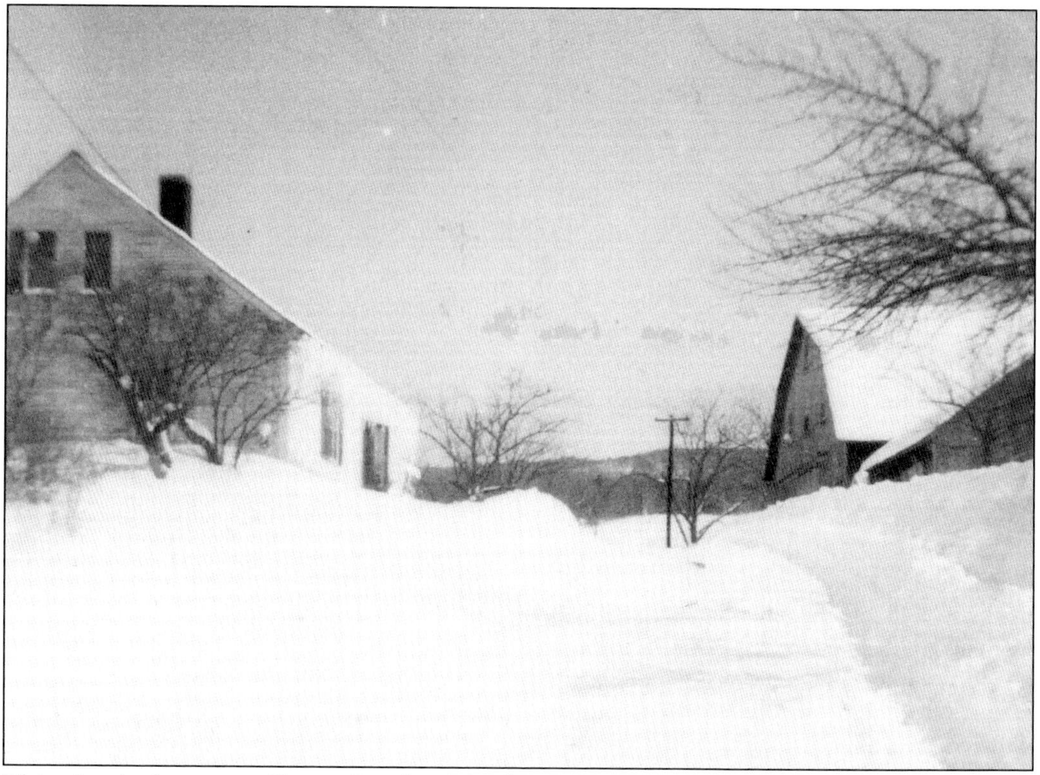

This view looks east up Ferson Road in March 1956. To the left is the residence of Earl and Millie (West) Farnham. This is believed to be a very early building, although little of the history is known. The barns on the right side of the road have since been removed.

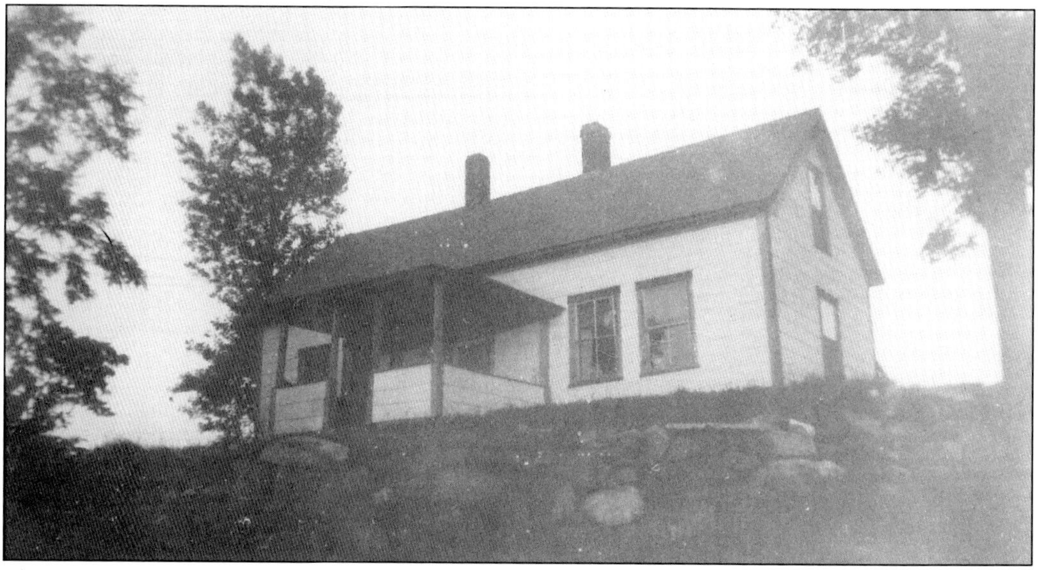

Elmer E. West bought this farm in 1942 from Arthur Elwin Fogg. The farmhouse, seen here in 1951, was located at the top of Ferson and Three Mile Road. The barns burned in August 1952, and the farmhouse burned in December 1954. Today the residence of Richard Neroni occupies the site at 185 Three Mile Road.

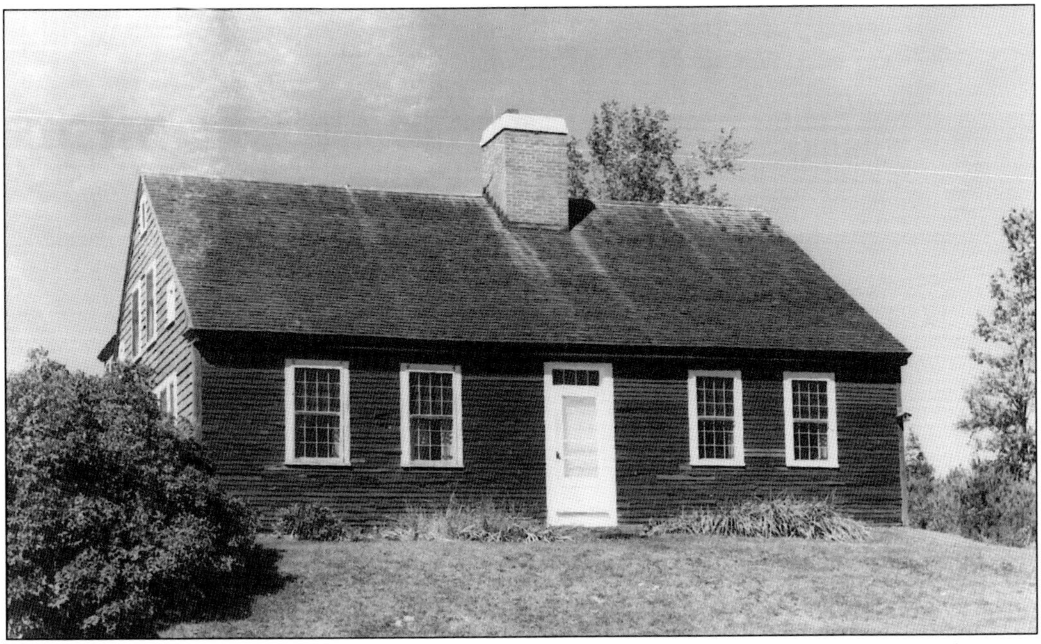

John Tenney arrived in Hanover by ox team in June 1770, having traveled up along the river from lower Connecticut. Shortly thereafter, he settled along the western slopes of Moose Mountain and constructed this fine cape home, still standing at 80 Three Mile Road. This photograph was taken in 1960.

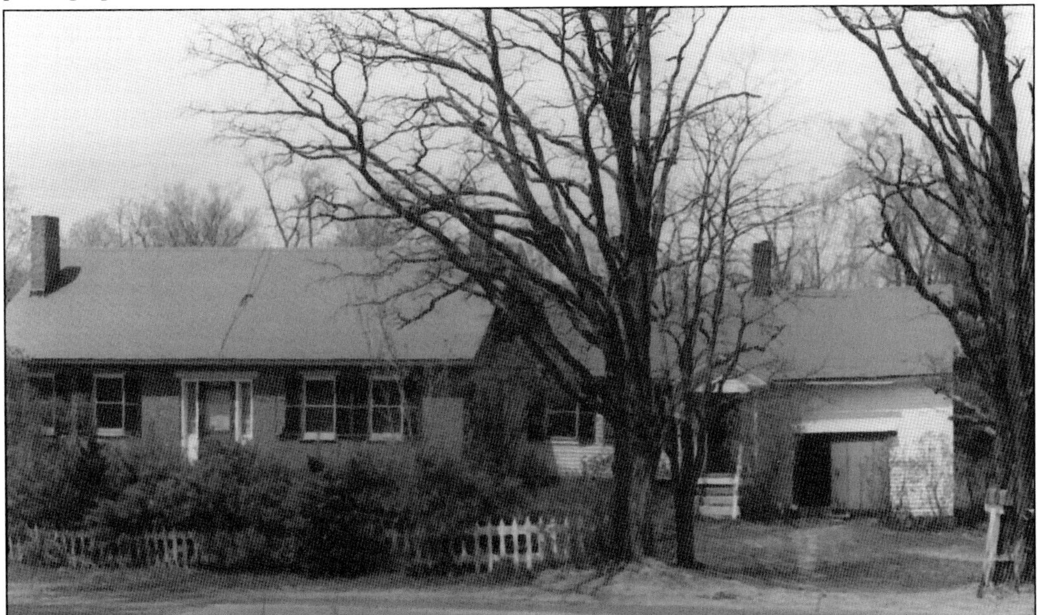

Andrew Boyd came from Malone, New York, in 1892 and purchased this brick house at 612 Hanover Center Road and its 160 acres from Hanna Topliff. The Topliffs were early settlers in the North Neighborhood, and in 1917, Elijah M. Topliff—then of Manchester, New Hampshire, but of the Class of 1852 at Dartmouth—bequeathed $240,000 to the college for a new dormitory named in his honor.

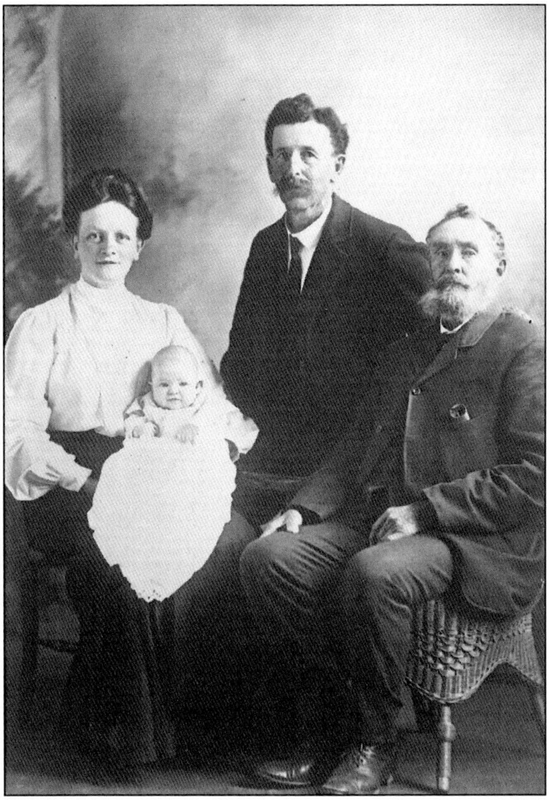

Four generations of Rennies are present in this early-twentieth-century view. From left to right are Marjorie Emerson (later Simonds), Edith (Rennie) Emerson, Alexander James Rennie, and Andrew Rennie. Alexander James Rennie migrated to Hanover from Rockburn, Quebec, in 1895 and settled in the North Neighborhood to farm the land. Today, Rennie Road takes its name from this family.

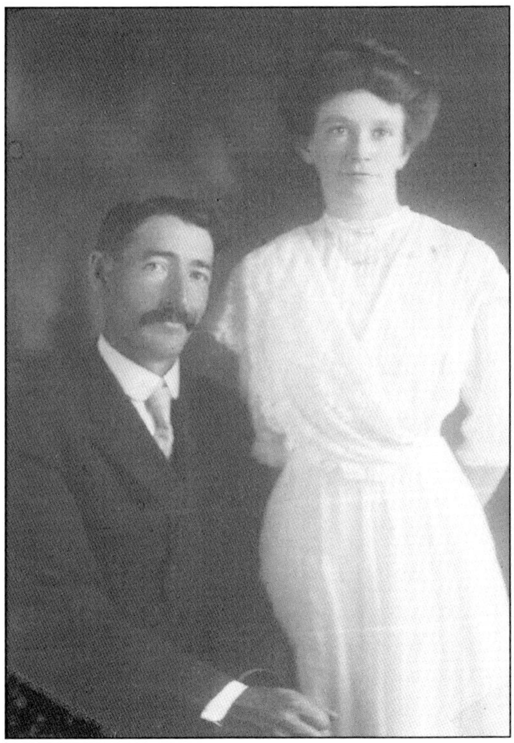

Henrietta Jane (Rennie) and William John Boyd are pictured here in 1913, the year they were married. During the decades surrounding the turn of the century, there was an influx of families with Scotch and French ancestry into Hanover from the Malone/Chateaugay area of Upper New York state and nearby Huntington County, Quebec. Names like Rennie, Boyd, Garipay, and LaBombard, now familiar to Hanover history, first appeared during that time.

Five

Back Down along the River

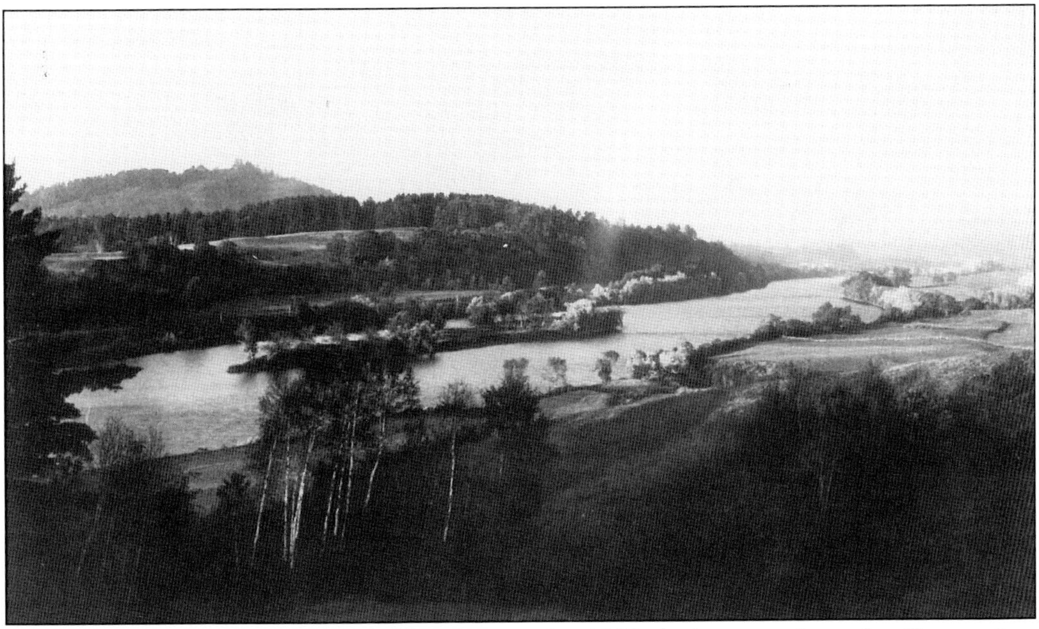

This beautifully scenic view, probably taken in the 1880s looking north up the Connecticut River from about the site of the present-day Chieftain Motel, shows the 40-mile stretch of river valley known years ago as Lower Coos Country. The word "Coos" was originally Native American and meant the place of the curved river. Today much of this view is different; the result of low-lying meadow land having been flooded due to the completion of Wilder Dam in 1950.

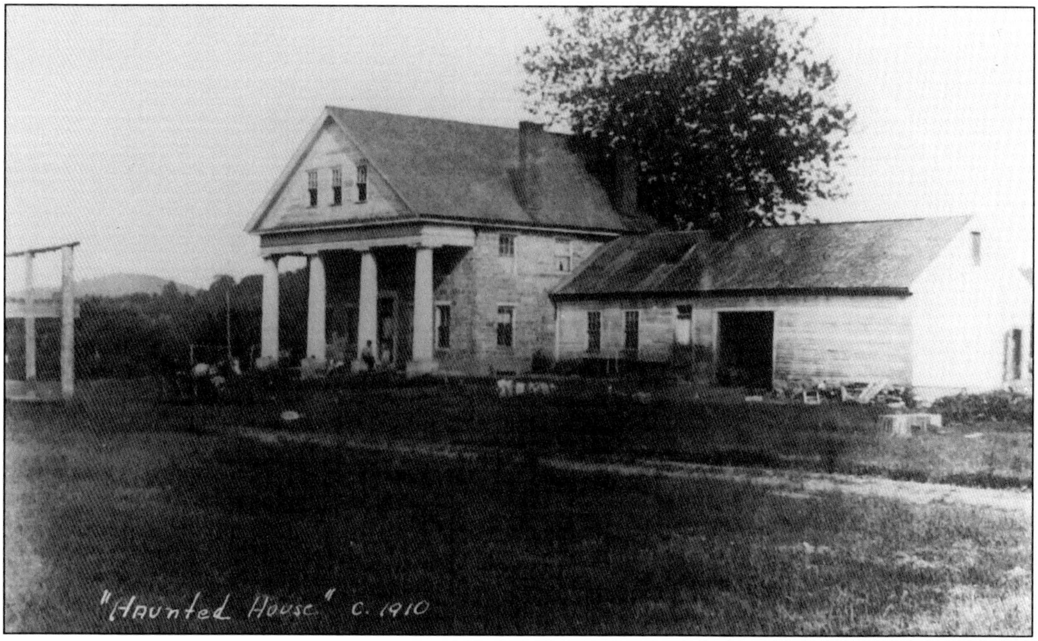

Luther Wood constructed this masterfully designed and beautifully proportioned Greek Revival-style stone tavern on the River Road in 1832. However, early in its short life as a hostelry, the building acquired a reputation of being haunted, and together with the construction of a new road to Lyme, which turned traffic away from the hostelry, and the opening of the railroad on the Vermont side of the river in 1848, the building began a long and sad period of decline.

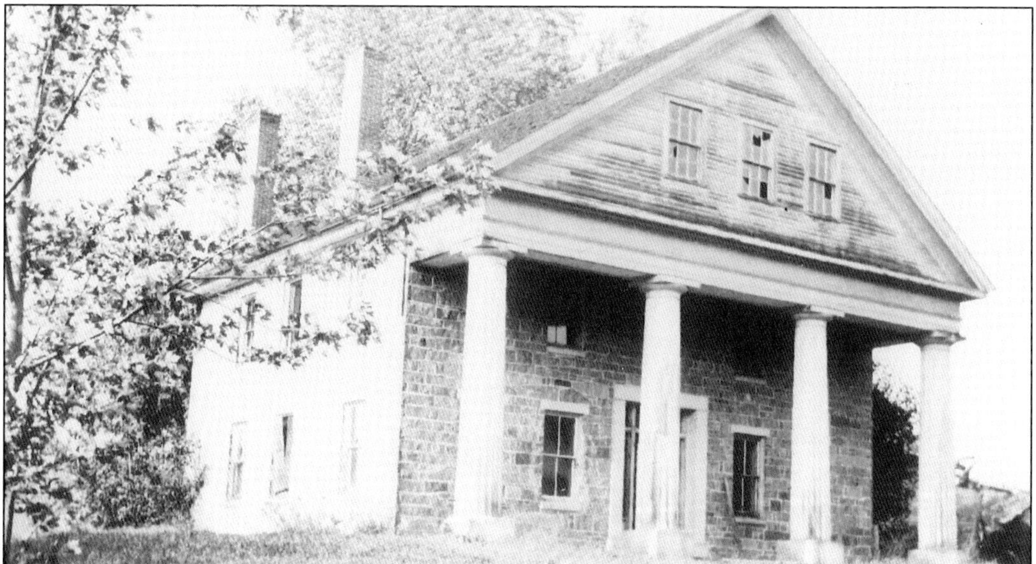

This view shows the magnificent building in 1925, now abandoned and no longer cared for. In 1958, the stone from the structure was donated by Mrs. Regina Stanhope to the new Lutheran Church in memory of her recently deceased husband, Ivan D. Stanhope, and today the site of the once commanding building is occupied by the new residence of John and Lois Stanhope at 66 River Road.

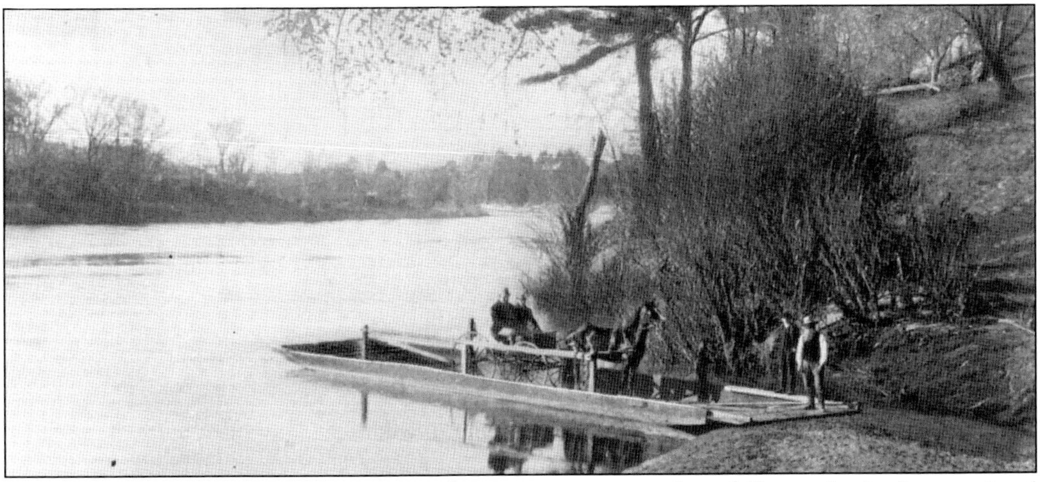

Since the earliest days of Hanover's settlement, as many as four different ferries have existed within the town, crossing the Connecticut River at equally as many different locations. Up until the very early years of the twentieth century, one ferry was chartered to cross between the village of Pompanoosuc, Vermont, and Hanover, landing near the River Road. The exact course of the Pompanoosuc ferry changed through the years; however, this *c.* 1900 view shows it landing at the Hanover shore.

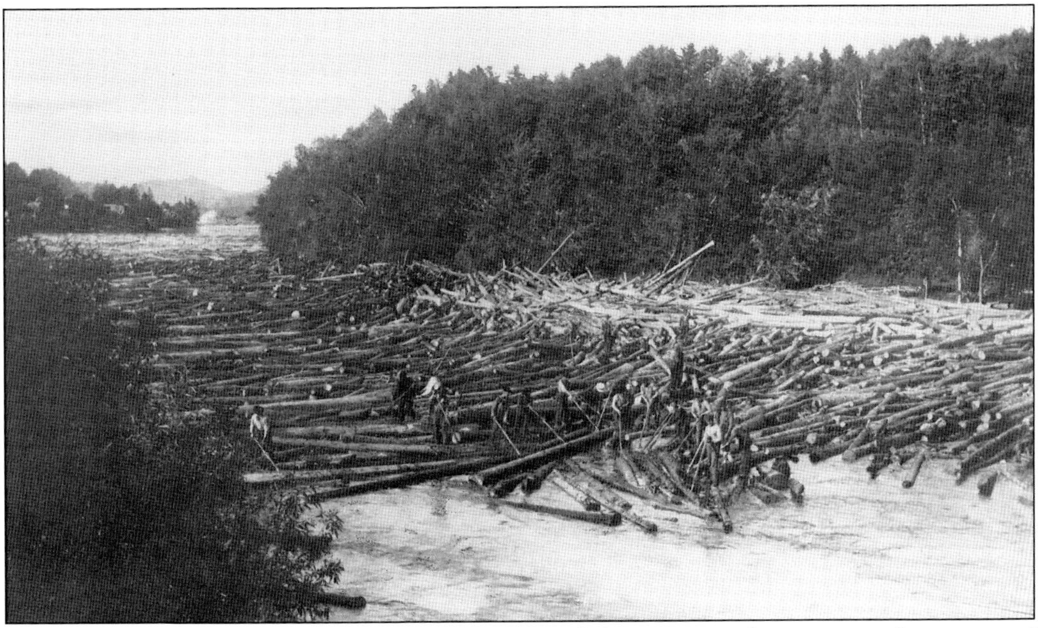

In the years following the American Civil War, until the 1920s, each spring saw the passing of huge log drives down the Connecticut River. The logs, cut from the forests of northern New Hampshire and Vermont during the winter months, were then floated downstream to saw and paper mills located in lower regions of the river valley. Here is a *c.* 1900 log drive passing by a section of rural Hanover shoreline.

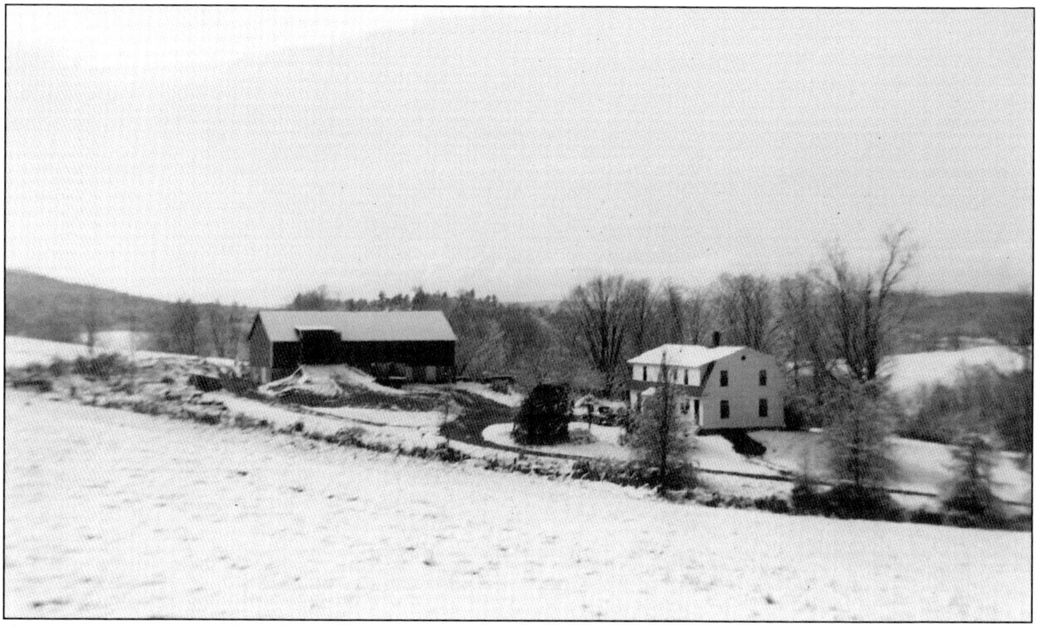

A wintry view *c.* 1950 of the Bollea farm, located along Lyme Road, looks southerly toward Goodfellow Road. This farm, once totaling approximately 300 acres, had been in the Arvin-Noonan-Bollea family for well more then 100 years before being sold in 1985. Today much of the land is the Montview Drive neighborhood, although the farmhouse, built in 1929, and barn, renovated in the early 1940s, still remain looking across into Vermont.

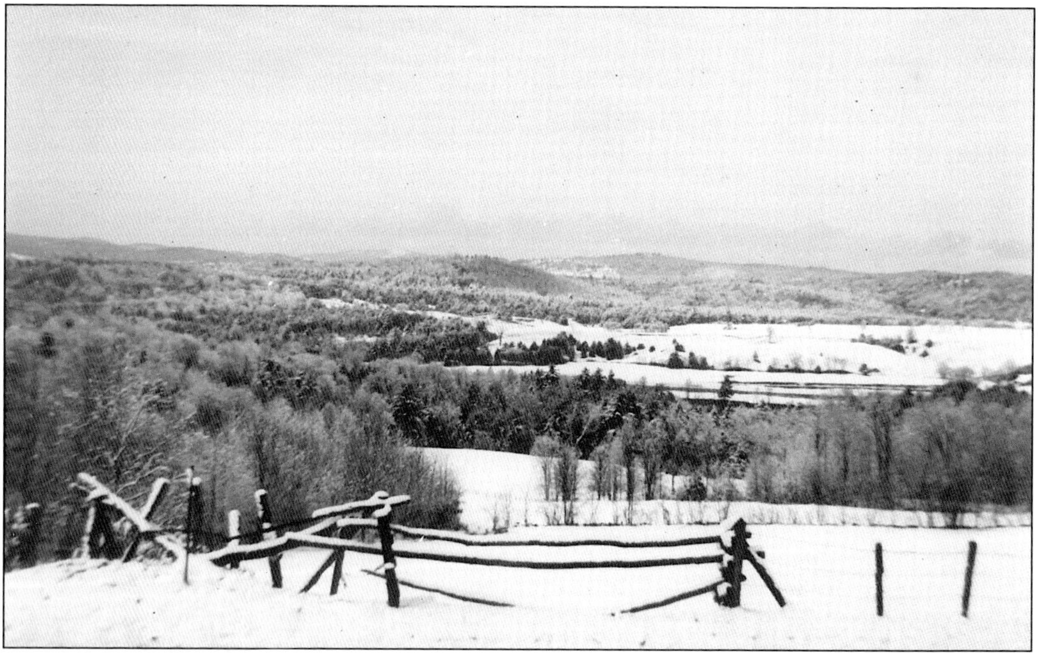

Seen here *c.* 1950, these fields located on the west side of Lyme Road were once part of the Bollea farm. In the distance are hills in Norwich, Vermont. Most of this area is now part of the Pete's Lane (named for Peter Bollea) and Heather Lane neighborhood developed in the late 1980s.

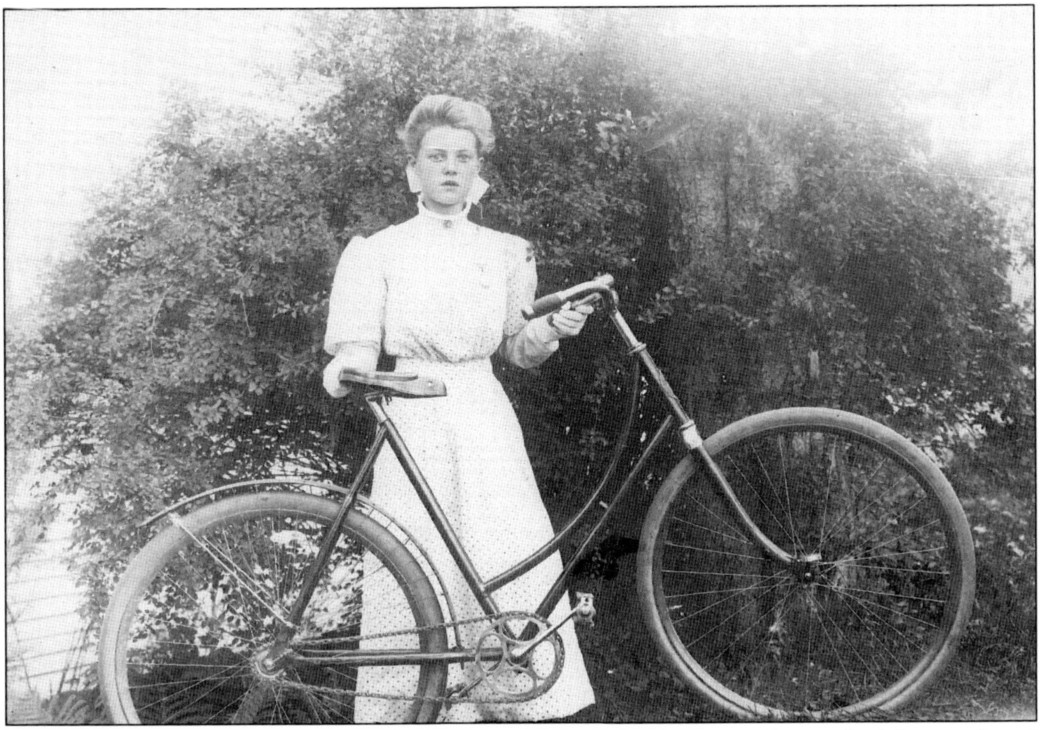

The mass-produced consumer goods that we now so take for granted were highly prized and considered very special by earlier generations of rural young people, as witnessed in this 1909 photograph of Medora G. Noonan (Bollea), age 16, with her new modern woman's bicycle.

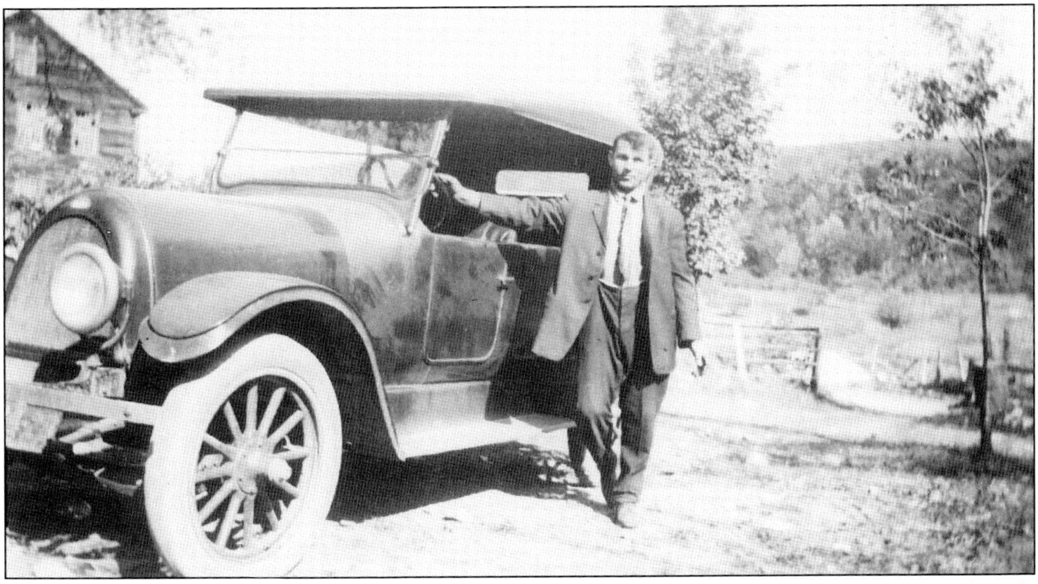

Peter Bollea has every reason to look proud in this mid-1920s photograph, standing beside his Franklin touring car in the driveway at the farm. Franklins were high-quality, expensive automobiles made in Syracuse, New York. Peter was born in northern Italy; however, he came to this country at a young age and married Medora Noonan in 1910. He worked the family farm on the Lyme Road until his death in 1960.

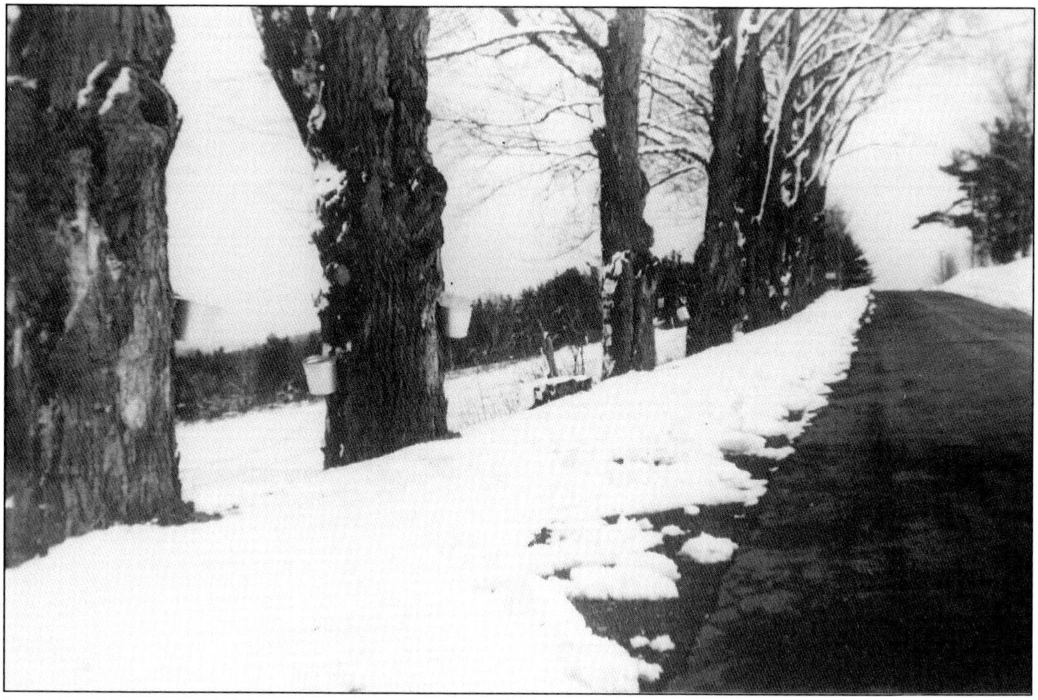

It is April 1948 and the Bolleas have their sap buckets hung and the maple trees tapped along Lyme Road, just a short distance north of Goodfellow Road and Piper's Lane.

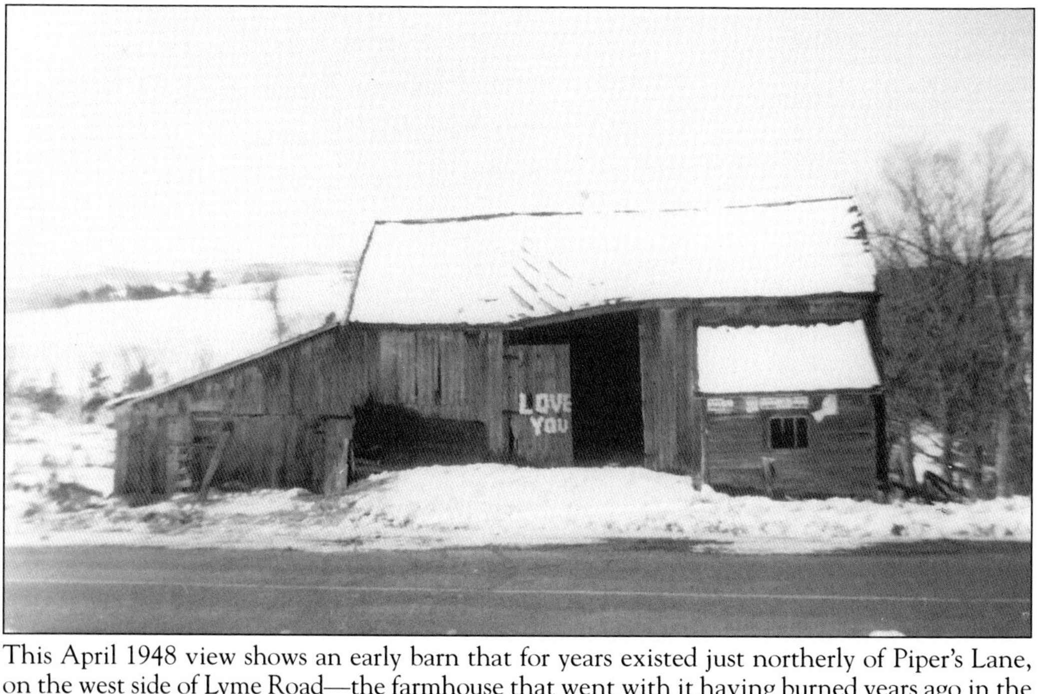

This April 1948 view shows an early barn that for years existed just northerly of Piper's Lane, on the west side of Lyme Road—the farmhouse that went with it having burned years ago in the early 1920s. Note the "snowball art" on the barn door.

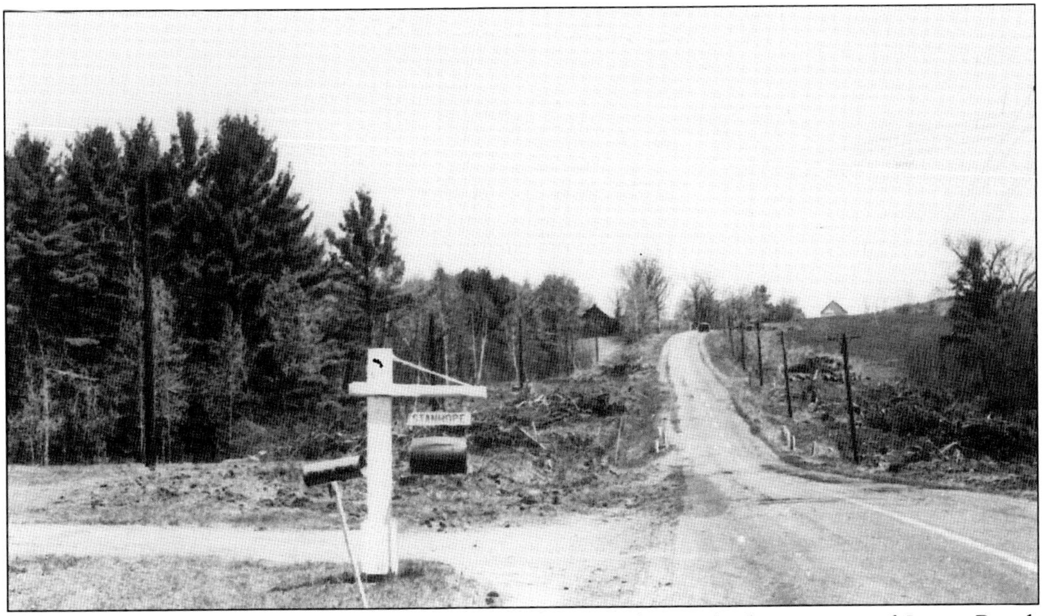

Gradually through the years, the State of New Hampshire rebuilt sections of Lyme Road, known to the State as Route 10. The greatest amount of this work was done in the 1950s and 1960s, a section at a time. Here work is just beginning in 1964 on a piece of the road south of the Hanover/Lyme town line, opposite the Stanhope residence at 182 Lyme Road. This view looks north.

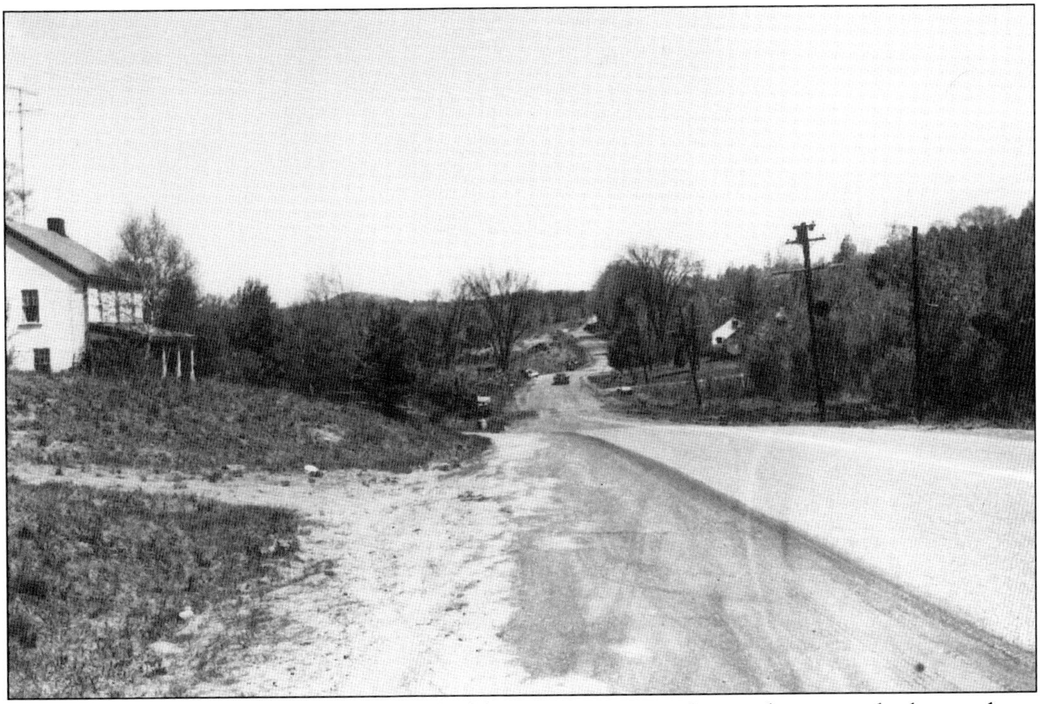

Another view of the same highway rebuilding project seen above, this scene looks north up Lyme Road from just south of Piper's Lane and Goodfellow Road. To the left is the Bernard Morse residence at 158 Lyme Road. Far up the road is the Bollea farm.

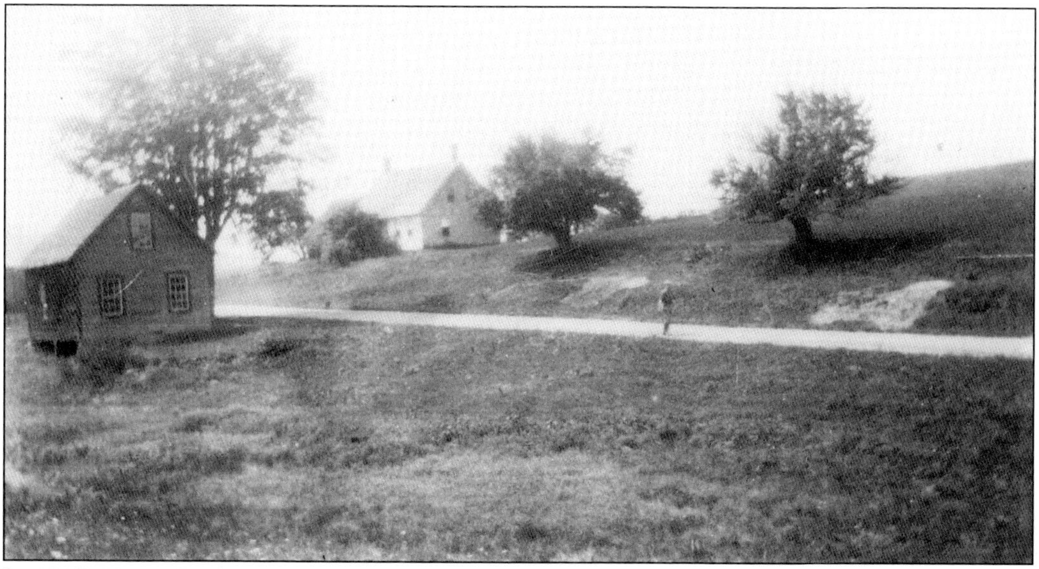

In 1917, Henry Buskey came up from Flushing, New York, and bought this farm on the Lyme Road, located immediately south of Goodfellow Road. This view looking westerly across Lyme Road toward the farmhouse was taken that fall. The farm's blacksmith shop is shown to the left.

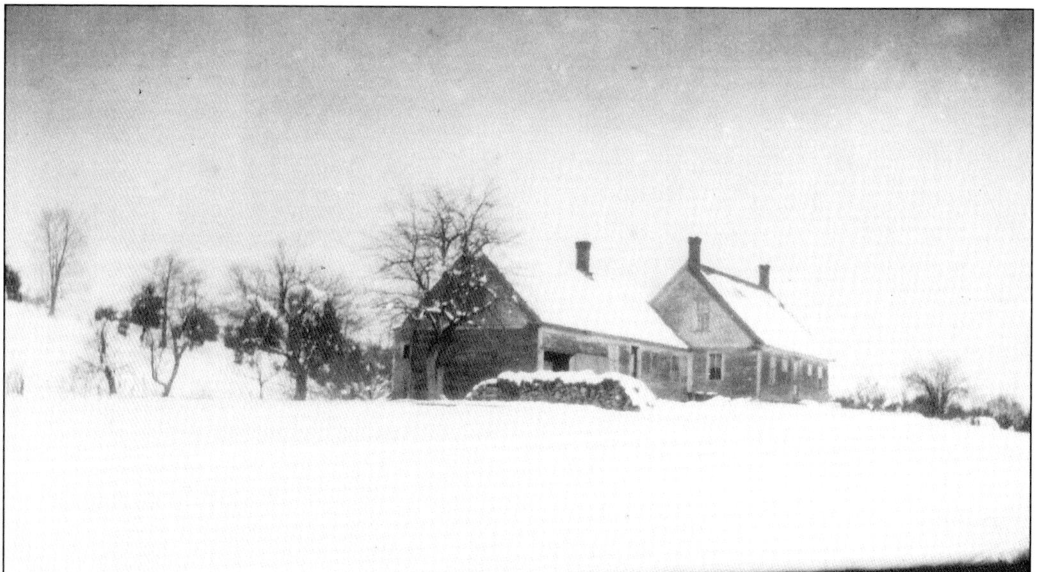

This view of Henry Buskey's farmhouse in the winter of 1918 looks northerly from Lyme Road. This house and attached el is thought to be of very early-nineteenth-century origins.

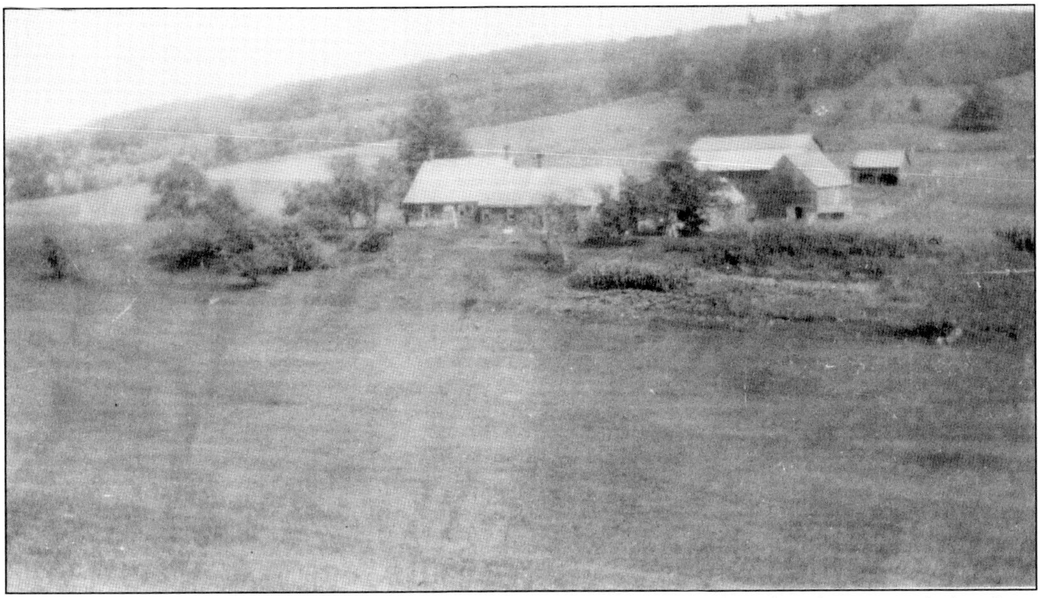

Looking easterly in 1917, this view shows the rear of the Buskey farmhouse and the farm buildings located on the opposite side of Lyme Road. The western slopes of Huntington Hill are in the background. At one time, this farm totaled about 140 acres.

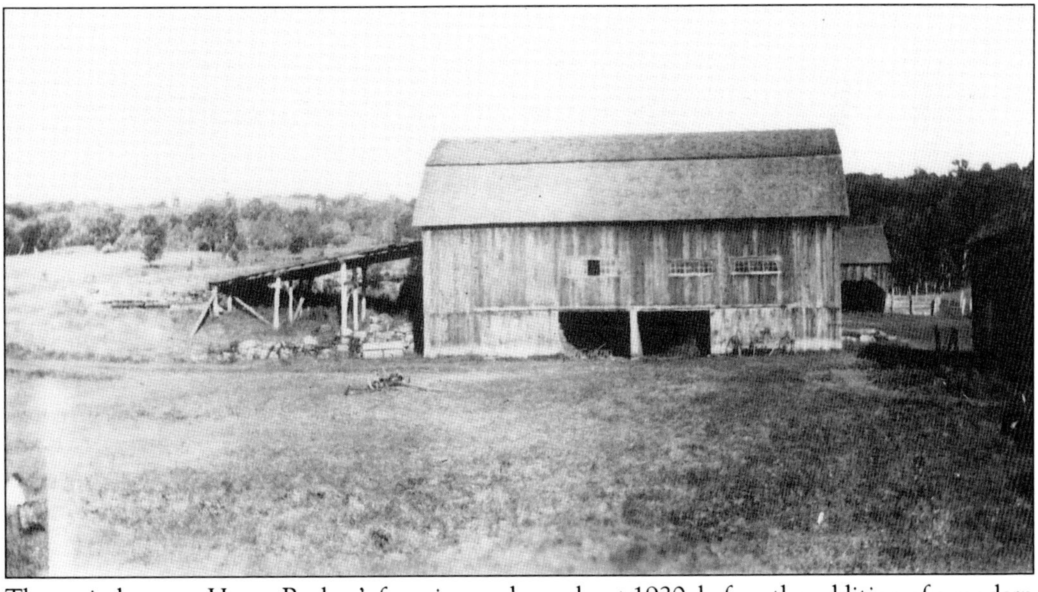

The main barn on Henry Buskey's farm is seen here about 1920, before the addition of a modern masonry tile silo in 1924—the first one built in the valley. Today the Mertz residence at 153 Old Lyme Road occupies the site of the old barn.

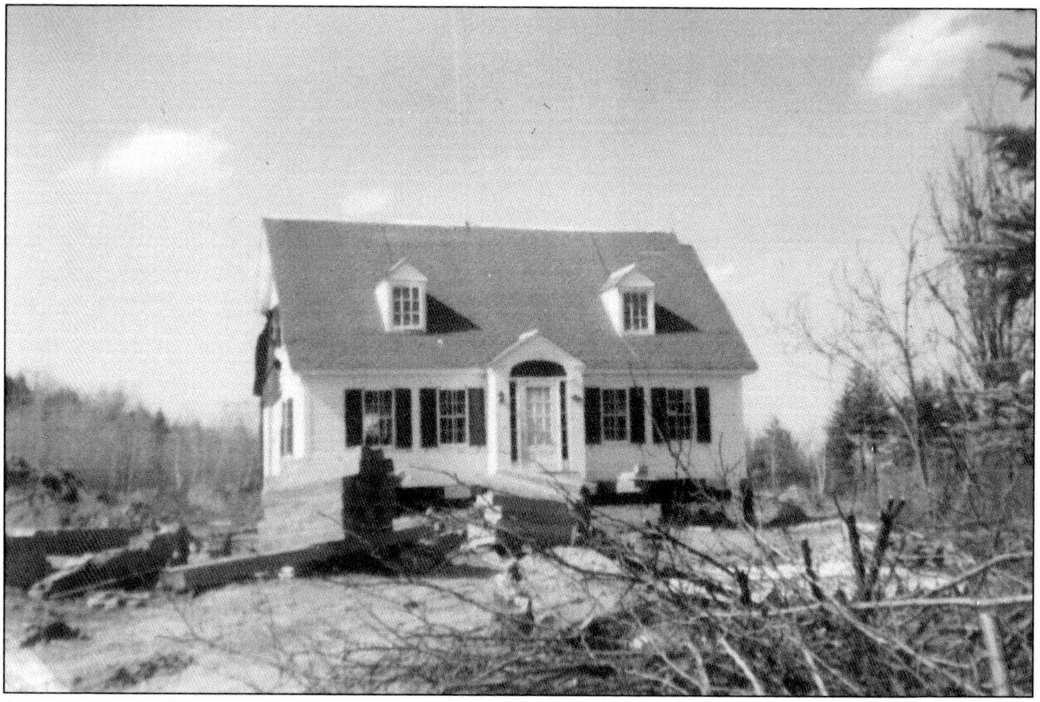

During the early spring of 1958, the Buskey residence was moved westerly to allow for the relocation of a section of Lyme Road. Today the home is the residence of Peter Landon, at 156 1/2 Lyme Road.

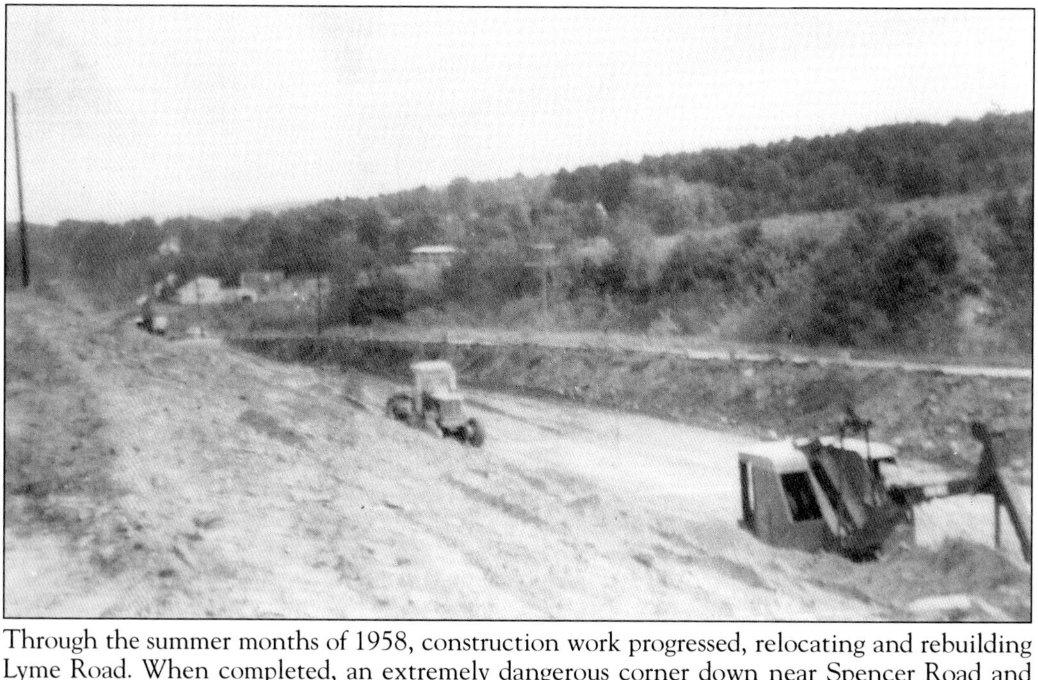

Through the summer months of 1958, construction work progressed, relocating and rebuilding Lyme Road. When completed, an extremely dangerous corner down near Spencer Road and Slade Brook had been eliminated. This view looks northeasterly toward Goodfellow Road.

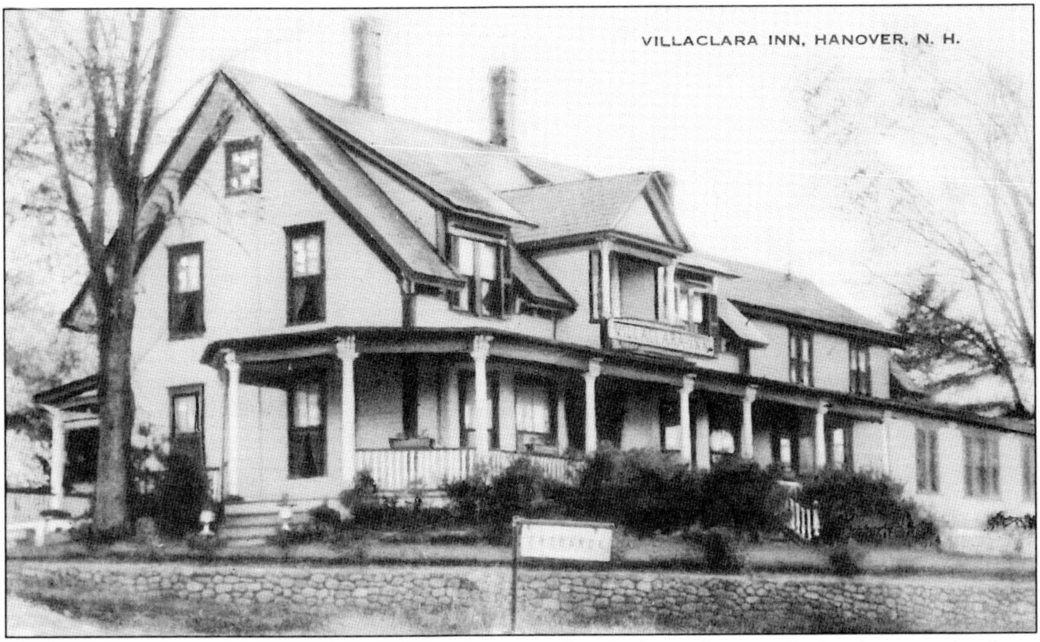

Miguel Rabassa and his wife, Clara, for many years kept a large farm with Ayrshire cattle along Lyme Road and the Connecticut River, and in addition, they operated the Villaclara Inn—seen here in this *c.* 1940 postcard view. The farmhouse/inn still stands at 113 Lyme Road and is now an apartment house.

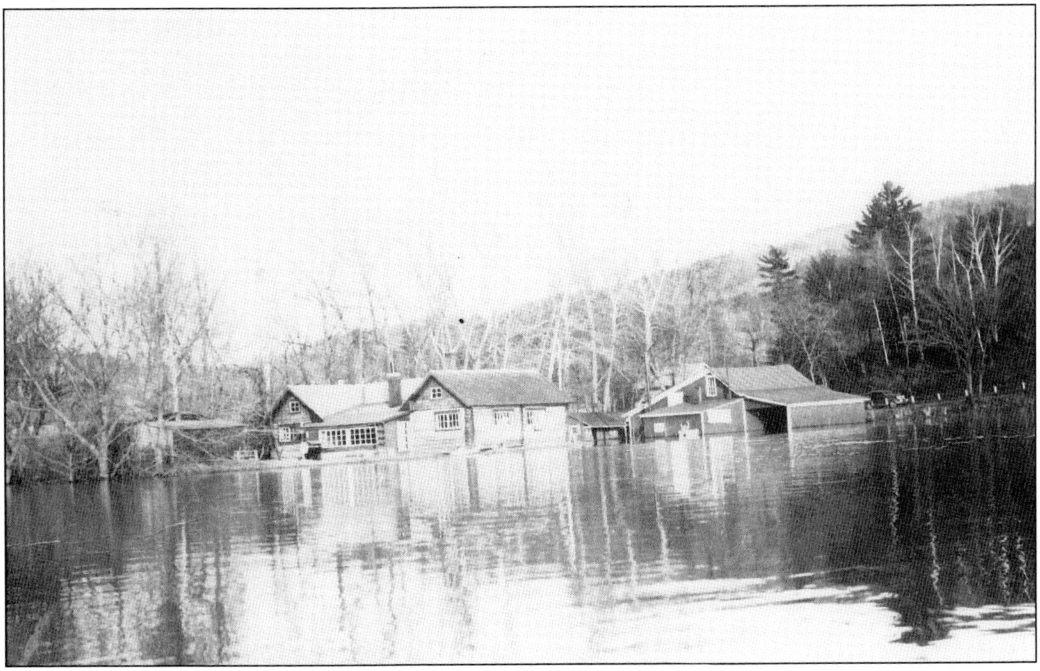

During the early weeks of March 1936, the northeast regions of the country received greater than average amounts of rainfall, and by the third week, extreme flooding was rampant. Here the complex of buildings at 96 Lyme Road sits surrounded by water from the Connecticut River. The road is to the far right of this view.

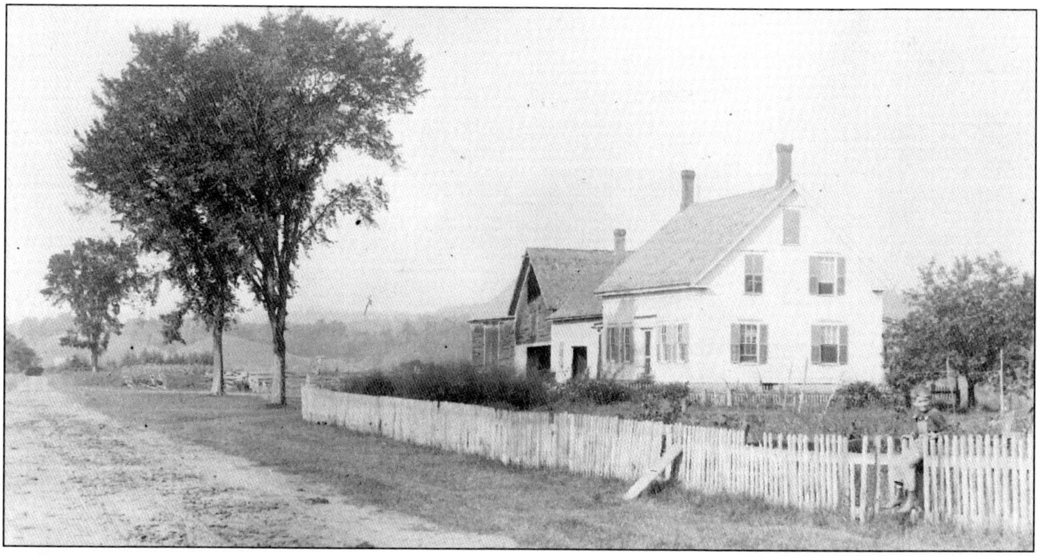

William R. Fullington migrated from England in the second half of the nineteenth century and bought this 220-acre farm that bordered the Connecticut River, along the Lyme Road. Fullington typically kept 200 head of registered Merino sheep, a breed prized for their fine wool, and also maintained an orchard of 120 sugar maple trees. This photograph, c. 1910, looking south shows the farmhouse still standing at 104 Lyme Road.

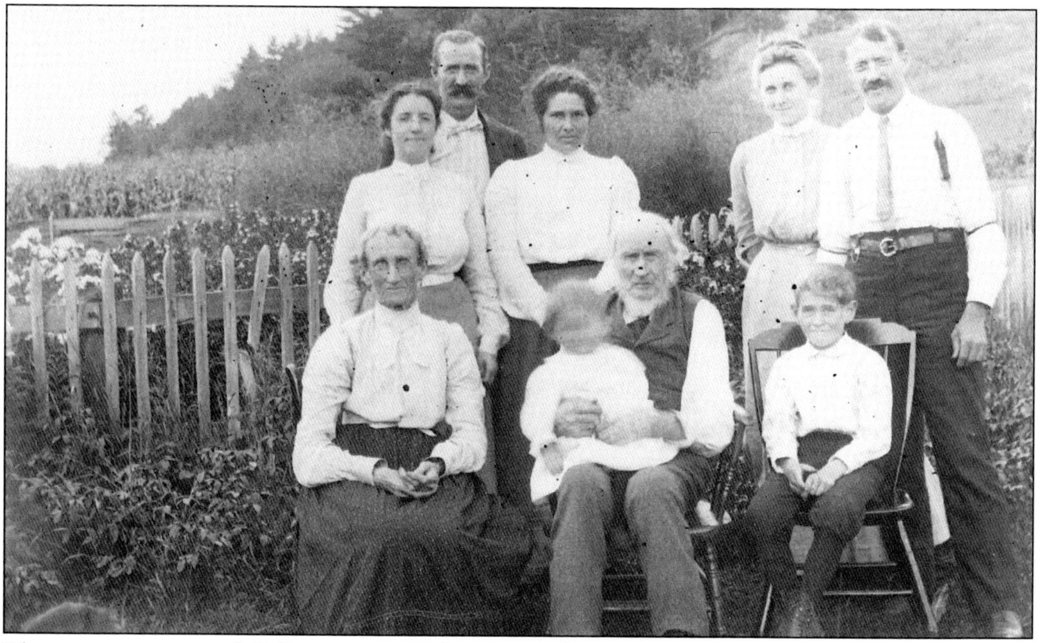

Three generations of Fullingtons are shown in this c. 1904 view. The elder William R. Fullington, originally from England, is seated in the middle holding his grandson, Haslett D. Fullington, who had a difficult time sitting still for the camera! To the left of William is his wife, and to the right, his oldest grandson, Oscar. Standing at the left rear is William's son, Harvey B. Fullington, who, years later in 1931, with sons Haslett and Wilson (the latter not yet born when this photograph was taken), went on to form Dartmouth Dairy, a major milk supplier to the area until the mid-1960s.

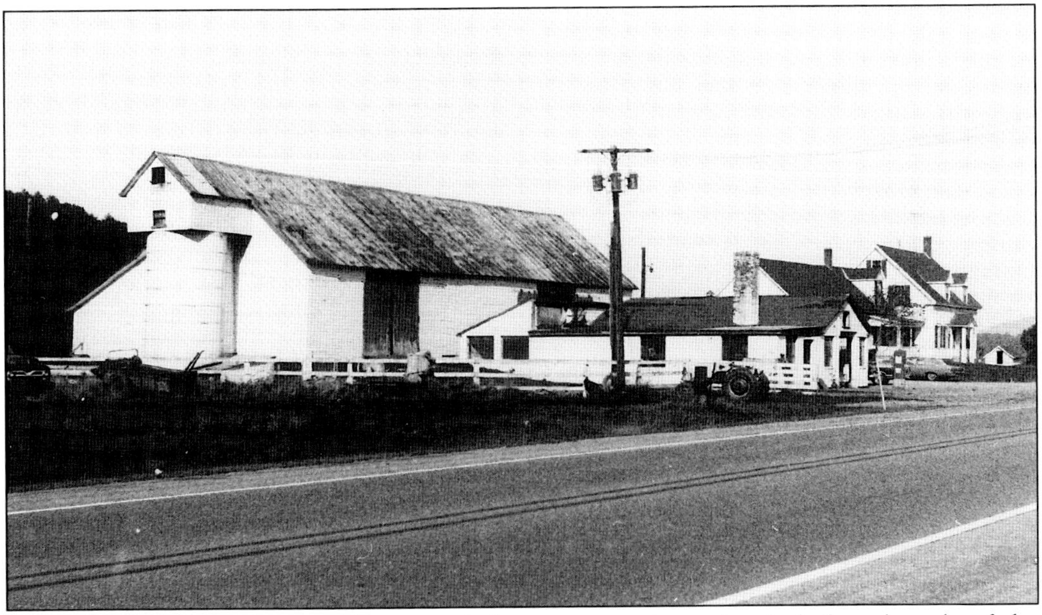

The Fullington farm, home of Dartmouth Dairy, is seen here shortly before the sale of the property to Dartmouth College in 1972. A little at a time, the twentieth century and its "progress" had been slowly chipping away at this farm. Like many family farms in the valley, some of its best meadows were flooded by the completion of Wilder Dam, and the straightening and rebuilding of Lyme Road (NH Route 10) took its share of land as well.

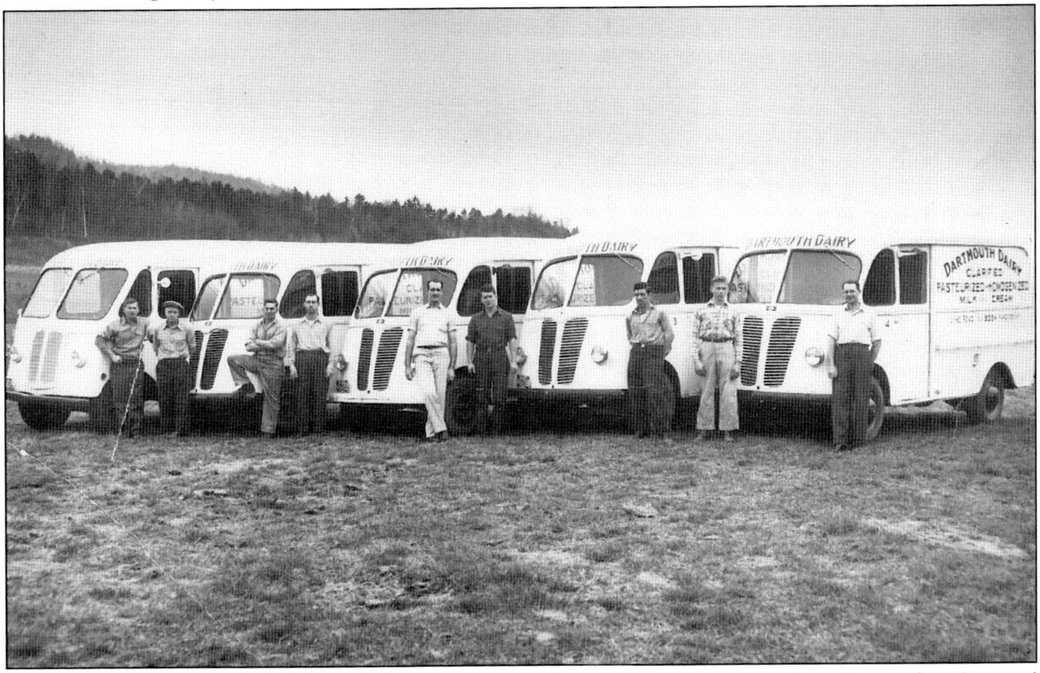

The Fullington's fleet of white Dartmouth Dairy delivery trucks were a familiar and welcomed sight on Hanover's roads and streets during the 1950s and 1960s. Each weekday morning, fresh milk from the dairy processing plant, located on the farm, was cheerfully delivered to Hanover families—brought right into their kitchens by the Fullingtons.

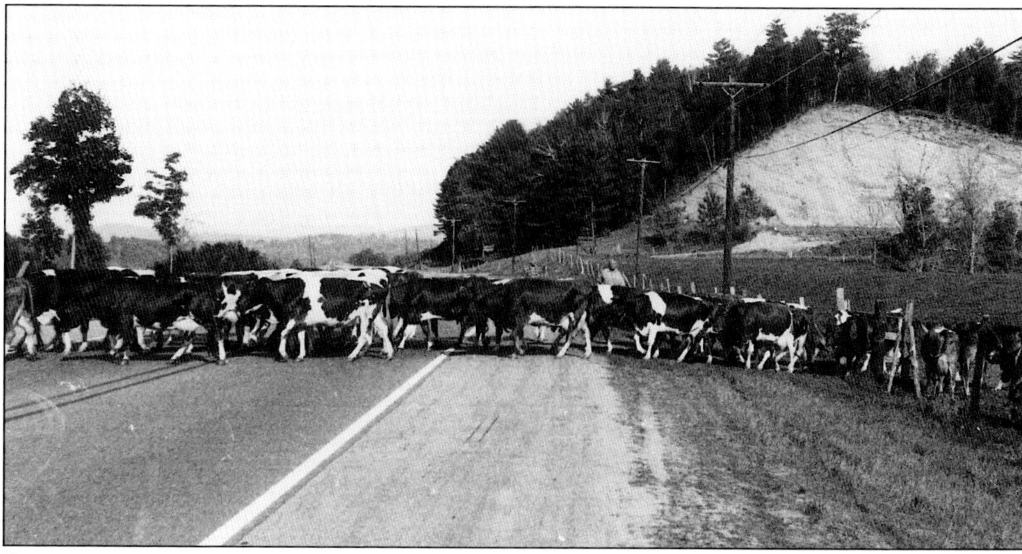

For many years cows crossing the Lyme Road were a familiar sight to many Hanover motorists, not only at the Fullingtons' farm, but at other locations along the river valley as well. This view records for posterity the last time Fullingtons' cows made their twice-a-day trek crossing the road, before being auctioned off when the farm closed in October 1971—and Hanover's last large working farm was gone.

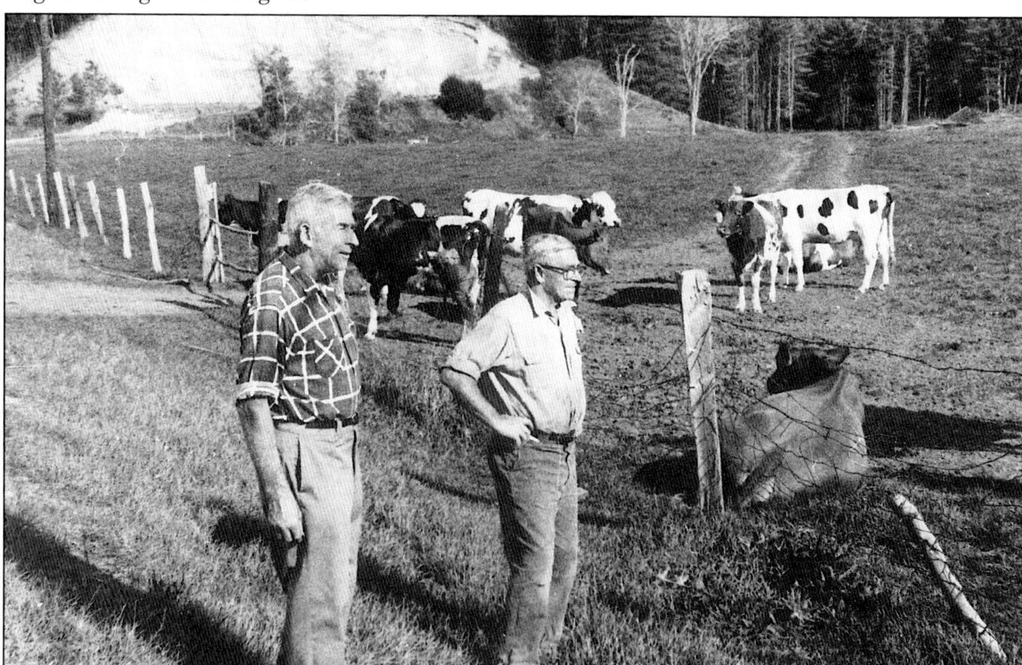

This scene captures the end of a way of life. Haslett D. and younger brother, Wilson W. Fullington, look out over their day pasture after having sold off the Dairy's herd of Guernsey cattle. At times they kept as many as 240 head, while milking 65 or more and buying additional milk to process from other surrounding farms as well. They were the third generation of Fullingtons to farm in Hanover.

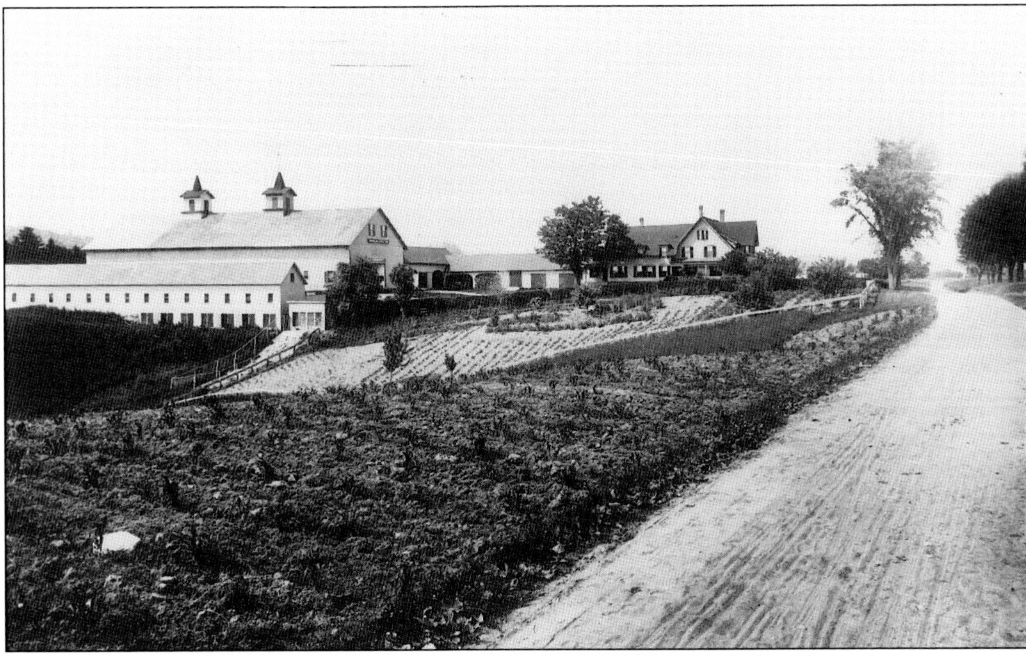

Frank Hutchinson was the enterprising farmer who is credited with building up the operation seen above, *c.* 1890, and known at that time as Grassland Stock Farm. Mr. Hutchinson died in the late 1890s, and within ten years or so, the 270-acre farm had been split up. Today the front part of the farmhouse still remains at 58 Lyme Road, and the once back el is now at 54 Lyme Road.

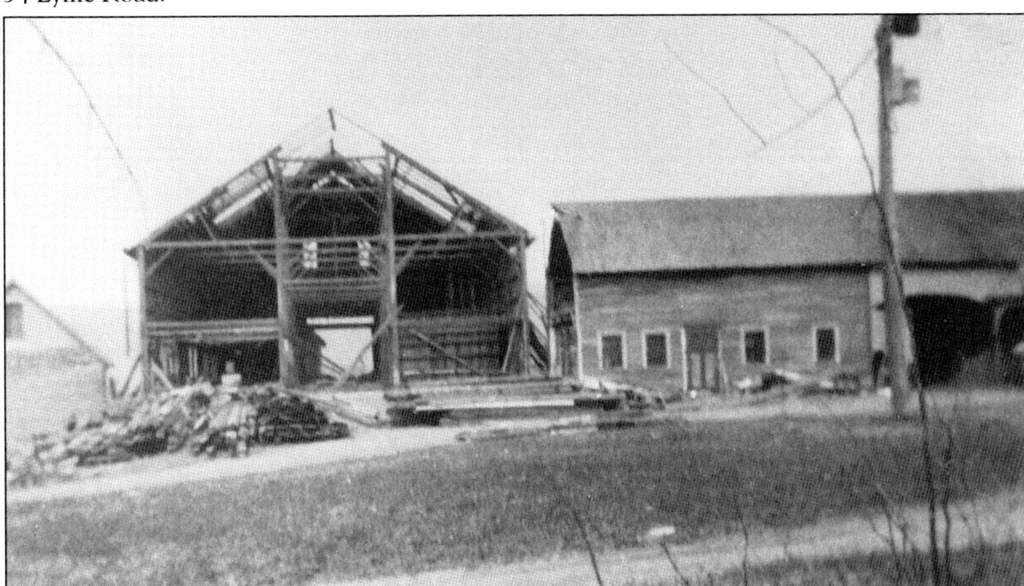

During the teens and twenties of this century, Perley M. Rich owned the Grassland Stock Farm complex on Lyme Road, but by about 1915, he began tearing the big barn down, as his hog and ice business did not require so large a structure. Here we see the east gable end removed from the main barn and the frame being dismantled for use elsewhere. Today Fletcher Circle occupies the site.

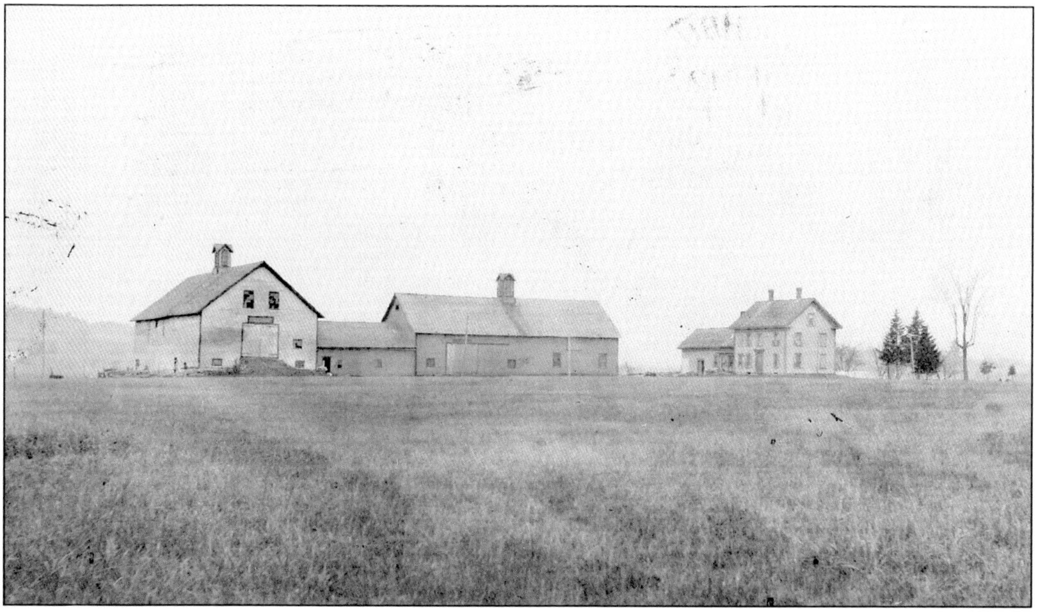

Until demolished in the early 1970s, this large complex of farm buildings existed on the south side of Reservoir Road—part of a 90-acre operation known as the Warden-Garipay Farm, shown here *c.* 1910. In 1891, Andrew A. Warden's eldest daughter, Christie, a beautiful young woman of 28, was the victim of a brutal and sensational murder by handsome, though sinister, Frank Almy—Mr. Warden's ex-farmhand.

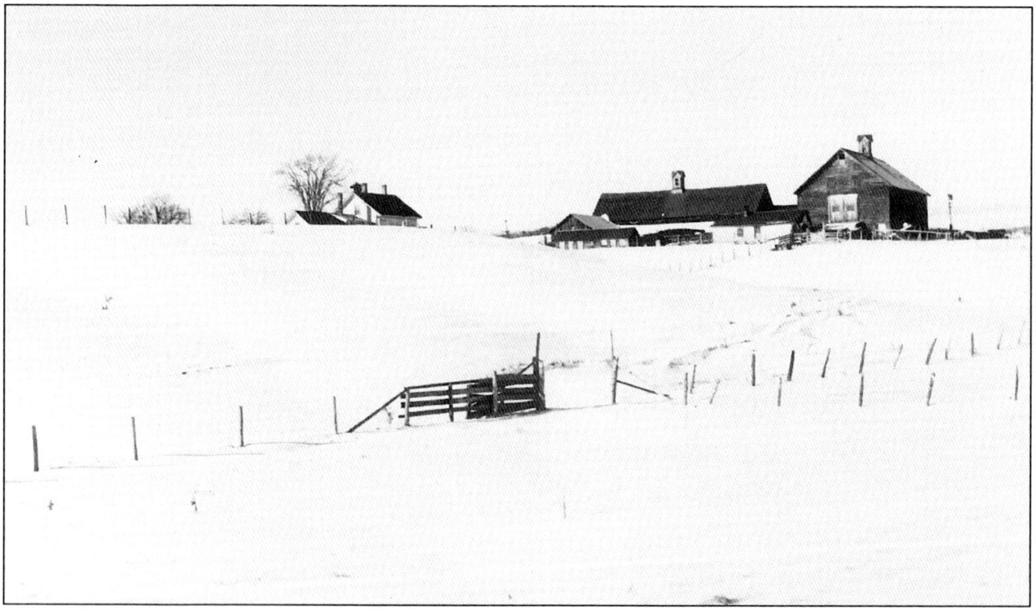

A beautiful wintry view shows the Garipay farm looking northerly, prior to the buildings being demolished in the early 1970s. In 1902, Louis Eugene Garipay and his wife, Louise (LaBombard), from upper state New York, purchased the farm from the Wardens. By 1957, after 55 years of farming, the Garipays sold the property to Dartmouth College, which for the next decade, utilized the building for storage. Today, not a trace of this once large farming operation remains.